Aim High

Student's Book 1

Tim Falla Paul A Davies
Paul Kelly Alistair McCallum

OXFORD
UNIVERSITY PRESS

CONTENTS

1 My network

THIS UNIT INCLUDES ●●●●

Vocabulary • family • possessive 's • everyday activities • sports and hobbies • collocations with *make, have* and *do* • expressions with *look* • *cloth* vs *clothes* etc. • phrasal verbs
Grammar • present simple affirmative and negative
Skills • reading, listening and talking about family and friends, and daily activities
Writing • an informal letter

Family life

BEFORE READING

LOOK at the photos. Discuss the questions.

1 In your country, are most families big or small?
2 Do you think people are happier in big families or small families? Why?
3 What are the advantages and disadvantages of having a big family?

READ

1   Read the text quickly. Are these sentences true or false?

1 Sue Povey has got thirteen children.
2 Sue's husband stays at home and looks after the children.
3 Sue is happy with her big family.

SUPERMUM!

Sue Povey gets up at six every morning and makes breakfast for fifteen people. Sue has a difficult job – she works hard every day. But she doesn't work in an office. She's a mother with fifteen children, and thirteen of them live at home. Sue's family is unusual – the average British family only has 1.8 children.

Sue Povey and her family live in Swindon, in the south of England. After breakfast her husband, Ian, goes to work. Sue drives the children to school. (She needs a minibus for this!) Nine children go to school and she drives home with the other four children. Every weekday she looks after the children and cleans the house. She does the washing eight times a day, and after lunch she irons clothes for three hours. Sue spends half her life in the kitchen.

Every afternoon at 3.30 she collects the children from school in the minibus. Then she helps them with their homework. After that she cooks dinner for fifteen. Her husband comes home at six. After dinner, she goes to the supermarket with two of her sons. They help her with the shopping. She buys 50 litres of milk a week!

Sue loves her big family. All the children help Sue and help each other. The house is always lively when it's full of children!

2 🎧 1.02 Read the *Reading tip*. Read the text again. Then choose the best answers.

1 Sue has a difficult job because
   a she makes breakfast every morning.
   b she has got a very big family.
   c two of her children don't live at home.

2 After breakfast, Sue
   a drives her husband to work.
   b drives the children to school.
   c looks after the children.

3 In the morning and afternoon, Sue
   a plays with the children.
   b goes shopping.
   c looks after the children.

4 The children come home from school
   a in the minibus.
   b with Sue's husband.
   c by bus.

5 Who helps Sue with the shopping?
   a Two daughters.
   b Two sons.
   c Her husband.

UNDERSTANDING IDEAS

Answer the questions. Look at the text, and use your own words and ideas.

1 Two of Sue Povey's children don't live at home. Think of two or three reasons why they don't.
2 Do you think Mr Povey sometimes helps his wife? How?
3 Do you think it's expensive to have a big family? Make a list of some of the things the Poveys need to buy.

VOCABULARY

Supermum!

1 Match the highlighted words in the text with these definitions.

1 You wear these.
2 To do something useful for someone else.
3 To take care of someone.
4 A big meal in the evening.
5 To pass time.
6 Get out of bed.
7 Full of energy.
8 A meal in the middle of the day.
9 To pick someone up.
10 Very loud and annoying.
11 The first meal of the day.
12 The opposite of 'noisy'.
13 Students have to do this after school.
14 Not interesting or exciting.
15 To control or operate a car.

2 Do you know these words?

argue   average   do the washing   iron   litre   south   unusual   weekday

For Ian, Sue's husband, family life is never boring. But they're all friends – everyone is too busy to argue. And when the children are all playing together, it can be very noisy.

Is the house ever quiet? Possibly – when all the children are in bed!

●●●○ Workbook: page 4

Supermum!

ACTIVATE

1 Sue Povey is talking about her family's daily activities. Match her sentences to the time of day.

MORNING	AFTERNOON OR EVENING

1 'We get up.'
2 'I cook dinner.'
3 'I drive the children to school.'
4 'We have breakfast.'
5 'I collect the children from school.'
6 'The children do their homework.'

2 Complete these sentences with the words from the box.

> quiet look after boring lunch spend lively clothes
> noisy help

1 Every day I _____ about an hour on my computer.
2 Peter lives near an airport. It's _____ in his garden!
3 I like wearing colourful _____.
4 I sometimes _____ my mum with the shopping.
5 This film is too long. It's _____!
6 When mum and dad go out, I _____ my little brother.
7 All the children are in bed. It's _____ in the house.
8 I usually have _____ at about twelve thirty.
9 All my cousins visit our house at the weekend, so it's very _____.

EXTEND

Collocations with *make*, *have* and *do*

1 Match the verbs with the nouns to make phrases.

make	have a celebration
	_____ the washing
	_____ a phone call
have	_____ your homework
	_____ a break
	_____ a lot of noise
do	_____ a shower
	_____ the shopping
	_____ your bed

Useful expressions: family and friends

2 What do you think the expressions in bold mean? Circle the correct option.

1 My brother and I **get on well**.
  a work hard   (b) are good friends
2 In the morning, my sister **spends ages** in the bathroom.
  a has a shower   b takes a long time
3 After school I sometimes **hang around** with my friends.
  a spend time   b go shopping
4 We're late for school. **Get a move on**!
  a hurry up   b stop talking
5 My little brother talks all the time. He **drives me crazy**!
  a makes me laugh   b annoys me
6 When my father cleans the car, I **give him a hand**.
  a help him   b talk to him

Expressions with *look*

3 Complete these sentences with the words from the box.

> round for ~~after~~ like at out

1 'Look after your little brother!'

2 'Look _____!'

3 'He looks _____ his father!'

4 'Let's look _____ the city.'

5 'Look _____ that picture!'

6 'Go and look _____ our suitcase!'

4 Can you find some more expressions using the verb *look*?

(●●●○○   Workbook: page 5)

Present simple: affirmative
EXPLORE

1 Read the text and find examples of the present simple affirmative.

Bart Simpson is the star of *The Simpsons*, a popular American TV programme. Eleven million Americans watch it every week. The Simpsons live in Springfield and Bart goes to Springfield Elementary School. He's very lazy and he isn't popular with the teachers, but his classmates like him. Bart has got two sisters, Lisa and Maggie. Lisa is very intelligent and she studies hard. Maggie is a baby. Bart's parents are Homer and Marge. Homer works at a power station from Monday to Friday and watches TV at weekends. Marge stays at home with Maggie.

2 Complete the table. How do we form the *third* person singular of the present simple?

Present simple: affirmative	
I work	we work
you work	you work
he / she / it _____	they work

LEARN THIS!

We use the **present simple** to talk about
1 something that happens always or regularly.
2 a fact that is always true.

⦿●●● Grammar Reference: page 94

EXPLOIT

1 Complete the sentences with the present simple affirmative of the verbs in the box. Then write which member of the Simpson family says it.

go   like   live   stay   study   ~~work~~

1 'I work at a power station.' Homer
2 'My brother and I _____ to Springfield Elementary School.'
3 'My little sister _____ hard at school.'
4 'My wife _____ at home with our baby.'
5 'My classmates _____ me.'
6 'I _____ in Springfield with my husband and children.'

2 🎧 (1.03) Listen and repeat.
1 /s/   likes   works
2 /z/   plays   goes   lives
3 /ɪz/   watches   finishes

3 🎧 (1.04) Listen and write the words in the correct group.

~~does~~   moves   drives   hates   listens   looks   loves
speaks   stays   teaches   tells   washes

/s/	/z/	/ɪz/
		does

4 Complete the text. Use the present simple affirmative.

My best friend

My best friend is called Jenny. She ¹lives (live) next door to me. We ²_____ (go) to the same school but we are in different classes. I ³_____ (walk) to school, but Jenny ⁴_____ (go) by bike, because she always ⁵_____ (get up) late.

After school we ⁶_____ (finish) our homework first and then we ⁷_____ (watch) TV.

I ⁸_____ (like) news programmes, but Jenny ⁹_____ (hate) them. She ¹⁰_____ (think) they're boring. She ¹¹_____ (love) chat shows.

5 Write five sentences about you or your family. Use the verbs in the box.

go   get up   like   live   play   watch   work   speak

My dad speaks French. I like reading.

⦿●●● Grammar Builder: page 95

⦿●●● Workbook: page 6

Talking about family and friends
VOCABULARY

1 Put the words in the box into the two groups below, A and B. Which word goes in both groups?

> **Family** ~~aunt~~ ~~brother~~ cousin daughter father granddaughter grandfather grandmother grandson husband mother nephew niece sister son uncle wife

A
aunt

B
brother

2 (1.05) Listen, repeat and check your answers.

3 (1.06) Listen to the pronunciation of the underlined vowels.

m<u>o</u>ther /ˈmʌðə/   c<u>ou</u>sin /ˈkʌzn/

4 (1.07) Which other words in exercise 1 have the sound /ʌ/? Listen and check your answers.

5 Read the *Look out!* box. Then complete the puzzles.

> **LOOK OUT!**
>
> **POSSESSIVE 'S**
> 1 We add **'s** after a name or a noun to show possession or a family relationship.
>   *my dad's computer   my uncle's wife*
> 2 After a plural noun ending in *-s*, we just add **'**.
>   *my parents' car   my cousins' grandfather*

1 My mother's brother is my _____.
2 My father is my cousins' _____.
3 My uncle's daughter is my _____.
4 My sister is my cousin's _____.
5 My nephews' sister is my _____.
6 My uncle is my mother's or father's _____.

6 Work in pairs. Write more puzzles for each other.

> Who is my dad's sister?

> Your aunt.

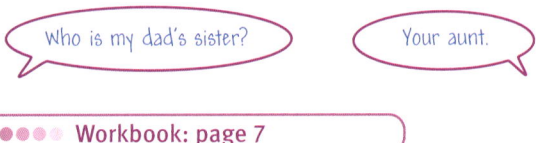

LISTEN

(1.08) Listen and complete Laura's network of people she meets regularly. Use the names in the box.

> Baker   Lisa   Hannah   Lucy   Molly   Sam

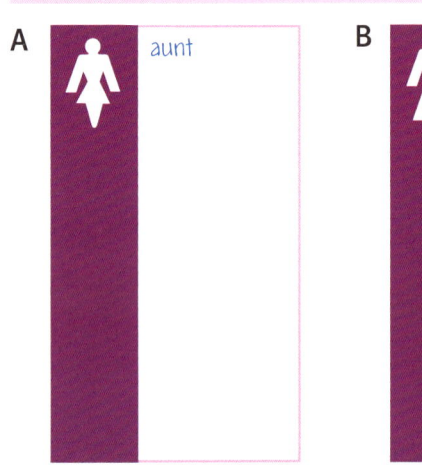
Janice
1 _____
volleyball team
Jane
book group
3 _____

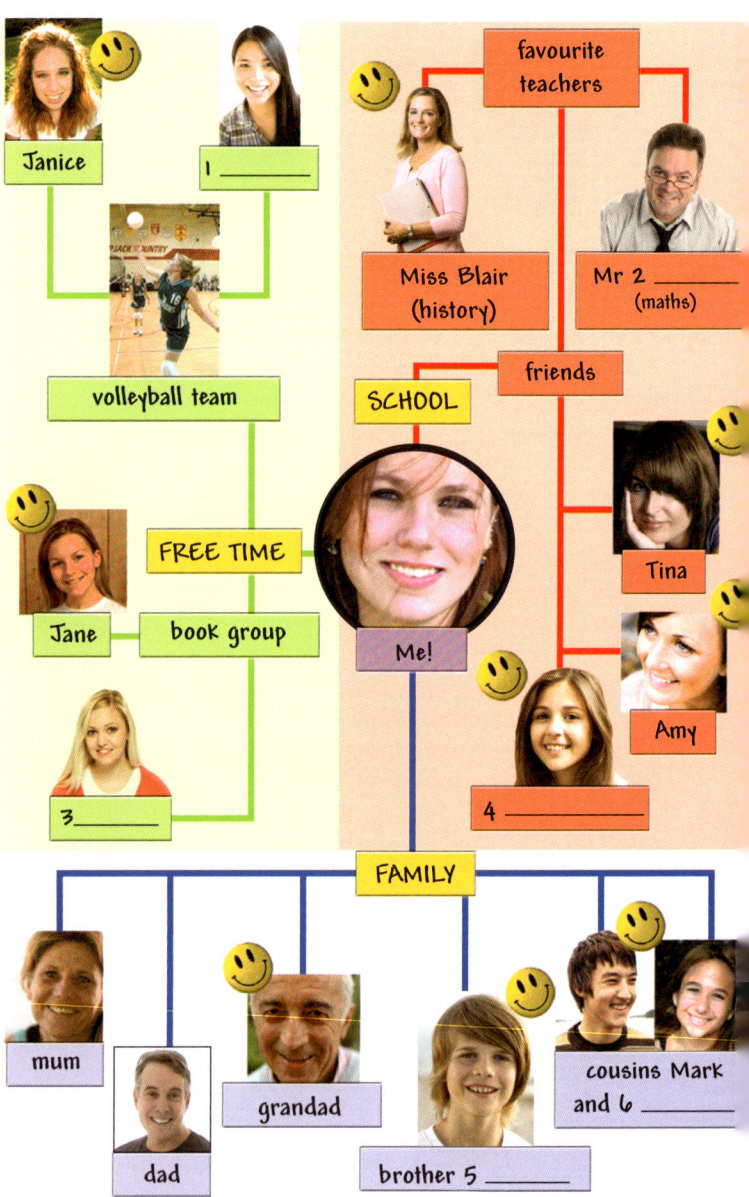
favourite teachers
Miss Blair (history)
Mr 2 _____ (maths)
friends
SCHOOL
FREE TIME
Me!
Tina
Amy
4 _____

FAMILY
mum
dad
grandad
brother 5 _____
cousins Mark and 6 _____

SPEAK

1 Draw a network of the people you meet regularly.

2 Work in pairs. Give your partner the names of six people from your network. Ask and answer about the people on your lists.

> Who's ...

> He's my cousin. He's 18 years old.

> She's my friend.
> She's in my volleyball team.

> ●●○○○ Workbook: page 7

Present simple: negative
EXPLORE

1 Read the text about two brothers. Find five examples of the present simple negative.

Josh and Ben are brothers. Both boys are athletic, but they don't like the same things. Ben loves football. He plays for two teams – his school team and his city team – and he trains every weekend. Josh trains a lot too, but he doesn't play football. He loves ice skating. He goes ice skating at an ice rink in the city.

'I want to be a professional ice skater,' says Josh. 'But Ben wants to play for Manchester United. I don't like football, but I think Ben is fantastic.'

'I don't like ice skating at all, but I know Josh is great,' says Ben. 'We don't like the same things, but we like each other.'

2 Read the *Learn this!* box and complete the sentences in the table below.

> **LEARN THIS!**
>
> We form the **present simple negative** with *don't* or *doesn't* and the base form of the verb.

Present simple: negative	
I ¹_____ play football.	We ³_____ play football.
You don't play football.	You don't play football.
He / She / It ²_____ play football.	They ⁴_____ play football.

●○○○○ Grammar Reference: page 94

EXPLOIT

1 Make the sentences negative.

1 I live in England.
   I don't live in England.
2 We come from London.
3 Karen studies science.
4 Mick plays ice hockey.
5 You like computer games.
6 Ben and I walk to school.
7 Mona gets up at five o'clock.

2 🎧 (1.09) Listen to Mark and Sally. Is the information in the table true (✓) or false (✗)?

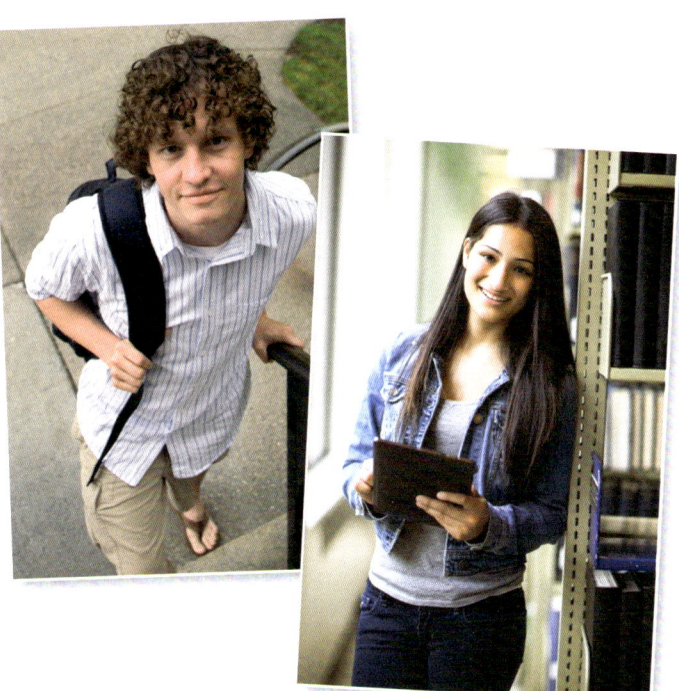

		Mark	Sally
1	comes from	Oxford ✗	Cardiff
2	lives in	Liverpool ✓	London
3	studies	maths	medicine
4	enjoys	playing the piano	shopping
5	plays	basketball	volleyball
6	works in	a restaurant	a shop

3 Write sentences about Mark and Sally. Use the information in the table and the present simple, affirmative or negative.

Mark doesn't come from Oxford.
He lives in Liverpool.

4 Write true sentences about yourself with the present simple affirmative or negative. Use the phrases below and your own ideas.

1 live in a flat
   I live in a flat. / I don't live in a flat.
2 study history
3 watch TV every day
4 speak Russian
5 walk to school
6 get up at seven o'clock on Saturdays
7 read in bed
8 play sport

●○○○○ Grammar Builder: page 95

●○○○○ Workbook: page 8

An informal letter
READ

Read the letter. Answer the questions below.

Dear Sam,

A My name is Robbie and I'm your new penfriend. This is a photo of me. I'm 16 years old and I'm from Manchester.

B I live in a flat with my parents and my sister Karen. She's 11 and she's usually a bit annoying. We've also got a dog called Rover.

C I go to Newtown Comprehensive School. After school, I take the dog for a walk, and then I do my homework. My parents don't get home until seven o'clock, so Karen and I cook dinner. After dinner, I watch TV or listen to music.

Write soon.

Best wishes,

Robbie

1 How old is Robbie?
2 Where is he from?
3 What is his sister's name?
4 How old is his sister?
5 What does he do after school?
6 Who cooks dinner at Robbie's house?

PREPARE

1 Read the letter. In which paragraph (A–C) does Robbie:

1 say how old he is? ___
2 say what he does after school? ___
3 say what his name is? ___
4 talk about his family? ___
5 say where he's from? ___
6 say which school he goes to? ___

2 Read the *Writing tip* and find words and phrases for beginning and ending letters in Robbie's letter.

Writing tip: beginning and ending letters

- We start an informal letter with Dear and the person's first name.
- We finish the letter with *Best wishes* and our first name. (We can use *Love* if we know the person very well.)

3 Read the *Look out!* box. Find the linking words in Robbie's letter.

Linking words
We use *and* to link two pieces of information.
We use *then* to show that one action happens after another.
We use *so* to explain the result or consequence of something.
We use *or* to show a choice of two or more things.

4 Circle the correct linking words in the sentences below.

1 In the evening we have dinner and **so** / **then** I do my homework.
2 My dad usually watches TV **and** / **or** listens to the radio.
3 At the weekend she helps her parents, **and** / **so** she can't meet her friends.
4 My cousin and I go to the same school **or** / **and** we are in the same class!
5 They never eat breakfast, **so** / **then** they are hungry before lunchtime.
6 For lunch we usually have sandwiches **or** / **so** pasta.

WRITE

Imagine you have a penfriend in Britain. Write a short letter to him or her. Use the writing plan to help you.

Dear _____

Paragraph 1
- Introduce yourself. Say how old you are and where you are from.

Paragraph 2
- Say something about your family. (How many brothers and sisters? Ages?)

Paragraph 3
- What do you do after school? What do you do after dinner?
Best wishes

_____

Check your work

Have you
- [ ] followed the writing plan?
- [ ] written 70–100 words?
- [ ] checked your spelling and grammar?

●●●○○ Workbook: page 9

My network
LANGUAGE SKILLS

1 🎧 (1.10) Complete the dialogue with the words from the box. Then listen and check your answers.

> doesn't don't friends go goes got how my see sister sister's you

Tony Hi! I'm a new student. ¹_____ name's Tony.
John Hello, Tony. Nice to meet ²_____. I'm John.
Tony Have you ³_____ any brothers or sisters?
John Yes, I've got a sister.
Tony ⁴_____ old is she?
John My ⁵_____ is 19. Her name is Cathy. She ⁶_____ go to this school. She ⁷_____ to university in London.
Tony What's your favourite sport?
John I love football! I ⁸_____ to the sports centre every weekend, and I play with my ⁹_____.
Tony What about your sister?
John My ¹⁰_____ favourite sport is tennis, but I ¹¹_____ like it. It's boring!
Tony That's the bell. I've got maths now. Bye, John.
John ¹²_____ you.

2 Read the dialogue again. These sentences are incorrect. Write two correct sentences, one negative and one affirmative.

1 Tony and John are teachers.
2 John has got a brother.
3 Cathy is eighteen.
4 Cathy goes to school.
5 John goes to the sports centre every evening.
6 John likes tennis.
7 Tony has got a French class now.

3 Circle the correct words in these sentences.

1 I've got one brother and two sisters. My **brother / brother's** name is Sam. My **sisters' / sister's** names are Ann and Emily. My brother is 4, so he **don't / doesn't** go to school. My sisters **is / are** 12 and 15. They **go / goes** to the same school as me.

2 Mr and Mrs Johnson **have / has** a big family. They've got seven **child / children**. Six of them **live / lives** at home. One of them is married. His name is Jack. He **visit / visits** his parents every weekend.

3 After school, I usually **meets / meet** my friends for half an hour. Then I **take / takes** the bus home. My brother and I **watch / watches** TV, or sometimes we play games on my **fathers / father's** computer. After dinner I do my homework, but my parents **help / helps** me if it's difficult. I **doesn't / don't** like homework!

What's the difference?

1 What's the difference between these words and phrases? Use your dictionary and write example sentences to show the difference.

1 cloth / clothes
This cloth is expensive.   Please put your clothes away.

2 housework / homework
_____. _____.

3 lunch / lunchtime
_____. _____.

4 sometime / sometimes
_____. _____.

5 teach / learn
_____. _____.

6 washing / washing-up
_____. _____.

7 wear / put sth on
_____. _____.

Phrasal verbs

2 Look up the phrasal verbs in the box and complete the sentences.

> ~~fill sth in~~ pick sth up put sth away take after sb
> take off try sth on turn sth down

1 What's your name? What's your address? Fill this form in, please.
2 The lesson's over. _____ your books _____.
3 _____ the television _____! It's too loud.
4 What time does the plane _____ _____?
5 _____ that cup _____, please. It's on the floor!
6 My mother is short and slim, and I am too. I _____ _____ my mother.
7 _____ these shoes _____. Are they the right size?

I CAN ...

Read the statements. Think about your progress and tick (✓) one of the boxes.

 I need more practice.  I sometimes find this difficult. No problem!

	✳	✳✳	✳✳✳
I can understand an article and talk about everyday activities.			
I can talk about my family and friends.			
I can talk about people I meet regularly.			
I can say what someone does and doesn't do.			
I can write an informal letter to a penfriend.			

●●●○ Workbook: Self check pages 10–11

2 Free time

Kung Fu

BEFORE READING

Discuss the questions.

1 Do you like watching sports? Do you like playing sports? Which ones?
2 How often do you exercise? Do you walk or cycle to school? Or do you go by car or bus?
3 Look at the photos. Where are these people? Are they at school, or on holiday? Which country are they in?

Reading tip

When you read a text for the first time, don't worry if you don't understand every word. Just try to understand the general meaning.

READ

1 Read the *Reading tip*. Then read the text quickly. Which sentence is true?

1 David trains only in the mornings.
2 David trains only in the afternoons.
3 David trains in the mornings and afternoons.

No pain, no gain

David Simmons comes from London, but he's in China for three months. He's a student at the Dengfeng Kung Fu School. In this interview with *Martial Arts Monthly* (MAM) David talks about life at the school.

MAM Tell me about a typical day. What time do you get up?
David Our routine is the same every day. We get up at five o'clock and start training immediately. We haven't got time to wash or have breakfast. If we're late, the teachers hit us with sticks.
MAM How do you train?
David First we train our legs, arms and stomachs. We run up and down 1000 steps and do press-ups. The training is very, very hard.
MAM How do you understand the teachers? Do you speak Chinese?
David A little, yes. But the teachers speak English, so I don't have a problem.
MAM When do you have breakfast?
David At half past seven. We have rice and soup. Training starts again at nine o'clock. We practise hitting with our hands. We learn to jump high and to kick, too. At eleven o'clock we take a break for ten minutes and then training starts again.
MAM When do you stop for lunch?
David At twelve thirty. But of course, our arms and legs hurt after all the training. So we stretch for ten minutes, and then we have lunch. After lunch we have a long rest.
MAM Do you train in the afternoons too?
David Yes. I like the afternoons because we train with sticks and swords.
MAM Is it dangerous?

David No, not really, because we don't fight. We learn how to defend ourselves, not to hurt other people.
MAM When does training finish?
David At six o'clock. We have a shower, and have dinner at half past six – rice and soup again – then we go to bed.
MAM What do you want to do when you go back to Britain?
David I want to start a Kung Fu school in London and teach people Kung Fu. I also want to appear in films as a Kung Fu fighter!

2 🎧 **1.13** Read the text again. Then choose the best answers.

1 Every day at the Dengfeng School, the students
   a practise their English.
   b do the same things.
   c learn to fight.
2 At eleven o'clock the students have a
   a meal.
   b long rest.
   c short break.
3 The students eat rice and soup
   a three times a week.
   b before they start training.
   c for breakfast and dinner every day.

4 David has a shower
   a after training.
   b before breakfast.
   c before lunch.
5 When he goes back to London, David wants to be a
   a soldier.
   b teacher.
   c doctor.

3 Are these sentences true or false? Correct the false sentences.

1 David Simmons works in China.
2 He has breakfast before he starts training.
3 David speaks a little Chinese.
4 In the mornings they practise fighting with swords.
5 They have a long rest just before lunch.
6 David wants to teach Kung Fu when he goes back to Britain.

UNDERSTANDING IDEAS

Answer the questions. Look at the text, and use your own words and ideas.

1 What does David like about the Dengfeng School, and what do you think he dislikes?
2 Do you think David wants to fight people?
3 Why do some people want to study Kung Fu? Try to think of three or four reasons.

VOCABULARY

No pain, no gain

1 Match the highlighted words in the text with these definitions.

1 To move suddenly into the air.
2 Difficult, tiring.
3 A short period when you stop your normal activity.
4 To do exercise regularly, to become stronger.
5 Not safe.
6 To protect yourself.
7 Usual, normal.
8 To do something regularly, to become good at it.
9 A period of relaxing, sleeping or doing nothing.
10 To touch, suddenly and violently.
11 To try to hurt someone.
12 To move quickly, using your legs.
13 To push out your arms and legs as far as possible.
14 The things that you normally do every day.
15 To hit with your foot.

2 Do you know these words?

   appear in   go back to   immediately   interview
   monthly   press-up   stick   sword

●●○○   Workbook: page 12

No pain, no gain

ACTIVATE

Complete these sentences with the words from the box.

break dangerous defend fight hard hit jump kick practise rest routine run stretch train typical

1. _____ the ball to me!
2. After a game of basketball, I'm usually tired and I want a _____.
3. There are a lot of difficult questions in this exam. It's _____!
4. Boxers _____ with their hands. They don't use sticks or swords.
5. I like sport. I can _____ a kilometre in four minutes, and I can _____ two metres into the air.
6. They're professional footballers. They _____ six days a week.
7. I get up at seven, have breakfast and get the bus to school at eight. That's my _____ every morning.
8. Don't drive so fast! It's _____!
9. When I get up, I usually _____ my arms and legs.
10. It's difficult to score a goal against that team. They _____ very well.
11. Don't _____ your little brother with your book! Be kind to him!
12. I want to be a professional musician, so I _____ every day.
13. On a _____ day, I drink three or four cups of tea.
14. At my school, we start lessons at 8.30, and at 10.30 we take a _____ for ten minutes.

EXTEND

Opposites

1 Find highlighted words in the text on page 12 that mean the opposite of these words.

1	safe	*dangerous*	4 easy	_____
2	unusual	_____	5 activity	_____
3	attack	_____		

Parts of speech

2 Find these highlighted words in the text on page 12. Are they used as verbs, adjectives, or nouns? Write the words in the correct box.

dangerous practise rest train hard break ~~jump~~

verbs	jump	_____ _____
adjectives	_____ _____	
nouns	_____ _____	

Verbs for walking and running

3 These verbs are used for different kinds of walking and running. Can you match them to the pictures?

march jog ~~sprint~~ stroll rush hike

a sprint   b _____

c _____   d _____

e _____   f _____

4 Write sentences using these verbs. Can you think of any other verbs for running or walking?

I can sprint very fast.

Useful nouns

5 These are nouns about routines and activities. Complete the sentences, using the nouns.

interval calendar holiday ~~break~~ timetable appointment

1. After two hours of studying English I need a break!
2. What day is 23rd July this year? Is it a Monday or a Tuesday? Check the _____.
3. I feel terrible. I want to make an _____ to see the doctor.
4. Every August, we have a _____. We usually go to Italy for two weeks.
5. This concert is very long. When is the _____?
6. What time is the next train? Let's look at the _____.

●●●●○ Workbook: page 13

Present simple: interrogative
EXPLORE

1 🎧 (1.14) Look at part 1 of an interview with 17-year-old snowboarding star, Jed Bright. Put the interviewer's questions in the correct places. Listen and check your answers.

a Do your parents travel with you?
b Do you do any other sports?
c Do you enjoy competitions?
d Does Nathan take part in the competitions?

Interviewer	¹_____
Jed	Yes, I do. I love the excitement – and the travelling.
Interviewer	²_____
Jed	No, they don't. I travel with my trainer, Martin Atkins, and my brother Nathan.
Interviewer	³_____
Jed	No, he doesn't. He just watches.
Interviewer	⁴_____
Jed	No, I don't. I haven't got time!

2 Complete the examples in the *Learn this!* box. Use the questions from exercise 1 to help you.

> **LEARN THIS!**
>
> We form **present simple questions** with *do* or *does* and the base form of the verb.
> ¹_____ you go snowboarding?
> Yes, I ²_____. / No, I ³_____.
> ⁴_____ she play chess?
> Yes, she ⁵_____. / No, she ⁶_____.

● ○ ○ ○   **Grammar Reference: page 96**

EXPLOIT

1 Write questions in the present simple.

1 you / go snowboarding?
   Do you go snowboarding?
2 your friends / like computer games?
3 your grandmother / play football?
4 you / watch a lot of films?
5 your best friend / do athletics?
6 you / like drawing?

2 Answer the questions in exercise 1.

Do you go snowboarding?
Yes I do. / No I don't.

3 Study the *Learn this!* box. Complete part 2 of the interview with the question words in the box.

> **LEARN THIS!**
>
> *Wh-* questions
>
> We can use the question words *how, what, when, where* and *who* to ask for information. We put the question word at the beginning of the question.
> *Where does your dad work?*
> *Who do you sit next to in class?*

Interviewer	¹Where do you live?
Jed	I live in Vancouver, in Canada.
Interviewer	²_____ do you live with?
Jed	My parents and my brother.
Interviewer	³_____ do you relax?
Jed	I read.
Interviewer	⁴_____ books do you like?
Jed	Crime stories are my favourites.
Interviewer	⁵_____ do you see your friends?
Jed	In the evenings and at weekends.

4 🎧 (1.15) Listen to part 2 of the interview and check your answers. Practise reading the interview in pairs.

5 Work in pairs. Match the beginnings and endings of the questions. Then ask and answer them.

1 What books do you	a get up in the morning?
2 Where do you	b do?
3 When do you	c read?
4 What sport do you	d sit next to in class?
5 Who do you	e buy your clothes?
6 How do you	f travel to school?

6 Work in pairs. Prepare an interview. Write five questions for your partner. Use the questions from exercises 3 and 5 to help you.

What books do you read?

7 Write answers to your partner's questions.

I read adventure stories.

8 Tell the class about your partner.

> *My partner doesn't do any sport but he watches football.*

● ○ ○ ○   **Grammar Builder: page 97**

● ○ ○ ○   **Workbook: page 14**

Free-time activities
VOCABULARY

1 Label the photos with eight of the words from the box.

> **Sports and hobbies** athletics basketball books chess computer games cycling films football gymnastics ~~ice skating~~ jogging music photography rollerblading swimming

1 ice skating

2

4

3

7

5

6

8

2 🎧 (1.16) Listen, repeat and check your answers.

3 Which sports and hobbies can you do:

1 at home?   3 on your own?
2 outside?   4 in a team?

●●●●○ Workbook: page 15

LISTEN

1 🎧 (1.17) Listen to four teenagers. Which sport or hobby is each person interested in?

1 Oliver _____   3 Nick _____
2 Lauren _____   4 Rachel _____

2 🎧 (1.17) Listen again. Complete the sentences with the correct name from exercise 1.

1 _____ visits chat rooms.
2 _____ goes to a club near her home.
3 _____ has got a collection of DVDs.
4 _____ meets friends after school every day.
5 _____ has got a brother, Michael.
6 _____ has lessons on Thursdays.
7 _____ reads film magazines.
8 _____ has got an expensive bike.

3 Put the sports and hobbies from Vocabulary exercise 1 into four groups, according to your own opinion.

1 I really like …
2 I quite like …
3 I don't like …
4 I hate …

SPEAK

1 Work in pairs. Tell your partner your opinions of the sports and hobbies. Tick the ones that are the same for both of you.

> I really like basketball, football, computer games and music. I quite like …

2 Do a class survey. Which sport or hobby is:

1 the most popular in the class?
2 the most popular with the boys?
3 the most popular with the girls?

GRAMMAR

Adverbs of frequency
EXPLORE

1 🎧 (1.18) Read and listen to what two teenagers say about their Saturdays. Match them with the pictures.

Jacob I always have football practice on Saturday morning, so I get up early and have a big breakfast. After football practice, I go home for lunch. In the afternoon, I usually do homework, but I sometimes play tennis at the sports club. I hardly ever watch TV during the day – the programmes are always really boring. In the evening, I always go out with friends. We often go bowling. I'm usually in bed before midnight.

Kirsty I usually get up late on Saturday morning. I never have breakfast. I watch TV for an hour and then I usually check my emails or visit a chat room. After lunch, I go shopping. I look at the new mobile phones, but I never buy a phone – they're always very expensive. I always go out with friends on Saturday evening. I'm often out until eleven o'clock.

2 🎧 (1.19) Complete the chart with the adverbs of frequency from the box. Listen, repeat and check your answers.

Adverbs of frequency always   usually   often   never   ~~sometimes~~   hardly ever

0%					100%
1 ____	2 ____	sometimes	3 ____	4 ____	5 ____

3 Find all the examples of adverbs of frequency in the texts in exercise 1.

4 Circle the correct words in the rules in the *Learn this!* box. Use the examples in the texts in exercise 1 to help you.

LEARN THIS!

1 We use **adverbs of frequency** to say how often something happens.
2 We normally put an adverb of frequency:
   a **before** / **after** the verb *be*
   b **before** / **after** most other verbs

●●●○○ Grammar Reference: page 96

EXPLOIT

1 Write sentences about Jacob and Kirsty, using adverbs of frequency and a phrase from the box.

on Saturday afternoon	on Saturday evening
on Saturday morning	on Saturday night

1 Jacob / have football practice …
   Jacob always has football practice on Saturday morning.
2 Kirsty / get up late …
3 Kirsty / have breakfast …
4 Jacob / play tennis …
5 Kirsty / buy a mobile phone …
6 Jacob and Kirsty / go out with friends …
7 Jacob / be in bed before midnight …
8 Kirsty / is out …

2 Look at the chart. How often do you do these activities? Complete the chart.

Activity	How often?	When?	Who with?
visit relatives	sometimes	at the weekend	my parents
do homework			
cook dinner			
do the washing-up			
listen to music			
watch TV			
go shopping			
play computer games			

3 Write sentences, using the information in the chart.
I sometimes visit relatives at the weekend with my parents.

4 Compare your sentences with the rest of the class. Which things are the same and which are different?
I sometimes visit relatives at the weekend.
My partner usually visits relatives after school.

●●●○○ Grammar Builder: page 97

●●●○○ Workbook: page 16

An announcement
READ

Film Club

Are you interested in films? We are! We meet at Lauren's house every Thursday at four o'clock to watch and talk about our favourite DVDs.

Every month, we meet to decide the next four films. We usually bring the DVDs, but we sometimes rent them.

Come to Film Club!
Call Lauren White on 07756 277382.

Chess ♛ Club

Are you a chess player? Good or bad, you're welcome at our club. We meet every Tuesday at six o'clock in Gino's Café to play chess. We usually play for fun, but we also have a competition every year. You can win great prizes.

Use your head. Play chess!

Don't wait. Phone Lewis Connor today on 07710 767262 or visit our website: www.chessatginos.com

Read the announcements. Answer these questions for each club and write your answers in the table.

1 When do they meet?
2 Where do they meet?
3 What do they do every week?
4 What do they do every month / year?
5 Who do you phone about the club?

Film Club	Chess Club
1 Thursday at 4 o'clock	
2	
3	
4	
5	

PREPARE

1 Read the *Writing tip* box. How many imperatives can you find in the announcements? Which imperative is negative?

Writing tip: using imperatives

1 We often use imperatives in announcements. They're direct and easy to understand.
   Don't forget! Call this number: 674583.
2 We form the affirmative imperative with the base form of the verb.
   We form the negative imperative with *don't* + base form.

2 Complete the imperatives with the words from the box.

come   don't forget   don't   stay   learn   meet   play   visit

1 Come and join the fun.
2 _____ basketball and get fit.
3 _____ _____ at home.
4 _____ people with the same hobby.
5 _____ new languages.
6 _____ our website.
7 _____ _____ to tell your friends.

WRITE

1 Invent a club. Use one of the names from the box or your own idea.

art club   basketball club   book club   computer club
gymnastics club   photography club   running club

2 Make notes about your club. Use the plan to help you.

- when it meets
- where it meets
- what they do
- who to phone
- phone number
- website

3 Write an announcement for your club. Use your notes from exercise 2.

Check your work

Have you
☐ used some imperatives?
☐ written 50–70 words?
☐ checked your spelling and grammar?

●●●○○   Workbook: page 17

Free time
LANGUAGE SKILLS

1 🎧 [1.20] Complete the dialogue with the words from the box. Then listen and check your answers.

> come do does doesn't don't never often on us
> usually where you

Jenny What's your favourite sport?
Kate I love tennis!
Jenny Really? How ¹_____ do you play?
Kate I ²_____ play every week, ³_____ Saturdays.
Jenny ⁴_____ do you play? In the park?
Kate No. I go to the sports centre with my brother. Mum drives ⁵_____ there.
Jenny ⁶_____ she play tennis too?
Kate Oh, no! She ⁷_____ play. She just watches. I play with my brother.
Jenny ⁸_____ you usually win?
Kate No, I don't. He's a really good player. What about you?
Jenny Well, I like watching tennis, but I ⁹_____ play it. I ¹⁰_____ know how to play.
Kate ¹¹_____ with us next Saturday! My brother can give ¹²_____ a lesson!

2 Read the dialogue again. Answer the questions.

1 When does Kate usually play tennis?
2 Where does she play tennis?
3 Who does she play with?
4 Does she usually win?
5 How do Kate and her brother get to the sports centre?
6 What does Kate's mum do at the sports centre?
7 Is Kate's brother a good player?
8 How often does Jenny play tennis?

3 Write questions for these answers. Use the question words in the box.

> how when who where how often what

1 I meet my friend Anna after school.
2 My mum works in a hospital.
3 I go swimming three times a week.
4 I usually have a sandwich for lunch.
5 I get to school by bus.
6 Jim gets up at seven thirty.

4 Circle the correct words in these sentences.

1 My sister **don't / doesn't** like computer games, but I love **they / them**!
2 That's your sister's DVD. **Give / Gives** it to **she / her**!
3 **Do / Does** your brother like soccer? **How / When** often does he play?
4 Bye! See you **on / at** Sunday. **Don't / Doesn't** be late!

Collocations

1 All these verbs are about using your hands. Match the verbs with the nouns. Make sentences, using the verbs and nouns.

1 catch ———————— at the door
2 knock a tube of toothpaste
3 shake to a friend
4 squeeze a ball
5 wave orange juice

Can you catch the ball?

Plurals

2 What are the plurals of these words? Use your dictionary to check.

1 foot *feet*   5 wife _____
2 baby _____   6 businesswoman _____
3 tooth _____   7 mouse _____
4 child _____   8 fireman _____

Idioms: parts of the body

3 What do the expressions in **bold** mean? Look up the parts of the body in the expressions.

1 Who's talking about me? My **ears are burning**!
   Someone's talking about me.
2 **Keep an eye on** your little sister. She sometimes runs out of the house, and the road is dangerous.
3 Tony's a good guitarist, but he doesn't practise enough. He doesn't want to be a musician. His **heart's not in it**.
4 I want to go out with my friends, but I've got hours and hours of homework to do. I'm **up to my neck** in work!
5 My brother always **looks down his nose at** me. He thinks he's better than me at everything!
6 After work, my dad likes to **put his feet up** and watch TV.

I CAN ...

Read the statements. Think about your progress and tick (✓) one of the boxes.

✳ I need more practice. ✳✳ I sometimes find this difficult. ✳✳✳ No problem!

	 ✳	 ✳✳	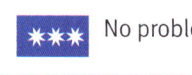 ✳✳✳
I can understand an article about sport.			
I can ask about people's hobbies and interests.			
I can talk about sports and hobbies.			
I can talk about daily routines.			
I can write an announcement for a club.			

● ● ○ ○ **Workbook: Self check pages 18–19**

VOCABULARY

1 Choose the correct ending.

1 My uncle is my …
   a father's brother.   b brother's father.
2 My grandmother is my …
   a father's mother.   b mother's father.
3 My niece is my …
   a daughter's sister.   b sister's daughter.
4 My cousin is my …
   a son's uncle.   b uncle's son.
5 My grandson is my …
   a daughter's son.   b son's daughter.

Mark [ ] /5

2 Write the plural form of these words.

1 wife _____   4 potato _____
2 husband _____   5 bus _____
3 photo _____   6 family _____

Mark [ ] /6

3 Complete the text.

My name is Angela. Mary and Jim are my mother and
[1]_____. My mother's brother is called John. John is my
[2]_____. John has got one child, David. David is my
[3]_____. My mother's mother and father, my [4]_____
and [5]_____, live in David's house. My sister has got two
children. Her daughter is my [6]_____ and her [7]_____ is
my nephew. I am their [8]_____.

Mark [ ] /8

4 Complete the sports and hobbies.

1 basket_ _ _ _   4 ice s _ _ _ _ _ _
2 computer g _ _ _ _   5 photog _ _ _ _ _
3 gymn_ _ _ _ _ _   6 rollerb _ _ _ _ _ _

Mark [ ] /6

5 Complete the sentences with the names of sports and hobbies.

1 There are eleven people on a _____ team.
2 We go _____ at the pool in town.
3 You play _____ with a friend or a computer!
4 I watch a lot of _____ on DVD.
5 I love _____ and I've got a good camera.
6 He often goes _____ on my bicycle!
7 In winter I go _____ on the lake.
8 He listens to _____ in his room.

Mark [ ] /8

GRAMMAR

1 Complete the sentences with the correct affirmative form of the verbs in the box.

get up	go	live	play	study	watch

1 My sister _____ French at school.
2 My brother and I _____ tennis.
3 My best friend _____ to a different school.
4 My dad _____ television every evening.
5 We _____ in Cambridge.
6 My mum _____ at six o'clock every morning.

Mark [ ] /6

2 Write two sentences in the present simple: affirmative (✓) and negative (✗).

1 they / listen to: ✗ chat shows ✓ the news
2 she / sit: ✗ next to Emma ✓ next to Sue
3 I / play: ✓ golf ✗ tennis
4 he / go: ✗ swimming ✓ cycling
5 they / come from: ✓ Jordan ✗ Egypt
6 she / teach: ✓ physics ✗ sport
7 he / speak: ✗ Welsh ✓ English
8 we / like: ✓ pizza ✗ rice

Mark [ ] /8

3 Complete the questions (1–6). Then match them with the answers (a–f).

1 _____ _____ you live?
2 _____ he like sport?
3 _____ _____ she study?
4 _____ _____ you get to school?
5 _____ she get up early?
6 _____ you know Lucas?

a History and German.
b No, she doesn't. She gets up late.
c Yes, he loves it.
d I walk.
e Yes, I do. He's in my class.
f In New York.

Mark [ ] /6

4 Rewrite the sentences to include the adverb of frequency in brackets.

1 I have cheese for breakfast. (often)
2 She's late for school. (hardly ever)
3 I play computer games. (often)
4 He does his homework on the bus. (never)
5 It's cold in January. (usually)
6 School finishes at quarter past four. (always)
7 We have lunch at school. (sometimes)

Mark [ ] /7   TOTAL [ ] /60

Sport in Australia

Sun, sea and sport!

Australians love sport. They play it, they talk about it and they watch it on TV. Australian weather is perfect for sport, and there are thousands of great beaches, so swimming is very popular. The population of Australia is only about 20 million, but many of the best sportsmen and sportswomen in the world come from Australia.

Young people in Australia are very active. More than 60% of children go to sports clubs. They also do activities with friends: for example, skateboarding, cycling and rollerblading.

The top four sports for boys are:

Activity	Participation (%)
football	22.2
swimming	15.7
tennis	9.5
cricket	9

Other popular sports for boys are basketball, martial arts, hockey and athletics.

The top four sports for girls are:

Activity	Participation (%)
swimming	17.5
tennis	7.8
basketball	6.9
gymnastics	5.4

Other popular sports for girls are football, athletics, martial arts, hockey and horse riding.

READ

Read the text and answer the questions.

1. What do Australians think of sport?
2. Why is swimming popular?
3. Which two sports are popular only with boys?
4. Which two sports are popular only with girls?

LISTEN

1. 🎧 (1.24) Listen to the information about swimmer, Ian Thorpe. Which Olympic Games are his medals from?

   a 2000   b 2004   c 2000 and 2004

2. 🎧 (1.24) Listen again. Are the sentences true or false?

   1. Ian Thorpe is from Sydney, Australia.
   2. He is very tall but he's got small feet.
   3. Ian's sister, Christina, is a tennis player.
   4. Ian is an Olympic champion and has got two gold medals.
   5. Ian holds two world records.
   6. Ian is interested in a lot of different sports.

WRITE AND SPEAK

1. How much do you know about Australia? Answer the questions.

   1. Can you name any Australian cities?
   2. Can you name any famous Australians?
   3. What's the name of the place in the photo? Why do people visit this place?

2. Work in groups. What sports and places are popular in your country? Write a 'top four' list of things for visitors to do.

3 School life

High flyers

BEFORE READING

Imagine that you don't have to go to school, and you study at home instead. What are the advantages and disadvantages of studying at home? Use the phrases in the box and your own ideas.

compare ideas   think   get up early   have fun
talk about your ideas   make friends   travel to school
discuss problems with the teachers

You don't have to get up early.
There isn't a gym.

READ

1 Read the *Reading tip*. Then look through the text quickly and find the answers to these questions.

  1 How many people live in Australia?
  2 How many Schools of the Air are there?
  3 How often do teachers visit their students?

Reading tip

When you're looking through a text for specific information, use subheadings to help you and read the first sentence of each paragraph.

2 🎧 ⌈1.25⌉ Read the text again. Then choose the best answers.

  1 Some students in Australia can't go to normal schools because
    a their parents work on farms.
    b they want to study unusual subjects.
    c they live hundreds of kilometres away from a school.
  2 There are about
    a 12,000 students in the Schools of the Air.
    b 1,000 students in the Schools of the Air.
    c 20 million students in the Schools of the Air.
  3 Once a week, students
    a send work to the teachers.
    b meet their teachers.
    c borrow books from the library.
  4 Students discuss their work with a teacher
    a on the phone.
    b by radio or on the internet.
    c once a year.
  5 A teacher and student meet when
    a the teacher visits the student's home.
    b the student visits the teacher's home.
    c they go to a school in the city.
  6 The Sports Carnival happens once a year and is
    a only for teachers.
    b compulsory.
    c optional.

THIS UNIT INCLUDES ●●●

Vocabulary • school subjects • in the classroom • prepositions of place • places in school • expressions with *take* • verbs for talking • capital letters • nouns from verbs • synonyms: big or small?
Grammar • *there is / there are* • *have to*
Skills • reading, listening and speaking about schools, subjects and timetables • describing a room
Writing • a note

SCHOOL OF THE AIR

Big country, small population

Australia is an enormous country, but it has a population of only 20 million. Some families live on big, isolated farms, hundreds of kilometres from a town or city. Children from these families can't travel to school every day, so many of them use a special school: the Australian School of the Air.

Schools without classrooms

There are twelve Schools of the Air in Australia and over 1,000 students use them. Students of the School of the Air study the same subjects as other Australian students, but they don't have lessons in classrooms with other students. They study at home on their own. The teachers

UNDERSTANDING IDEAS

Answer the questions. Look at the text, and use your own words and ideas.

1 Describe a typical day for a student of the School of the Air.
2 How do teachers check students' work?
3 Do you think life is easy or difficult for students of the School of the Air? Why?
4 Think of three or four things that a student's parents have to do.

at the School of the Air prepare lessons and send them to the students by post or email. The students have to work on these lessons for five or six hours a day, Monday to Friday. They send their work to the teachers once a week and discuss it by radio or over the internet. They can also borrow books from the school library. The books arrive by post.

A chance to meet

Once or twice a year, a teacher visits every student at home. The teacher spends a day with the student, helps them with their work and discusses problems. The teacher often has dinner with the family and stays for a night at the student's house. Teachers and students can also meet at the Sports Carnival. This takes place once a year on playing fields in Alice Springs. Students don't have to go, but it is a great way for them to do sport together and to make friends. 'I study on my own,' says one student, 'but I'm not lonely. My teachers are very friendly, and I chat to them quite often. I email other students most days, too. And I love the annual Sports Carnival!'

VOCABULARY

School of the air

1 Match the highlighted words in the text with these definitions.

1 A system for delivering letters and packages.
2 By themselves, not with other people.
3 A collection of books that students can use.
4 Happening once a year.
5 A long way from other people or places.
6 To take something for a short time (and give it back later).
7 Very big.
8 Unhappy because you are not with other people.
9 Maths, English, and the other things that you study at school.
10 To happen.
11 To go from one place to another.
12 To get ready.
13 To talk in a relaxed, friendly way.
14 To talk about something serious or important.
15 The number of people in a country.

2 Do you know these words?

carnival   kilometre   make friends   over   playing field
quite often   special   twice

●●●○   Workbook: page 20

School of the air
ACTIVATE

Complete these sentences with the words from the box.

> annual borrow chats discuss enormous isolated
> library lonely on his own population post prepare
> subject takes place travel

1 It's my grandma's birthday next week. She lives a long way away. I can't _____ to her house, so I want to send her a present by _____.
2 Russia is an _____ country. It takes about eight hours to fly across it. It has a _____ of about 145 million.
3 Tom lives in an _____ village in the country. He hasn't got any brothers or sisters, so he spends a lot of time _____. Sometimes he feels _____ at weekends, so he _____ to his friends on the phone.
4 There's a geography exam next month. I think geography is a difficult _____. I have to _____ for the exam. I think it's a good idea to visit the _____ so I can _____ some books.
5 Do you find the lessons difficult? Why don't you _____ it with the teacher?
6 Our school concert is an _____ event. It _____ in November every year.

EXTEND

Places in schools

1 These are some of the places you can find in a school. Complete the sentences, using the nouns.

> canteen corridor ~~gym~~ hall library playing fields
> staff room stairs

  1 You can do exercises and play basketball in the gym.
  2 You walk up or down the _____ to get to another floor.
  3 The whole school can meet in the _____.
  4 You can play football or hockey on the _____.
  5 Before you go into the classroom, you sometimes have to wait outside in the _____.
  6 When the teachers have a break, they usually go to the _____.
  7 You have lunch and snacks in the _____.
  8 Students can borrow books from the _____.

2 **Does your school have all these places? What other places are there in your school?**

Expressions with *take*

3 Match these sentences with the pictures.

 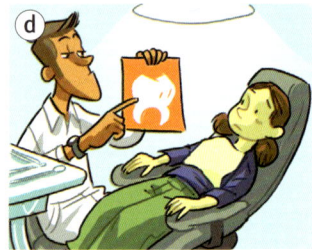
 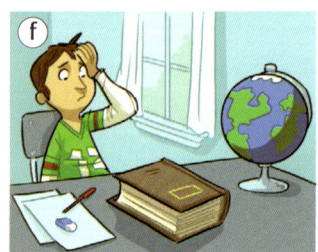

1 'I don't like it. Take it down!'   e
2 'I have to take it out.'   ____
3 'It looks terrible. Take it off!'   ____
4 'Don't take it apart!'   ____
5 'It's too long. I can't take it in.' ____
6 'Take it away!'   ____

Verbs for talking

4 **These verbs are used for different kinds of talking. Match them with the definitions.**

> shout announce discuss gossip whisper interview
> argue

1 To talk about something serious or important.
  discuss
2 To have an angry conversation with someone.
  _____
3 To talk very quietly to someone, so that other people can't hear.
  _____
4 To talk in a very loud voice.
  _____
5 To ask someone a list of questions.
  _____
6 To talk about other people's private lives.
  _____
7 To say something important to a large number of people.
  _____

●●●○○ Workbook: page 21

GRAMMAR

there is / there are
EXPLORE

1 Read the text. Which country is this classroom in?

Look around your own classroom. <mark>Are there</mark> any desks? <mark>Is there</mark> a noticeboard? The answer is probably yes. Schools in large cities in India are the same. But outside the cities, they're often very different. The children in the photo go to a small school in India. Their classroom is outside. <mark>There isn't</mark> a noticeboard. <mark>There's</mark> a desk for the teacher, but there aren't any desks for the children. In fact, <mark>there aren't</mark> any chairs – the children sit on the ground. But <mark>there are</mark> some books – and a lot of motivation!

2 Complete the table with the highlighted words from the text.

there is	there are
singular	**plural**
affirmative There's a teacher.	**affirmative** ¹_____ some students.
negative ²_____ a TV.	**negative** ³_____ any CDs.
interrogative ⁴_____ a noticeboard? No, there isn't.	**interrogative** ⁵_____ any children? Yes, there are.

LOOK OUT!

We use *Is there a / an …?* to ask about singular nouns.
We use *Are there any …?* to ask about plural nouns.

●●○○○ Grammar Reference: page 98

EXPLOIT

1 Look at the photo in Explore exercise 1 again. Complete the sentences with the correct form of *there is / there are*.

1 There are some students.
2 _____ a teacher.
3 _____ a computer.
4 _____ any posters.
5 _____ a noticeboard.
6 _____ a TV.
7 _____ any shelves.
8 _____ some trees.

2 Write sentences about your classroom. Use the words in the box and your own ideas.

> computer   shelves   desks   chairs   posters
> CD player   TV   noticeboard

There isn't a computer in our classroom.

3 Look at the picture of a bedroom and complete the questions with *Is there a / an …?* or *Are there any …?*

1 Is there a   bed?
2 _____ chairs?
3 _____ desk?
4 _____ CD player?
5 _____ shelves?
6 _____ TV?
7 _____ books?
8 _____ window?
9 _____ CDs?
10 _____ posters?
11 _____ bin?
12 _____ clock?
13 _____ plants?
14 _____ cupboard?

4 Ask and answer the questions in exercise 3. Use the prepositions from the box.

> behind   in front of   next to   near   on   under

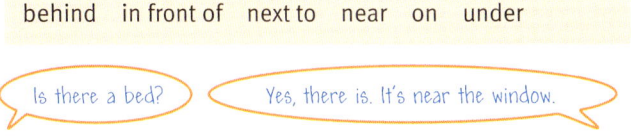

Is there a bed?   Yes, there is. It's near the window.

●●●○○ Grammar Builder: page 99

●●●○○ Workbook: page 22

Talking about school
VOCABULARY

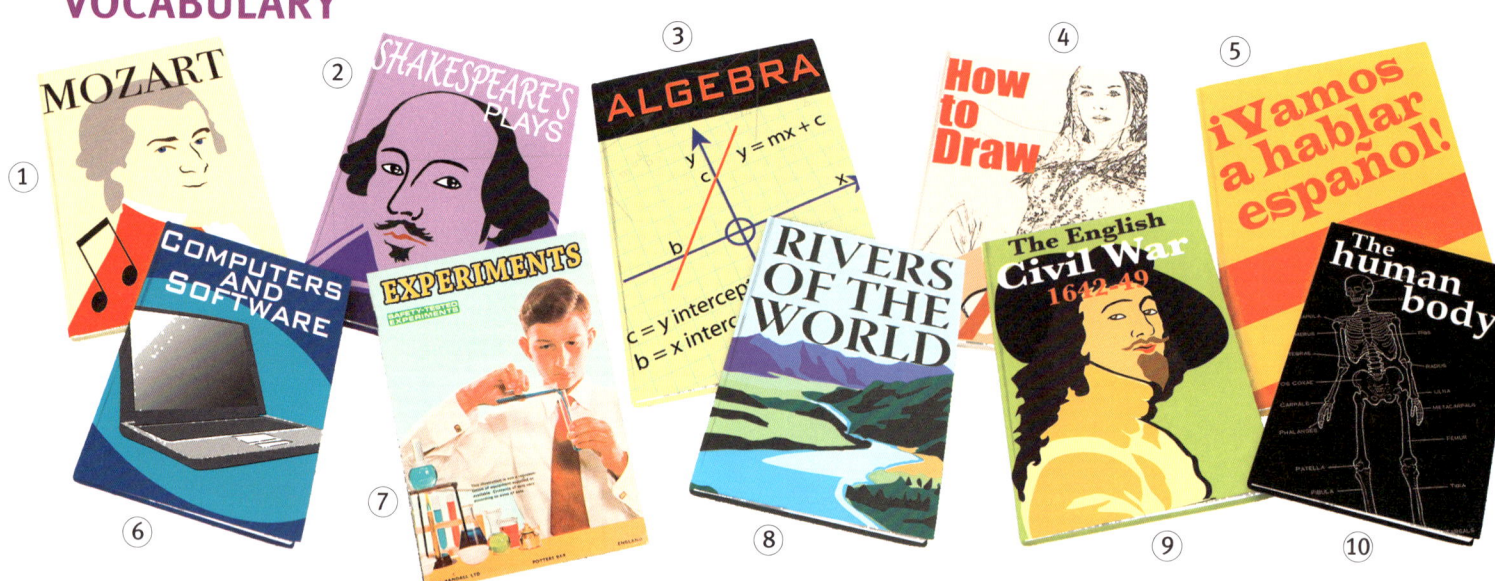

1 Match the textbooks with ten of the school subjects from the box.

1 music

School subjects Arabic   art and design   biology chemistry   design and technology (D.T.)   English French   geography   German   history information and communications technology (I.C.T.) maths   ~~music~~   physical education (P.E.)   physics science   Spanish

2 🎧 (1.26) Listen, repeat and check your answers.

3 Which of the subjects from exercise 1 do you study? Do you study any others that are not in the list?

(●●●●○ Workbook: page 23)

LISTEN

🎧 (1.27) Read the *Listening tip*. Then listen and complete the timetable for Mondays with school subjects from Vocabulary exercise 1.

Listening tip
When you listen, don't worry or stop if you miss an answer. Just move on to the next question. You'll have a chance to complete the missing answers when you listen again.

1	8.45–9.30	maths
2	9.35–10.20	
	10.25–10.45	MORNING BREAK
3	10.45–11.30	
4	11.35–12.20	
	12.20–1.30	LUNCH BREAK
5	1.30–2.15	
6	2.20–3.05	
7	3.10–3.55	

SPEAK

1 Work in pairs. Which subjects do you like? Ask and answer questions, using the phrases in the box to help you.

I love it. / It's great.   It's all right / OK / not bad.
I hate it. / I can't stand it.

(Do you like art and design?)   (It's OK.)

2 Write your perfect timetable for one day. Copy the timetable in Listen and complete it with your favourite subjects.

3 Work in pairs. Ask and answer questions about your partner's timetable. Can you copy it correctly?

(What lesson have you got at quarter to nine?)   (Art and design. What lesson have you got …?)

GRAMMAR

have to

EXPLORE

1 Read the text. What do students at Summerhill School have to do?

Summerhill School in England is a private school, and it's very different from most other schools. There is a timetable, but students don't have to go to the lessons. They sometimes play football instead! There's a meeting every week for all the children and teachers at the school, and they vote to decide the school rules there. The teachers and students all have to follow the rules. Does the head teacher have to follow the rules? Yes, she does!

2 Study the information in the *Learn this!* box. Complete the examples, using the highlighted words from the text in exercise 1.

LEARN THIS!

1 We use **have to** (or *has to*) to say that something is necessary or compulsory.
2 We use **don't have to** (or *doesn't have to*) to say that something is not necessary (but it isn't against the rules).

We ¹_____ be at school before 9 o'clock.
We ²_____ have lunch at school. Some people go home for lunch.
Do you have to study French? Yes, I do. / No, I don't.
³_____ she have to do P.E.? Yes, she ⁴_____. / No, she doesn't.

● ● ● ● ● Grammar Reference: page 98

EXPLOIT

1 Complete the sentences with the correct form of *have to*, affirmative or negative.

1 My brother has to wear a school uniform: black trousers and a green sweatshirt, but I _____ wear a uniform.
2 We _____ take exams every term – only at the end of the year.
3 I _____ be at school by 8.50 because the first lesson starts then.
4 We _____ study a foreign language: French, Spanish or German.
5 I don't like geography, but I _____ study it.
6 My sister is at a normal state school – she _____ pay.

2 🎧 (1.28) Listen, repeat and check your answers. How are the words *have to* (or *has to*) pronounced? Try to copy what you hear.

3 Look at the chart. Are these things compulsory or not compulsory at your school? Choose yes or no. Then write sentences with *have to* or *don't have to*.

We have to / don't have to wear a uniform.

		Compulsory?
1	wear a uniform	yes / no
2	study a foreign language	yes / no
3	take exams	yes / no
4	do homework	yes / no
5	get to school before 9.00	yes / no
6	stay at school after 3.00	yes / no

4 Read and complete one student's description of an ideal school. Use *have to* and *don't have to*.

We ¹don't have to get to school early in the morning – 10.30 or 11.00 is OK. We ²_____ wear a uniform – we can wear what we like. Every morning the teachers ³_____ ask the students what they want to study. There are classrooms, but we ⁴_____ go to lessons. We sometimes go to the computer room or the library instead. We ⁵_____ be quiet in the library – we can sit and talk with friends. There's a canteen where students have a snack or lunch. We ⁶_____ buy the food – it's all free.

5 Think about your ideal school. Write a short description, using *have to* and *don't have to*.

We don't have to....

● ● ● ● ● Grammar Builder: page 99

● ● ● ● ● Workbook: page 24

WRITING

A note
READ

1 Read the four parts of a note to a new student at a secondary school. Number them in the correct order.

☐ Lunch is at 12.30. You don't have to buy lunch in the canteen. There's a shop next to the gym and it sells sandwiches and other snacks.

☐ Lessons start at 8.45 in the morning, and you have to be at school before 8.30. There are four lessons in the morning, two before the morning break and two after the break. The morning break is from 10.20 to 10.50.

☐ Lessons start again at 1.45 and finish at 3.30. On Tuesdays, you have to go to the gym for P.E. before 1.45. On Thursdays school finishes an hour early, at 2.30.

☐ Welcome to Cheney Secondary School! I hope that you enjoy your first week.

2 Answer the questions about Cheney Secondary School.

1 What time do lessons start in the morning?
2 What time is the morning break?
3 Where is the shop?
4 When is P.E.?
5 When does school finish on most days?
6 When does school finish on Thursdays?

PREPARE

1 Read the *Writing tip* below. Write examples for each of the rules in the *Writing tip*.

Writing tip: punctuation
We use capital letters in English for:
• the personal pronoun *I*
• days and months
• names
• languages and nationalities
• towns and countries

2 Rewrite the sentences, using the correct capital letters.

1 the new school year starts on monday 6th september.
2 your first lesson on thursday is history.
3 our spanish teacher is from lima, in peru.
4 my brother james and i go to eton college.
5 our geography teacher's name is george white.

WRITE

1 Prepare a note for a new student at your school. Write down information about your school.

• lessons start – what time?
• lessons in the morning – how many?
• break – what time?
• lunch – where? what time?
• buy snacks, drinks – where?
• lessons finish – what time?
• sports and games – what? where? when?

2 Write the note, using the information in exercise 1.

Check your work
Have you
☐ used capital letters correctly?
☐ written 80–100 words?
☐ included all the information in exercise 1?

●●●○○ Workbook: page 25

School life
LANGUAGE SKILLS

1 🎧 (1.29) Complete the dialogue with the words from the box. Then listen and check your answers.

> a   any   are   aren't   don't   have   is   near   there   to

Nicola What's your school like? How many students ¹_____ there?

Carla It's quite a big school. There are about eight hundred students.

Nicola Do you ²_____ to wear a uniform?

Carla Yes, we do. We have to wear black skirts and white blouses.

Nicola What about sports? ³_____ there ⁴_____ gym?

Carla Yes, there is. We sometimes play basketball there. But my favourite sport is swimming. ⁵_____ isn't a swimming pool at the school, but there's a sports centre ⁶_____ the school, and we go there twice a week to use the pool.

Nicola And what's your favourite subject?

Carla I love French. We ⁷_____ have to study French – some students prefer to learn Spanish. But French is my favourite subject.

Nicola Are there ⁸_____ computers in your classroom?

Carla No, there ⁹_____. But the computer room is next ¹⁰_____ our classroom, so we go in there if we need to use the computers.

2 Read the dialogue again. Are these sentences true or false? Correct the false ones.

1 There are about eight thousand students at Carla's school.
2 Carla has to wear a uniform to school.
3 At Carla's school, the girls have to wear white skirts.
4 There's a gym at Carla's school.
5 There's a swimming pool at Carla's school.
6 The students at Carla's school have to study French.
7 French is Carla's favourite subject.
8 There are some computers in Carla's classroom.

3 Complete these questions.

1 What time _____ _____ _____ _____ get up?
2 _____ _____ _____ swimming pool at your school?
3 _____ you _____ _____ wear a uniform to school?

4 Rewrite these sentences, using the negative form of the verb.

1 There are some Chinese boys in my class.
2 We have to go to school seven days a week.
3 There's a TV in my bedroom.
4 My brother has to do homework every evening.
5 There are some students in the hall.

DICTIONARY CORNER

Exploring vocabulary: education

1 Match the definitions with words and phrases about education.

> ~~boarding school~~   field   head   public school   term

1 A school where students study, live and sleep. *boarding school*
2 The teacher in charge of a school.
3 An area of study or knowledge.
4 The period when students have classes at school.
5 A school where students have to pay to study.

Making nouns from verbs

2 Look up the verbs and find the noun form. Complete the sentences.

1 I want to **invite** Sarah to the party. Let's send her an *invitation*.
2 We have to **prepare** for the party next week. We have to do some _____.
3 We can **discuss** this problem with our teacher. We can have a _____.
4 He has to **pay** this bill. He has to make a _____.
5 I have to **revise** for the exam tomorrow. I have to do some _____.
6 My two brothers often **argue**. They often have an _____.
7 My dad likes to **collect** old coins. He has a good _____.

Synonyms: big or small?

3 These adjectives are about size. Put them in the correct column.

> colossal   ~~enormous~~   huge   little   massive   minute   tiny

big		small	
¹*enormous*		⁵_____	
²_____		⁶_____	
³_____		⁷_____	
⁴_____			

●●●○○ Workbook: Self check pages 26–27

4 Celebrate!

Time to celebrate!

BEFORE READING

Look at the photo of the woman. Read the *Speaking tip*. Then ask and answer the questions.

1 Where is the woman?
2 What's she doing?
3 What's she wearing?

READ

1 Read the text quickly and answer the questions.

1 What's Meg's job?
2 Does she like her job?

2 🎧 ⟨1.34⟩ Read the text again. Then choose the best answers.

1 Why do some people ask Meg to organize their party?
   a Because Meg's parties are always exciting.
   b Because they're very busy.
   c Because they've got a lot of money.
2 Meg can help people who want
   a a wedding party.
   b an unusual party.
   c all types of parties.
3 At the moment, Meg is organizing
   a a party for a person who lives on a Caribbean island.
   b a big party in a castle.
   c a party for a well known person.
4 Why doesn't Meg tell the interviewer the person's name?
   a She can't remember the name.
   b She's not allowed to.
   c She doesn't know the name.
5 What does Meg think of her job?
   a She enjoys it because she travels a lot.
   b She likes it, but it's boring sometimes.
   c It's difficult, but she enjoys it because it's interesting.

THIS UNIT INCLUDES ●●●●

Vocabulary • clothes • types of celebration • describing events • parts of speech • expressions with *get* • weddings • prefixes: opposites • idioms
Grammar • present continuous • *can / can't* • adverbs
Skills • reading and listening about organizing a celebration • describing clothes • talking about the clothes you are wearing
Writing • an invitation

Party planner

Meg Burton has an unusual job. She's a party planner. Our reporter, Jenny Lane, interviewed her.

Jenny **What do you do in your job, Meg?**
Meg I organize parties. Some people want a small, simple party, and they don't need any help. But other people want to have a big, extravagant wedding party, for example, in a memorable place. It takes a lot of time to organize a party like that. These days people don't have much time, so I do it for them.

Jenny **What kinds of parties do you organize?**
Meg Oh, all sorts of parties! Lots of people want to get married in a Scottish castle, for example. Most people love nature, and some people want to have parties outdoors. I sometimes organize parties in a forest or on a mountain.

Jenny **What other unusual places are popular?**
Meg Well, some people love swimming and diving, and they want to celebrate underwater! Believe it or not, trips in hot-air balloons are very popular for special occasions too! People want a day to remember.

Jenny **And how do you help?**
Meg Oh, there's a lot to do! I organize the invitations, the food, the music … sometimes the guests have to travel from another country, so I book flights for them.

Jenny **What are you doing at the moment?**
Meg I'm planning a party for a very well known person. He's English, but he's having a party abroad. He's flying to an island in the Caribbean next week. He's having a party in an enormous tent on the beach next to the sea.

Jenny **That's fantastic! Who is this well known person? And why is he having this big party?**
Meg Sorry! I can't tell you!

Jenny **Do you enjoy your job?**
Meg I love it. I have to work very hard and very fast, and there are always problems. But it's never boring!

UNDERSTANDING IDEAS

Answer the questions. Look at the text, and use your own words and ideas.

1 Meg tells the interviewer that there are always problems. What problems can happen when you're organizing a party?
2 Do you think it's expensive to organize a party? Why?
3 What kind of party is Meg organizing at the moment? Make a list of some of the things she has to do.

VOCABULARY

Party planner

1 Match the highlighted words in the text with these definitions.

1 In a different country, not in your own country.
2 The people at a party or celebration.
3 In the open air, not inside a building.
4 A large building that was built to defend people.
5 This is tall, and it's cold at the top.
6 To show that you are happy about something.
7 Worth remembering.
8 To keep something in your mind.
9 There are a lot of trees here.
10 Costing a lot of money.
11 To plan or arrange an event.
12 The opposite of 'slowly'.
13 You live in this when you're camping.
14 There's water all around this place.
15 To reserve a place – for example, on a flight or at a restaurant.

2 Do you know these words?

diving flight hot-air balloon nature special occasion
underwater wedding well known

> ●●●   Workbook: page 28

Party planner
ACTIVATE

Complete these sentences with the words from the box.

abroad book castle celebrate extravagant fast
forest guests island memorable mountain
organize outdoors remember tent

1 There are thousands of beautiful trees in that _____.
2 Cyprus is an _____ in the Mediterranean Sea.
3 Queen Elizabeth often spends the summer in a _____ in Scotland.
4 I want to fly to London next month. I have to _____ a ticket.
5 Who's that girl? I know her face, but I can't _____ her name.
6 We usually have a special dinner to _____ my grandmother's birthday.
7 Inviting a celebrity chef to prepare the food for the party was very _____, but it was a very _____ dinner!
8 Be careful! Don't drive too _____!
9 I'm not staying in this country for my holiday. I'm flying _____.
10 It's my brother's birthday next week. Let's _____ a celebration!
11 The weather's beautiful today. I don't want to stay at home. I want to go _____.
12 They're having a camping holiday. They're sleeping in a _____ next to the river.
13 This is a big wedding. There are a hundred _____!
14 Kilimanjaro is a very tall _____. It takes about five days to climb to the top.

EXTEND

Adjectives describing events

1 The vowels are missing from the adjectives in these sentences. Write the correct adjectives.

1 It's an **u n u s u a l** wedding. They're getting married in a park!
2 There are hundreds of people in this hall. It's **c r _ w d _ d**!
3 This is an **_ n c r _ d _ b l _** concert. The singer is brilliant!
4 What a **t _ r r _ b l _** match! Our team is playing really badly.
5 There are only three people in this restaurant. It's very **q _ _ _ t**.
6 It's an **_ m _ z _ n g** event. All my friends are here!
7 I can't stand this film. It's **b _ r _ n g**!
8 We're watching a **f _ s c _ n _ t _ n g** TV programme. It's about the pyramids.

Parts of speech

2 Find these words in the text on page 30. Are they used as verbs, adjectives, nouns or adverbs? Write the words in the correct box.

hard extravagant book island ~~remember~~ guest fast
memorable

verbs	1 remember	2 _____
adjectives	3 _____	4 _____
nouns	5 _____	6 _____
adverbs	7 _____	8 _____

3 Some English words can be used as verbs **and** nouns. Are the words in bold verbs or nouns?

1 That restaurant is always busy. You have to **book** if you want to eat there. verb
2 I'm reading a **book** about life in England.
3 There's a new car in your **drive**. Is that your brother's car?
4 My parents always **drive** carefully.
5 What have you got in your **hand**?
6 Can you **hand** me that DVD, please?
7 There's a fantastic film on TV tonight. Let's **watch** it!
8 I don't know what time it is. I haven't got my **watch** with me.

Expressions with *get*

4 Match the sentences with the pictures.

1 They're getting married. e
2 She's getting tired. ___
3 Get ready! ___
4 He gets dressed at seven thirty. ___
5 Get well soon! ___
6 They get together once a year. ___

●●●○○ Workbook: page 29

Present continuous
EXPLORE

1 🎧 (1.35) **Read and listen to the dialogue. Find examples of the present continuous.**

Jane	Hi Sue. Where are you?
Sue	I'm at Sarah's house, but I'm not having a good time.
Jane	Why not?
Sue	I don't know many people here.
Jane	Is Kate there?
Sue	Yes. She's chatting. What are you doing?
Jane	I'm sitting in the living room with my parents. We're watching TV. It's a boring documentary.
Sue	Do you want to meet up for a coffee?
Jane	Sure. Where shall we meet?
Sue	At the café near the cinema.
Jane	OK. I'm leaving the house now. See you in about fifteen minutes.

2 **Read the rule and complete the table with verbs from the text.**

Present continuous
Present continuous We form the present continuous with the verb *be* and the verb + *-ing*.
affirmative I'm ¹_____ the house now. She ²_____ chatting. We're ³_____ TV.
negative I ⁴_____ _____ having a good time.
interrogative What ⁵_____ _____ doing?
Use We use the present continuous to talk about actions that are happening now.

3 **Read the spelling rules for the present continuous in the *Look out!* box. Find more examples of the rules in the dialogue in exercise 1.**

LOOK OUT!

> **Spelling rules: verb + *-ing***
> - Most verbs: + *-ing*
>   *watch → watching*
> - Verbs ending in *-e: e → -ing*
>   *write → writing*
> - Verbs ending in short vowel + consonant: double consonant + *-ing*
>   *swim → swimming*

●●○○○ Grammar Reference: page 100

EXPLOIT

1 **Write true sentences about what is happening now. Use the present continuous, affirmative or negative.**

1 I / wear a sweatshirt
   I'm wearing a sweatshirt. / I'm not wearing a sweatshirt.
2 I / sit next to my friend
3 the teacher / smile
4 we / study / maths
5 the sun / shine
6 I / wear / trainers
7 my parents / work
8 my friends and I / eat

2 **Ask and answer questions about the people in the picture. Use verbs from the box.**

> carry   chat   drink   eat   laugh   play   sit   smile   stand   walk   wear

What's the woman doing?   *She's carrying a baby.*

3 **Write a short description of one of the people in the photo. Include this information:**

- his or her physical appearance (tall, short, short / long hair, etc.)
- his or her clothes
- what he or she is doing

David has short hair ...

●●●○○ Grammar Builder: page 101

●●●○○ Workbook: page 30

Describing clothes
VOCABULARY

1 Match the clothes in the picture with the words from the box. Which items aren't illustrated?

Clothes blouse boots cap cardigan dress headscarf jacket jeans jumper shirt shoes shorts skirt socks sweatshirt T-shirt tie top tracksuit bottoms trainers trousers

2 🎧 1.36 Listen, repeat and check your answers.

3 Match the clothes in the picture with the colours.

Colours pink red purple blue green yellow orange brown white grey black

Sally's blouse is red.

4 Write some questions about what the people in the picture are wearing.

Who's got a ...?
What colour is ...?

5 Play a memory game. Look at the picture in exercise 1 for a minute and then close your book. Try and answer your questions in exercise 4.

Who's got a pink dress?   Laila

6 Write sentences describing three people in the picture in exercise 1.

Sally is tall. She has got black hair and a red blouse.

●●●●● Workbook: page 31

LISTEN

1 🎧 1.37 Listen to four teenagers talking about their clothes. Which two have to wear a uniform for school?

1 David   2 Maria   3 Peter   4 Fiona

2 🎧 1.37 Listen again. What do they wear when they go out with friends? Complete the sentences with the correct clothes.

1 David usually wears _____ or jeans, and a sweatshirt or a _____.
2 Maria wears jeans or a _____, and sometimes a _____ if it's a special occasion.
3 Peter usually wears a _____ and a jacket, and _____.
4 Fiona usually wears jeans and a _____, and sometimes a _____ if it's cold.

SPEAK

1 Work in pairs. Ask and answer the questions.

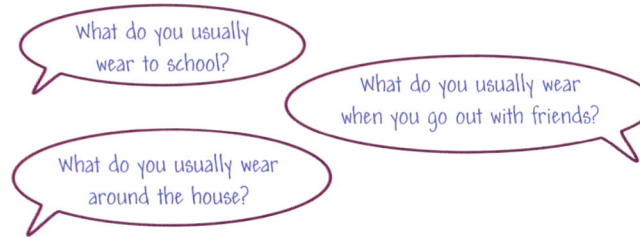

What do you usually wear to school?

What do you usually wear when you go out with friends?

What do you usually wear around the house?

2 Imagine you are going on one of these holidays. What clothes do you take?

1 A trip across the desert.
2 A beach holiday.
3 A trip to the mountains.

can and adverbs
EXPLORE

1 Read the text and find examples of *can*.

Sarah Michelle Prinze is an American actress. As an actress she can do lots of things that she can't do in real life, but she can do martial arts in real life. She's very good at martial arts. She's got a brown belt in tae kwon do. What else can she do? She really likes sport. She can ice-skate really well and she can rollerblade.

2 Complete the table with the correct forms of *can*.

can
affirmative
I / You / He / She / It / We / They can sing.
negative
I / You / He / She / It / We / They ¹_____ sing. (Full form: *cannot*)
interrogative and short answers
²_____ I / you / he / she / it / we / they sing? Yes, I can. / No, I can't.
Use
We use *can* to talk about ability.

3 Read the *Learn this!* box. Do you know any other adjectives that don't change?

LEARN THIS!

Adverbs

1 We form most adverbs by adding *-ly* to the adjective.
slow→slowly careful→carefully easy→easily

2 Some adjectives don't change.
fast late early

3 The adverb form of *good* is *well*.

4 We use adverbs with verbs to say how something happens.
He drives slowly. She can sing beautifully.

● ○ ○ ○ Grammar Reference: page 100

EXPLOIT

1 Complete the sentences. Use *can* and *can't* and the verbs from the box.

> count do play ~~ride~~ talk type drive speak swim

1 Jake can ride a bike but he _____ a car.
2 I don't like computers because I _____ very well.
3 She's a good sportsperson. She _____ volleyball and she _____ gymnastics.
4 He _____ French, but he wants to learn.
5 She's only three years old but she _____ from one to twenty.
6 I have swimming lessons every Saturday, but I _____ very well!
7 Emily is one year old. She can walk but she _____.

2 Complete each sentence with an adverb from the *Learn this!* box.

1 He's a slow driver. He drives slowly.
2 This is important, so listen _____.
3 I've got an exam tomorrow so I have to go to bed _____.
4 We're waiting for Jim. He always arrives _____.
5 She's good at volleyball. She plays very _____.
6 The exam isn't difficult. All the students pass _____.

3 Complete the table. Tick the things that you can do.

		You	Your partner
1	play chess well		
2	type quickly		
3	speak Japanese fluently		
4	remember names easily		
5	run fast		
6	do maths easily		
7	read quickly		
8	eat chocolate slowly		

4 Complete the table for your partner.

Can you play chess well?   Yes, I can. / No, I can't.

5 Write about what you and your partner *can* and *can't* do, using the table in exercise 3. Tell the class.

We can both play chess well.
Hana can type quickly, but I can't.
We can't speak Japanese fluently.

● ○ ○ ○ Grammar Builder: page 101
● ○ ○ ○ Workbook: page 32

WRITING

An invitation
READ

1 Look at the photo and answer the questions.

1 Where is the boy?
2 What is he wearing?
3 What is he doing?

2 Read the emails. Match the invitations with three types of event from the box.

> football match   graduation party   picnic   dinner
> volleyball match   ice skating   barbecue   film

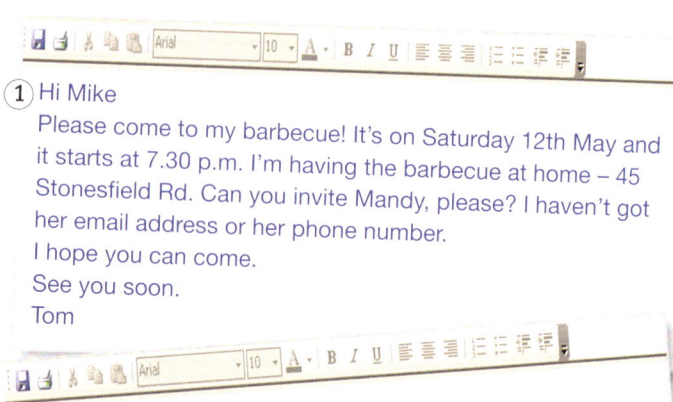

① Hi Mike
Please come to my barbecue! It's on Saturday 12th May and it starts at 7.30 p.m. I'm having the barbecue at home – 45 Stonesfield Rd. Can you invite Mandy, please? I haven't got her email address or her phone number.
I hope you can come.
See you soon.
Tom

② Dear Kate,
Jess and I are going for a walk next Monday – it's a holiday, so we're not going to school! We're walking to Old Park, and then we're having a picnic. We're meeting at about 10 o'clock at my house. Can you come with us? Can you bring something to eat?
I hope to see you there.
Love
Sally

③ Liam
Dave and I are organizing a volleyball competition next Saturday afternoon, starting at two o'clock. It's at Newtown Sports Centre. Can you bring your trainers?
Hope you can come.
Cheers
Joe

PREPARE

1 Study the information in the *Look out!* box. Find three examples of *can* for requests in the invitations.

LOOK OUT!

> **can for requests**
> We can use *can* for requests.
> *Can you help me, please?*

2 Put the information below in the order that it appears in the invitations.

- [ ] the time
- [ ] the event
- [ ] the place
- [ ] extra information or request
- [ ] the day

3 Find two different ways of starting an email, and three ways of finishing an email.

4 Read the *Writing tip*. Find five mistakes in this invitation.

> **Writing tip: finding mistakes**
> When you have finished a piece of writing, ask your partner to look for mistakes. It's often easier to find mistakes in somebody else's work.

> Dear Tina
> We're play tennis in Saturday. The match start at ten therty. After the match we're having lunch at my house. I hope you can to come.
> Love
> Anna

WRITE

1 Write an invitation. Include this information:

- the event (for example a game, meal or party)
- when it starts (time / day)
- the place
- some extra information or a request

2 Work in pairs. Swap your invitations. Check each other's work for mistakes and help each other to correct them.

> **Check your work**
> **Have you**
> - [ ] included all the information in exercise 1?
> - [ ] used *can* for requests correctly?
> - [ ] written 40–60 words?

●○○○○ Workbook: page 33

Celebrate!
LANGUAGE SKILLS

1 🎧 (1.38) Complete the dialogue with the words from the box. Then listen and check your answers.

> let's   well   can   good   at   are   can't   watch   watching   do

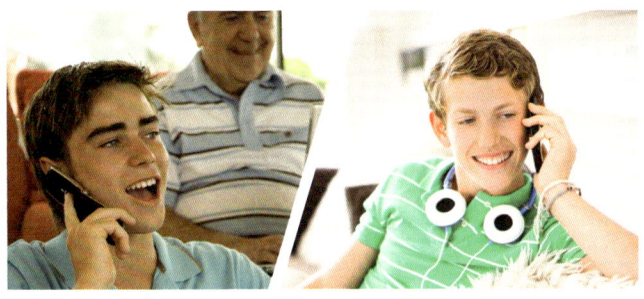

Jim	Hi, Martin. How are you? What ¹_____ you doing?
Martin	Hi, Jim. I'm fine. I'm at the sports stadium with Terry. We're ²_____ a football match.
Jim	Wow! Who's playing?
Martin	It's Newtown against Stamford. It's a ³_____ match! Newtown are winning. They're playing ⁴_____. It's 2–0.
Jim	⁵_____ you want to come to my house this afternoon?
Martin	I'm sorry, I ⁶_____. I'm visiting my grandfather after the match. What about this evening?
Jim	OK. ⁷_____ meet at my house ⁸_____ eight o'clock. We can ⁹_____ a DVD.
Martin	¹⁰_____ Terry come with me?
Jim	Of course he can. See you later. Bye!
Martin	Bye, Jim!

2 Read the dialogue again, and then correct the mistakes in these sentences.

1 Terry and Martin are watching a volleyball match.
2 Newtown are playing badly.
3 Martin is visiting his grandmother after the match.
4 Jim and Martin are meeting at seven o'clock this evening.
5 Terry can't go to Jim's house in the evening.

3 Circle the correct words in the email.

Hi Mary
How are you? I'm working ¹ **hard** / **hardly** right now.
² I **study** / **I'm studying** French. There's an exam tomorrow. I'm worried! I can't write French very ³ **good** / **well**. The spelling is difficult! I'm trying to learn a lot of new words, but it's ⁴ **noisy** / **noisily** in my house. My brother ⁵ **is playing** / **plays** the guitar right now. He always plays ⁶ **loud** / **loudly**! ⁷ **I don't** / **I'm not** like his music. What about you? Are you studying too? Or ⁸ **do** / **are** you enjoying yourself? Write soon!
Love
Anna

Exploring vocabulary: weddings

1 Match the definitions with these words about weddings.

~~bride~~   bridegroom   honeymoon   reception

1 The woman who is getting married. *bride*
2 The man who is getting married.
3 The party after the wedding.
4 The holiday after the wedding.

Prefixes: opposites

2 Find the opposites of these adjectives. Use the prefixes from the box.

dis- im- un- in- ir-

1 formal	*informal*	5	polite	_____
2 honest	_____	6	possible	_____
3 memorable	_____	7	regular	_____
4 necessary	_____	8	reliable	_____

Useful idioms

3 These sentences are about events, holidays and celebrations. What do the expressions in bold mean?

1 'Did you **make it** to the match? I was ill, so in the end I couldn't go.' *manage to go to*
2 The match starts at two o'clock **on the dot**. Don't be late!
3 It takes a lot of time to organize a wedding, and it **costs a fortune**!
4 I'm on holiday next week, but I'm not going anywhere. I'm **taking it easy**.
5 I had to make a speech at my sister's wedding. I was so nervous I **had butterflies** about it all day.

I CAN ...

Read the statements. Think about your progress and tick (✓) one of the boxes.

✴	I need more practice.	✴✴	I sometimes find this difficult.	✴✴✴	No problem!

	✴	✴✴	✴✴✴
I can understand a magazine article and describe photos.			
I can describe what is happening in a picture.			
I can describe what someone is wearing.			
I can say how well I can do something.			
I can write an invitation to a party.			

●●● Workbook: Self check pages 34–35

VOCABULARY

1 Complete the school subjects with the endings in the box.

| aphy   ic   ics   istry   ology   sign   tion   tory |

1 mus_____
2 phys_____
3 chem_____
4 physical educa_____
5 information and communications techn_____
6 geogr_____
7 art and de_____
8 his_____

Mark ___ **/8**

2 Write the names of the school subjects.

1 *Hola. Me llamo Jordi. Soy de Barcelona.* S _____
2 If w=5, d=20 and h=5, then V = 5×20×5 = 500.
  m _____
3 Columbus discovered America in 1492. h _____
4 To make this we need some pens, paper and paints.
  a _____ and d _____
5 We make the negative form with *don't* / *doesn't* and the base form of the verb. E _____
6 Now, I want you to use this computer to control this machine. d _____ and t _____

Mark ___ **/8**

3 Complete the words for clothes. Use *a, e, i, o* and *u.*

1 tr _ cks _ _ t
2 tr _ _ s _ rs
3 tr _ _ n _ r s
4 j _ _ ns
5 b _ _ ts
6 sk _ rt
7 j _ mp _ r
8 sw _ _ tsh _ rt

Mark ___ **/8**

4 Complete the lists.

1 Things you wear on your feet: socks, _____ and _____.
2 Clothes only a girl wears: a blouse, a _____ and a _____.
3 A thing you wear on your head: a _____.
4 Things men sometimes wear with a shirt: a jacket and a _____.
5 Trousers you wear to play sport: shorts and _____.
6 Tops that a lot of young people wear with jeans: a sweatshirt or a _____.

Mark ___ **/6**

GRAMMAR

1 Write sentences with *there is / are*, affirmative (✓) and negative (✗).

1 a cupboard ✓   any shelves ✗
2 a gym ✗   a playing field ✓
3 a computer room ✓   a library ✗
4 any DVDs ✗   some videos ✓
5 a cinema ✓   a museum ✗
6 a café ✓   any restaurants ✗

Mark ___ **/6**

2 Write sentences with *have to*, affirmative (✓) and negative (✗). Use the prompts below.

1 Jack / do the washing ✗
2 Sue and Jenny / walk to school ✓
3 Karen / do a lot of homework ✗
4 my dad / get up early ✓
5 my grandparents / work ✗
6 their mum / cook dinner every night ✓

Mark ___ **/6**

3 Complete the sentences with the present continuous of the verbs in brackets.

1 She _____ to her friend. (chat)
2 They _____ their dinner. (not eat)
3 The dog _____ in the river. (swim)
4 I _____ a letter. (write)
5 He _____ to me. (not listen)
6 We _____ for our maths exam. (study)

Mark ___ **/6**

4 Write sentences using *can* or *can't.*

1 Lucy / play tennis ✗
2 Linda and Sarah / speak Italian ✓
3 I / do martial arts ✓
4 my sister / cook ✗
5 his cousins / swim ✗
6 your aunt / play the paino ✓

Mark ___ **/6**

5 Rewrite the sentences using the adverb from the adjective in brackets.

1 He's walking. (slow)
2 She's singing. (good)
3 They're playing football. (bad)
4 He speaks Chinese. (perfect)
5 She's eating. (fast)
6 I'm speaking. (quick)

Mark ___ **/6**   **TOTAL** ___ **/60**

Schools in England
READ

1 Look at the chart. How many years of compulsory education are there in England? Is this the same in your country?

The English Education System			
School	Number of years	Age	Compulsory?
Nursery	2	3 to 4	No
Primary	6	5 to 10	Yes
Secondary	5	11 to 16	Yes
College	2	17 to 18	No

2 Read the text. Match the paragraphs with three of the headings.

a Types of secondary school
b Subjects at secondary school
c University education
d British primary schools
e Exams at 16 and 18 years old

Secondary education in England

☐ In England, children start secondary school at the age of 11. In the first two years of secondary school, all the students study the same 12 subjects. They are: English, maths, science, design and technology, information and communication technology, history, geography, a foreign language, art and design, music, citizenship and P.E. When students are 14, they can choose the subjects that they like, but some subjects (e.g. maths, English, science and P.E.) are still compulsory.

☐ At the age of 15–16, students take national exams called GCSEs (General Certificate of Secondary Education exams). After these exams, about 25% of students leave school and find jobs. The other 75% stay at school. They study two, three or four school subjects and take advanced level exams ('A levels') when they are 18.

☐ Most students in England (about 90%) go to state secondary schools. State schools are free. The other 10% go to private schools. Some of these schools are very famous – and very expensive. For example, it costs about £24,000 a year to study at Eton College!

3 Are these sentences true for England? Then say what is true in your country.

1 Education is compulsory between the ages of 5 and 16.
2 Students start secondary school when they are 13 years old.
3 Students take national exams when they are 12 and 17 years old.
4 Most students go to state schools.
5 All students stay at school until they are 18 years old.
6 English is a compulsory subject at all secondary schools.
7 Some students go to private schools.

LISTEN

1 🎧 (1.41) Listen to two teenagers talking about their schools. Choose the correct answer.

1 Nick and Stephanie wear a school uniform.
2 Nick and Stephanie don't wear school uniforms.
3 Nick wears a uniform, but Stephanie doesn't.

2 🎧 (1.41) Listen again. Complete the table.

	Nick	Stephanie
Name of school	Abingdon	Oaklands
Private or state?		
Number of students		
Number of teachers		
Mixed (boys and girls)?	yes / no	yes / no
Wants to leave when?		

WRITE AND SPEAK

1 Answer the questions.

1 Is your school a state school or a private school?
2 How many students are there in your class?
3 How many teachers have you got?
4 Is it a mixed school (for both boys and girls)?
5 Do you wear a uniform?

2 Work in pairs. Make a chart for your country like the chart in Read exercise 1.

5 Wild!

Dangerous!

BEFORE READING

Answer the questions with a partner.
1. Make a list of dangerous animals and compare your list with your partner's. Do you have the same animals?
2. Do you know the names in English of the animals in your lists?
3. Are there dangerous animals in your country?

READ

1. Look through the text quickly and match the photos (1–3) with paragraphs (A–C). Where can you find these animals?

1 _____ 2 _____ 3 _____

THIS UNIT INCLUDES ●●●●
Vocabulary • geographical features • continents • prepositions of place • holiday accommodation • compound adjectives • suffixes: *-ful*, *-y*, *-able*, *-ly* • animals • synonyms: extreme adjectives • compound nouns: nature • holiday words
Grammar • comparative adjectives • superlative adjectives
Skills • reading an article • listening to a radio quiz • asking and answering quiz questions • giving opinions • describing a landscape
Writing • a postcard

2. 🎧 1.42 Read the text again and choose the best answers.

1. The hippos in cartoons are
   a like the hippos in real life.
   b very dangerous.
   c nice animals.
2. Hippos
   a run faster than people.
   b eat grass all day.
   c kill other African animals.
3. A box jellyfish's tentacles
   a are 60 centimetres long.
   b can hurt people a lot.
   c can kill a shark.

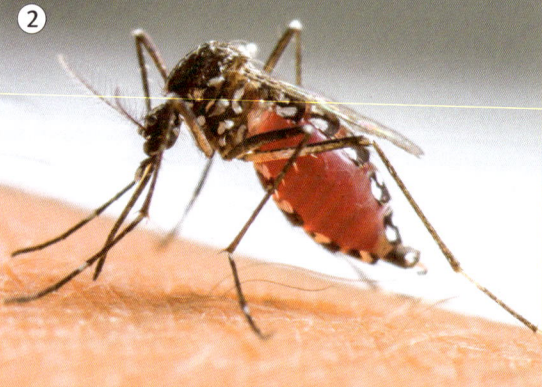

The world's deadliest animals

What do you think are the most dangerous animals in the world? Sharks? Snakes? Lions? These animals are very dangerous, it's true, but they are certainly not the most dangerous.

A Hippos

In cartoons, hippos are usually slow, happy and comical. But real hippos are bad-tempered and aggressive, and are certainly more dangerous than lions and tigers. Hippos spend all day in the mud of rivers and lakes, but they leave the water at dusk to eat 68 kilograms of grass. Hippos are very heavy – some are about 3,000 kilos. However, they can run faster than an Olympic sprinter and they don't like people. Hippos kill more people in Africa than any other animal.

B Box jellyfish

When people think of dangerous animals in the sea, they usually think of sharks. But sharks hardly ever kill people. The most dangerous sea animal isn't very big. It's a small jellyfish. The body of the box jellyfish is about 20 centimetres long. But it has got about 60 tentacles – and they are about three metres long. A sting from one of these tentacles is very painful and it can kill a human very quickly. Box jellyfish swim in the seas around Australia from October to April. When the jellyfish are there, nobody goes swimming.

C Mosquitoes

The animal with the most dangerous bite isn't a snake or a lion. It's an insect and you can find it all over the world: the mosquito. Mosquitoes take people's blood and they also give malaria to over 300 million people every year. Sadly, about three million of these people die. Forty per cent of the world's population is always in danger of malaria from mosquitoes. The mosquito is the world's most dangerous animal – and it's also one of the smallest. However, it's one of the strongest, too. Mosquitoes can fly for four hours continuously and they often travel 10 kilometres a night.

4 There are mosquitoes
   a in every country.
   b that eat people.
   c that bite lions and snakes.

5 The mosquito
   a kills forty per cent of the world's population.
   b can fly for a long time.
   c gives malaria to animals.

Reading tip
When you scan a text for numbers, remember that they can be written as words or figures, depending on the type of text.

3 Read the *Reading tip*. Find these numbers in the text. What do they refer to?

1 twenty *centimetres – the body of the box jellyfish is about 20 cm long.*
2 three hundred million
3 three thousand
4 three million
5 sixty-eight
6 sixty

UNDERSTANDING IDEAS

Answer the questions. Look at the text, and use your own words and ideas.

1 The text says hippos in cartoons and hippos in real life are very different. Can you think of any other animals that are in cartoons? Are they very different to the animals in real life? How?
2 Most people think hippos are slow, but they are very fast. What other things do you think are unusual about these three animals?
3 Can you think of another animal that people think is nice but that is dangerous?

VOCABULARY

The world's deadliest animals

1 Match the highlighted words in the text with these definitions.

1 In a way that shows you feel unhappy.
2 A runner who takes part in short fast races.
3 Hurting.
4 A small animal with six legs, and often with wings.
5 Very soft wet earth.
6 Films made with moving drawings.
7 In a way that happens without stopping.
8 A painful place on a person's body made by an insect or animal.
9 Angry and ready to attack.
10 Becoming angry very easily.
11 At the end of the day just before it becomes dark.
12 Long, thin parts like legs that some sea animals have.
13 The sharp pain that you feel when an animal, insect or plant hurts you.
14 The red liquid that is in a person's body.
15 To make a person or animal die.

2 Do you know these words?

certainly   comical   grass   hippopotamus   kilogram   malaria   per cent

3 🎧 (1.43) Match the photos with the words from the box. Listen, repeat and check your answers.

Wildlife   bear   eagle   elephant   hippo   jellyfish   lion   mosquito   shark   snake   tiger   whale

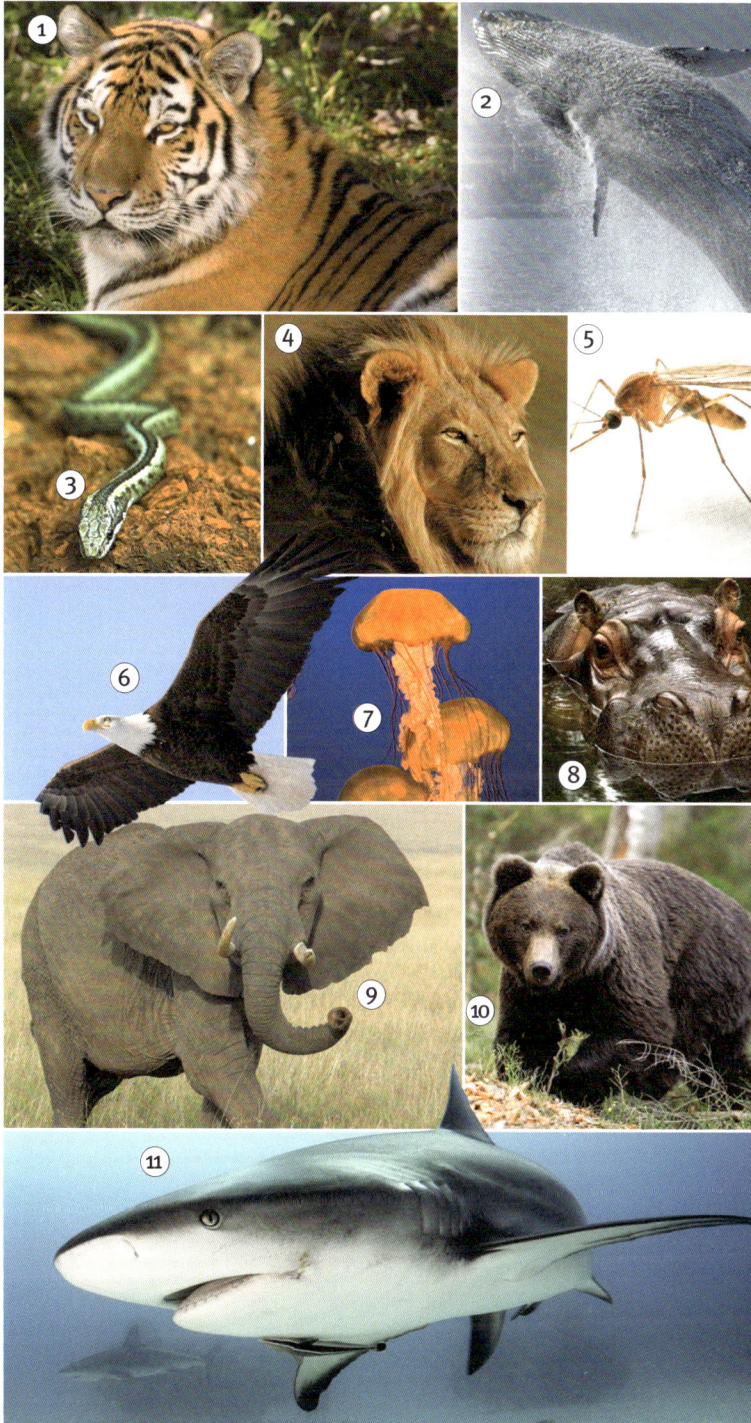

●●○○   Workbook: page 36

The world's deadliest animals
ACTIVATE

Complete these sentences with the words from the box.

> aggressive bad-tempered bite blood cartoons
> continuously dusk insects kill mud painful sadly
> sprinter sting tentacles

1 That plant is dangerous. A _____ from it can be very _____. It hurts a lot.
2 These _____ start to fly into people's houses at _____, when the sun goes down.
3 When I play rugby, my sports clothes are very dirty; they're full of _____. My mum becomes _____ when she sees them!
4 He never stops training and he runs _____. He wants to be a _____ for his country in the next Olympic Games.
5 She really likes watching _____. She's watching one now about a sea animal with long _____ that takes people's things from the beach.
6 Be careful with that dog. It's always angry and _____. Look at this _____ on my leg!
7 I go to the hospital to give _____ every month. _____, not many people do it and the doctors say they need more donors.
8 All jellyfish have painful stings, but not all of them can _____ humans.

EXTEND

Compound adjectives

1 Match the words on the left with the words on the right to make compound adjectives.

1	bad-	a	handed
2	well	b	working
3	second-	c	written
4	left-	d	hand
5	badly-	e	known
6	first-	f	tempered
7	good-	g	class
8	hard-	h	looking

Suffixes

2 Make the words in the box into adjectives by adding the correct suffix.

> friend help wash pain cloud rain enjoy live

-ful	-y	-able	-ly
painful	1_____	2_____	3_____
4_____	5_____	6_____	7_____

3 Complete the sentences with adjectives from exercise 2.

1 My dad's very friendly. He knows a lot of people.
2 You never see the sun in England. It's always _____.
3 My brother's really _____. I always speak to him when I have a problem.
4 I was at the dentist's this morning and my tooth hurts. It's quite _____.
5 His books are _____. We really like them.
6 Take an umbrella with you. It's _____ today.
7 You can't put this coat in the washing machine. It isn't _____.
8 She's really _____ and she's always playing sport.

Animals

4 Match the photos with the words in the box.

> lobster eagle goat parrot bee ox prawn bear
> rhinoceros whale octopus bat

5 Put the animals in the correct groups. How many more animals can you add to each group?

Land	Sea	Air
ox		

●●●○○ Workbook: page 37

GRAMMAR

Comparative adjectives
EXPLORE

1 Read the text. Underline the adjectives comparing the African elephant and the Asian elephant.

What is the difference between African and Asian elephants? African elephants are larger and heavier than Asian elephants, and they've got bigger ears. However, Asian elephants are more intelligent and better at following instructions.

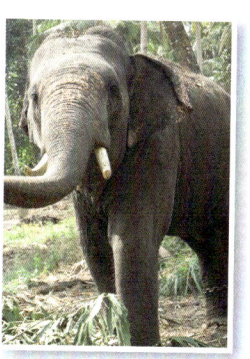

2 Complete the table with comparative adjectives from the text.

Short adjective	Comparative	Rule
long	longer	+ -er
large	¹_____	+ -r
heavy	²_____	-y → -ier
hot	hotter	double consonant + -er

Long adjective	Comparative	Rule
intelligent	³_____	*more* + adjective

Irregular adjective	Comparative	
good	⁴_____	
bad	worse	
far	further	

than

We use *than* to make comparisons.
Sue is taller than me.

● ● ● ● ● **Grammar Reference: page 102**

EXPLOIT

1 Complete the sentences with the comparative form of the adjectives in brackets.
1 Which ocean is *wider*, the Atlantic or the Pacific? (wide)
2 Which planet is _____ from the sun, Jupiter or Saturn? (far)
3 Which animals are _____, hippos or dolphins? (dangerous)
4 Which country is _____, Russia or Canada? (big)
5 Which animals are _____, cats or horses? (fast)
6 Which metal is _____, gold or silver? (expensive)
7 Which is _____, a litre of water or a litre of ice? (heavy)

2 Answer the questions in exercise 1.

The Pacific is wider than the Atlantic Ocean.

3 Look at the chart below and write sentences about the places. Use the comparative form of these adjectives and *than*.

1 cold	4 high
2 dry	5 hot
3 big	6 wet

1 The Atacama Desert is colder than the Arabian Desert.

	The Atacama Desert	The Arabian Desert
How much rain?	0–0.1 mm	35 mm
How hot? (maximum)	25° C	50° C
How cold? (minimum)	0° C	5° C
How high? (maximum)	2,400 m	3,700 m
How big?	181,300 km²	2,330,000 km²

Atacama Desert (Chile)

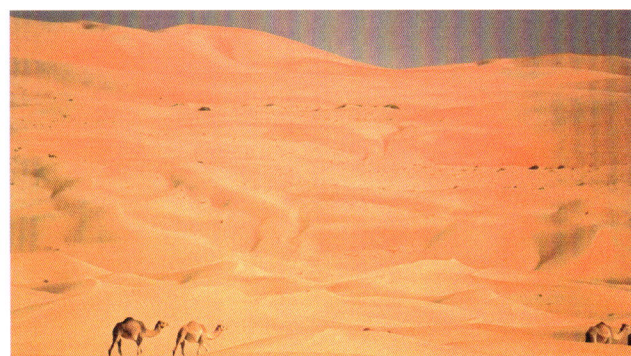

Arabian Desert

4 Compare places that you know. Use the comparative form of adjectives from the box.

beautiful big boring exciting
friendly hot small wet

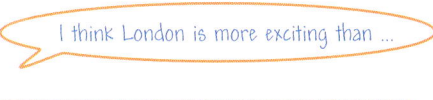

I think London is more exciting than …

● ● ● ● ● **Grammar Builder: page 103**

● ● ● ● ● **Workbook: page 38**

Our world
VOCABULARY

1 Match the photos with words from the box. Which word is not illustrated?

1 – island, sea

Geographical features beach desert forest hill ~~island~~ lake mountains ocean rainforest river ~~sea~~ valley waterfall

2 🎧 (1.44) Listen, repeat and check your answers.

> **1** We usually use *the* with
>   **a** the names of seas and oceans, rivers and deserts.
>   *the Mediterranean, the Nile, the Sahara Desert*
>   **b** the names of groups of islands and hills or mountains.
>   *the Canary Islands, the Cotswolds, the Himalayas*
> **2** We don't usually use *the* with the names of lakes, beaches, or single hills or mountains.
>   *Lake Garda, Bondi Beach, Primrose Hill, Mount Sinai*

3 🎧 (1.45) Complete the names of the places with the geographical features from the box. Listen and check your answers.

Desert island Lake Mountains ~~rainforest~~ River Sea

1 the Amazon rainforest
2 the Black _____
3 the _____ of Tasmania
4 the Atlas _____
5 the Euphrates _____
6 the Gobi _____
7 _____ Superior

4 🎧 (1.46) Listen and repeat the names of the continents.

Continents Africa Asia Australia Europe North America South America

5 Where are the places in exercise 3? Ask and answer, using the continents from exercise 4.

Where's the Amazon rainforest?

It's in …

● ● ● ○ ○ **Workbook: page 39**

LISTEN

1 🎧 (1.47) Listen and complete the questions from a radio quiz. Then try to answer them.

1 Are the Rocky Mountains in North America or _____?
2 Which sea does the _____ Danube flow into – the Black Sea or the Mediterranean?
3 Which _____ is between America and Asia?
4 Where's the Gobi _____ – in Africa or Asia?
5 Can you name two _____ in the Mediterranean Sea?
6 In which continent is _____ Victoria?

2 🎧 (1.48) Listen to the radio quiz and check your answers.

SPEAK

1 Work in pairs. Write three quiz questions about geographical features. Use the examples to help you.

Can you name two …?
Where's …? Is it in … or …?
In which continent is …?

2 Ask and answer each other's quiz questions.

Superlative adjectives
EXPLORE

1 Read the article and find the superlative form of these adjectives.

1 cold *the coldest* 3 low   5 dry
2 bad   4 wet   6 difficult

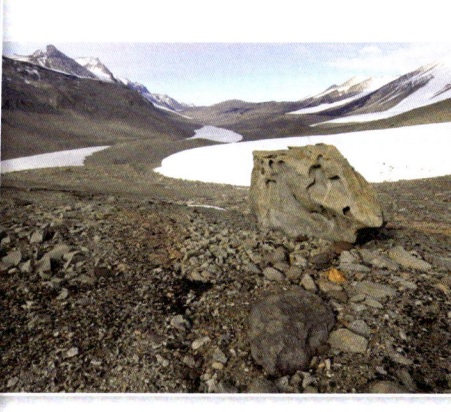

Extreme climate

Antarctica is the coldest place in the world and it has the worst weather. The lowest temperature on record is −89°C. Antarctica is also the wettest and the driest place in the world. How is this possible? It's the wettest place because 70 per cent of the world's fresh water is in Antarctica and 90 per cent of the world's ice. And it's the driest because in one place, The Dry Valleys, it never rains or snows. The Dry Valleys is the most difficult place in the world for plants and animals – nothing can live or grow there.

2 🎧 (1.49) Complete the table with the superlative form of the adjectives. Listen, repeat and check your answers.

Short adjective	Superlative	Rule
long	the longest	+ -est
large	¹_____	+ -st
heavy	²_____	-y → -iest
hot	³_____	double consonant + -est

Long adjective	Superlative	Rule
difficult	⁴_____	*most* + adjective

Irregular adjective	Superlative	
good	the best	
far	the furthest	
bad	⁵_____	

⬤⬤⬤⚬⚬ Grammar Reference: page 102

EXPLOIT

1 Complete the sentences. Use the superlative form of the adjectives in brackets. Which sentences do you agree with?

1 I'm *the funniest* person in the class. (funny)
2 June is usually _____ month of the year. (hot)
3 Money is _____ thing in the world. (important)
4 Brazil has got _____ football team in the world. (good)
5 Alexandria is _____ city in Egypt. (exciting)
6 English is _____ subject at school. (difficult)

2 🎧 (1.50) Complete the quiz questions, using the superlative form of the adjectives. Choose the correct answers. Then listen and check.

1 Which capital city is *the furthest* (far) north?
   a Reykjavik (Iceland)   **b** Ottawa (Canada)
   c Oslo (Norway)

2 Which ocean is _____ (deep)?
   a the Indian Ocean   **b** the Atlantic Ocean
   c the Pacific Ocean

3 Which animals are _____ (dangerous)?
   a crocodiles   **b** snakes   **c** elephants

4 Which is _____ (long) river in the world?
   a the Nile   **b** the Amazon   **c** the Yangtze

5 Which animal is _____ (fast)?
   a cheetah   **b** leopard   **c** lion

6 What is _____ (large) animal in the world?
   a African elephant   **b** blue whale   **c** giraffe

7 Which is _____ (big) continent?
   a Africa   **b** Asia   **c** North America

3 Write questions and answers. Use *who* or *what* in the questions, and use the superlative form of the adjectives.

1 beautiful / continent in the world?
   What's the most beautiful continent in the world?
2 interesting / city in your country?
3 good / way to travel?
4 bad / food in the world?
5 easy / subject at school?
6 good / football player in the world?
7 funny / person in the class?

⬤⬤⬤⚬⚬ Grammar Builder: page 103

⬤⬤⬤⚬⚬ Workbook: page 40

A postcard
READ

Hi Susan,
We're in Turkey. It's lovely here and the weather is fantastic. We're at a campsite in a small village. This is a picture of the beach near the campsite. We go swimming every morning and Kate goes sailing in the afternoon too.
Wish you were here!
Love
Dan & Kate xxx

Dear Mark
We're in Scotland. It's great here, but the weather isn't very good. We're in a youth hostel near Loch Ness. Do you know Loch Ness? It's famous for the monster! This is a picture of the loch. ('Loch' means 'lake.') There are lots of lovely mountains all round. We go walking in the mountains every day.
See you next week.
Bye for now
Sally

Read the postcards and answer the questions.

1 Where are they?
2 What do they think of the place?
3 What is the weather like?
4 Where are they staying (hotel, campsite, etc.)?
5 What is in the picture on the card?
6 What do they do every day?

PREPARE

1 Put the words in the correct order to make phrases from the postcards.

1 and is here it's weather fantastic the lovely
2 were wish here you
3 you see week next

2 Look at the prepositions of place in the box below. How many of the phrases can you find in the postcards? Underline them.

> **Prepositions of place** in the mountains on a lake/river by a lake/river in a village/town at the seaside in a hotel/youth hostel at a campsite/near the campsite

3 Match the types of holiday accommodation with the pictures.

> **Holiday accommodation** apartment cottage hotel villa youth hostel

WRITE

> **Writing tip: before writing**
>
> Before you begin to write, plan your writing: think about what you want to write and make notes.

1 Read the *Writing tip* above. Then imagine you are on holiday in one of the places in Prepare exercise 3. Make notes about:

1 the weather
2 the type of accommodation
3 the activities you can do there

2 Write a postcard to a friend. Use the writing plan to help you.

> • Start with *Dear …* or *Hi …*
> • Say where you are.
> • Say what the place is like and what the weather is like.
> • Say what type of accommodation you are staying in.
> • Say what the picture is of.
> • Say what you do every day.
> • Finish with *Love* or *Bye for now* and your name.

> **Check your work**
>
> **Have you**
> ☐ followed the writing plan?
> ☐ written 50–70 words?
> ☐ checked your spelling and grammar?

●●●○○ Workbook: page 41

Italy   Egypt   Spain   Finland   Austria

Wild!
LANGUAGE SKILLS

1 🎧 (1.51) Complete the dialogue with the words from the box. Then listen and check your answers.

> does sail apartment doing than that lovely like
> on seaside

Sara	What are you ¹_____?
Jane	I'm reading my emails. I've got one from Anne.
Sara	Is she ²_____ holiday?
Jane	Yes. She's in Malta with her family.
Sara	Oh, that's nice. What's the weather ³_____?
Jane	She says it's fantastic. It's hotter ⁴_____ here.
Sara	It's cloudy and rainy here every day!
Jane	She says they're staying in an ⁵_____ in a small village.
Sara	Is it near the ⁶_____?
Jane	Yes, it is. She's learning to ⁷_____!
Sara	Wow! I'd like to do that!
Jane	Look, there are some photos with the email, too.
Sara	Let me see! Oh, that beach looks ⁸_____.
Jane	Yes, it ⁹_____. And there aren't many people.
Sara	Click on the next one.
Jane:	OK. ¹⁰_____'s Anne's mum and dad and...

2 Read the dialogue again. Then answer the questions.

1 What is Jane doing?
2 Who has she got an email from?
3 Where is Anne?
4 What's the weather like there?
5 Where are Anne and her family staying?
6 What is Anne learning?
7 What would Sara like to do?
8 Who is in the second photo?

3 Complete the sentences with the correct comparative or superlative forms of the adjectives.

> good old interesting big bad happy nice intelligent

1 London is _____ city in Britain.
2 Reading is _____ than watching TV. TV is really boring!
3 Our team is _____ football team in the country. We always lose!
4 My sister is _____ than me. She hasn't got any exams this week!
5 I think a holiday at the beach is _____ than a holiday in the mountains.
6 Jack is _____ student in the class. He always passes his exams.
7 He says Mike is _____ than David but I like David. He's friendly.
8 My brother is _____ than me. He's 15 and I'm 13.

Compound words: nature

1 Look up the words in **bold**. Then make compound words by adding words from the box.

> anemone bank bank beam bed ~~berg~~ burn
> cap dune flower front gull rink side storm

1	ice:	iceberg	_____ _____
2	river:	_____	_____ _____
3	sand:	_____	_____ _____
4	sea:	_____	_____ _____
5	sun:	_____	_____ _____

Synonyms: extreme adjectives

2 Match the extreme adjectives with their synonyms.

1	hilarious	a	very cold
2	terrible	b	very hot
3	freezing	c	very good
4	furious	d	very wet
5	boiling	e	very funny
6	soaking	f	very angry
7	fantastic	g	very bad

Holiday words

3 Check the meaning of the words in the box and complete the text.

> books fortnight sightseeing half board ~~resort~~

We always stay at the same lovely hotel at a seaside ¹resort on the Red Sea. My dad always ²_____ two rooms for the last two weeks of April. We stay for a ³_____ but we'd like to stay for longer! My dad also asks for ⁴_____ so we have our breakfasts and dinners at the hotel. Every day we go to the beach but we also visit other places and go ⁵_____.

I CAN ...

Read the statements. Think about your progress and tick (✓) one of the boxes.

✳ I need more practice.	✳✳ I sometimes find this difficult.	✳✳✳ No problem!

	✳	✳✳	✳✳✳
I can understand an article about animals.			
I can make comparisons.			
I can talk about places around the world.			
I can describe people and things using superlative adjectives.			
I can write a postcard describing a place.			

●●○○ Workbook: Self check pages 42–43

6 Out and about

THIS UNIT INCLUDES ●●●
Vocabulary • places in town • • sequence words • expressions with *time* • prepositions + nouns • jobs: *-er* or *-or*?
Grammar • past simple: *be* and *can* • past simple affirmative (regular verbs)
Skills • reading, listening and talking about places in town • talking about past ability • memory game
Writing • phone messages

Around town

BEFORE READING

Look at the photos. Answer the questions.

1 What is happening in the pictures?
2 What do you think the dangers of this sport are?
3 What other dangerous sports can you name?
4 Do you do any dangerous sports?

READ

Reading tip

You can use the context of a text to help you find the meaning of new words. By reading the text you can guess that the word *skydiver* is the name for someone who jumps out of planes with a parachute.

1 **Read the *Reading tip*. Read the text quickly. What is a *freefall*?**

a The moment when a skydiver finishes the jump.
b The part of a jump from a plane before the parachute is open.
c The part of a jump from a plane when the parachute is open.

2 🎧 (2.02) **Read the text again. Then choose the best answers.**

1 By the age of 19, Michael Holmes
a was an instructor.
b was an experienced skydiver.
c worked in New Zealand.
2 Holmes prepared for the jump at Lake Taupo
a quickly.
b in a special way.
c in the usual way.
3 The students and instructors planned to open their parachutes at
a 4,500 metres.
b 3,000 metres.
c 1,500 metres.
4 Holmes couldn't open the safety parachute because
a there was a problem with the cords from the safety parachute.
b it was too late.
c there was a problem with the main parachute.
5 Before he landed, Holmes could see
a bushes in the park.
b the hospital.
c some cars.

A FLYING VISIT TO THE PARK

Michael Holmes first jumped from a plane when he was 16. Holmes loved the experience and he started skydiving frequently. He jumped 1,000 times before he was 19!

Later Holmes studied to become an instructor and he worked in New Zealand. One morning at an airport near Lake Taupo, he prepared for a routine jump. First of all, Holmes checked his equipment: his jumpsuit, goggles, gloves, helmet and boots. After that he checked the most important parts of a skydiver's equipment: his harness and his two parachutes. There was a main parachute and a smaller safety parachute. Finally, he looked at his altimeter. There weren't any problems and he was ready for the jump.

There were 16 students and instructors and the pilot on the plane. The plane climbed slowly to 4,500 metres and then one of the instructors opened the door; it was time to jump! There was a small camera on Holmes' helmet so that he could film the instructors with their students. They wanted to freefall for 3,000 metres and then open their parachutes.

As soon as Holmes jumped out of the plane, he filmed the skydivers. Then he looked at the altimeter on his wrist. It was time to open his own parachute, but he couldn't! The cords from his parachute were stuck together. It was impossible to open! Then he quickly tried to open the safety parachute but there was a problem. He couldn't open it because of the cords from the main parachute. He was only 1,000 metres from the ground and his life was in danger. He decided to cut the cords with a penknife but it was too late.

Holmes looked down at the ground. He could see a car park and a park next to it. He talked to the camera on his helmet. 'I'm dead. Bye,' he shouted. Suddenly, he landed in some bushes in the park. However, he wasn't dead! His left ankle and a lung were hurt but he was alive thanks to the bushes. He was in hospital for only two weeks!

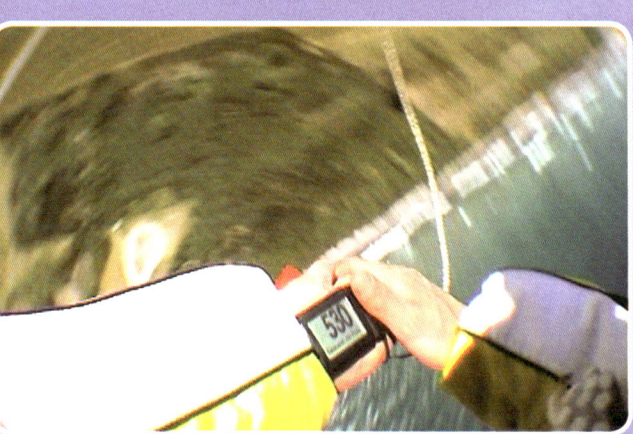

UNDERSTANDING IDEAS

Answer the questions. Look at the text, and use your own words and ideas.

1 Why do you think people like skydiving? Try to think of three or four reasons.
2 There was a camera on Holmes' helmet. Why do you think he filmed the instructors and the students?
3 Holmes is alive today because of the bushes. Why?

VOCABULARY

A flying visit to the park

1 Name the seven pieces of skydiving equipment with words from the reading text.

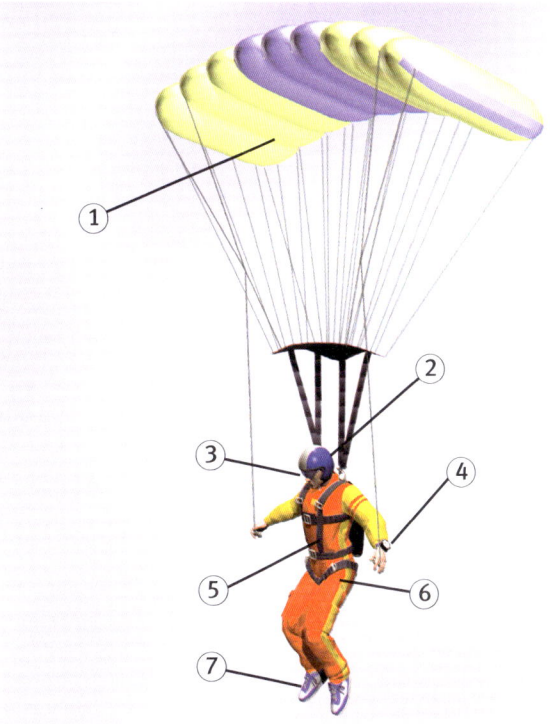

2 Match the highlighted words in the text with these definitions.

1 Prepared to do something.
2 The surface of the earth.
3 One of the two organs that take air in and out of the body.
4 The things you need to play a sport, to do an activity etc.
5 A small knife that closes.
6 A thing that you have done in your life.
7 A person who teaches a sport or activity.
8 Strong, thick strings.
9 The opposite of 'dead'.
10 The most important.
11 Came down from the sky.
12 Something you can't do.
13 Small, thick trees.
14 A person who flies a plane.
15 To make a film.

●●○○ Workbook: page 44

A flying visit to the park
ACTIVATE

Complete these sentences with the words from the box.

> alive bush cord equipment experience film ground impossible instructor land lungs main penknife pilot ready

1 I can _____ my brother's wedding with my dad's new camera.
2 We've got a big tent and a lot of camping _____.
3 I passed my driving test but I haven't got any _____ of driving. I've got to practise a lot.
4 I studied all my books carefully and I think I'm _____ for the exam.
5 We always sit on the _____ after playing football and eat a sandwich.
6 He couldn't run faster in the race. He couldn't take any more air into his _____!
7 He was in a very bad car accident but he's _____.
8 My skiing _____ was really good. I could ski after only three lessons with him.
9 We _____ at the airport at 10 o'clock this evening.
10 There was a _____ between me and the next climber when we climbed the mountain.
11 This maths homework is really difficult! It's _____ to do.
12 There's a _____ in the middle of our garden.
13 Can I borrow your _____ to cut this stick?
14 He wants to be a _____ and fly planes.
15 The most important meal in Britain is dinner. It's the _____ meal of the day.

EXTEND
Sequence words

1 Look back at the text on page 48 and find sequence words that match the definitions.
  1 Following another action. After that
  2 To introduce the last in a list of things.
  3 The first thing to be done.
  4 To introduce the next thing that happens.
  5 Happening some time after something else.
  6 When one thing happens and another starts.

2 Circle the correct word or words.
  1 First I have breakfast. Then I have a shower. **Later** / **Finally**, I brush my teeth.
  2 **First of all** / **After that**, we stayed in Rome. Then we visited Florence.
  3 **As soon as** / **First of all** we arrived home, we cooked dinner.
  4 First you stretch out your arm. **Then** / **After**, you open your hand.
  5 David was at Marlowe secondary school. **As soon as** / **Later** he studied at Oxford University.
  6 We visited the museum. **As soon as** / **After that**, we returned to school.
  7 I studied French at school. **Later** / **First of all**, I worked in Paris.
  8 **Then** / **First of all** he asked some questions. Then I replied.

Expressions with *time*

3 Match the sentences with the expressions with *time*.

> at times   run out of time   on time   time flies   waste time   take your time

  1 The holidays finish very quickly. time flies
  2 We arrived at the start of the film.
  3 I sometimes like cooking.
  4 You don't have to hurry.
  5 Finish the exam now!
  6 He doesn't do any work!

Preposition + noun

4 Match the nouns with the correct prepositions.

> the seaside   home   a newspaper   night   TV   the mountains   the morning   my own

at	in	on
1 at the seaside	4 _____	7 _____
2 _____	5 _____	8 _____
3 _____	6 _____	

5 Complete the sentences with the prepositions *by*, *for*, *in*, and *on*.
  1 Our lives were in danger!
  2 He's not in the office this week. He's _____ holiday.
  3 Her dad takes us to school _____ car.
  4 Let's go _____ a walk in the park after lunch.
  5 I can't chat now. I'm _____ a hurry.
  6 My brother goes to work _____ foot.
  7 I always listen to the news _____ the radio.
  8 They make these clothes _____ hand.

●●●●○ **Workbook: page 45**

Past simple: *be* and *can*
EXPLORE

1 🎧 (2.03) Listen to the dialogue and find examples of *be* and *can*.

Tom	Hi, Cathy. Are you having a good holiday?
Cathy	Yes, we're in Abu Dhabi now with Uncle Jack.
Tom	Were you there last weekend?
Cathy	No, we weren't. We were in Dubai.
Tom	What was it like?
Cathy	It was amazing. On Saturday we were at the Emirates Towers. They're two of the tallest buildings in Dubai. We had dinner in the hotel restaurant on the 50th floor.
Tom	Really? What could you see?
Cathy	We could see the skyscrapers along the Sheikh Zayed Road but we couldn't see anything else because they are so high!

2 Complete the table with past simple forms of *be* and *can* in the dialogue.

Past simple: *be*
affirmative
I / He / She / It ¹_____ in Dubai.
We / You / They ²_____ in Dubai.
negative
I / He / She / It ³_____ in Dubai.
We / You / They ⁴_____ in Dubai.
interrogative and short answers
⁵_____ he in Dubai?
Yes, he ⁶_____. / No, he ⁷_____.
⁸_____ you in Dubai?
Yes, we ⁹_____. / No, we ¹⁰_____.

Past simple: *can*
affirmative
I / He / She / It / We / You / They ¹¹_____ see it.
negative
I / He / She / It / We / You / They ¹²_____ see it.
interrogative and short answers
¹³_____ I / he / she / it / we / you / they see it?
Yes, she ¹⁴_____. / No, she ¹⁵_____.

LOOK OUT!

We always use a base form after *could*, not an infinitive (with *to*).

● ● ● ○ ○ Grammar Reference: page 104

EXPLOIT

1 Complete the sentences with *was*, *were*, *wasn't* or *weren't*.

1 They were at school, but they weren't in the classroom.
2 I _____ at home on Sunday morning. I was on holiday.
3 Today is Wednesday. Yesterday _____ Tuesday.
4 You _____ at the art gallery. Where were you?
5 The weather _____ very nice yesterday. It was wet and cold.
6 We _____ at the cinema last night. The film was great.
7 My grandparents _____ teachers. They were doctors.
8 Our last lesson _____ geography. It was maths.

2 Write sentences about the people below. Use *could* and *was*.

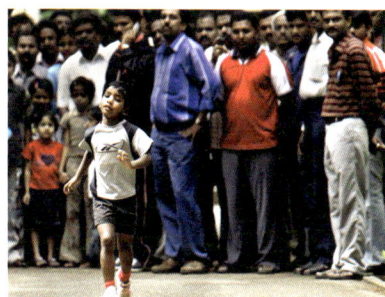

1 Budhia Singh / run marathons / three
  Budhia Singh could run marathons when he was three.
2 Maria Sharapova / play tennis / four
3 Vanessa Mae / play the violin and piano / five
4 Michael Schumacher / drive / four
5 Sergey Karjakin / play chess / four

3 Write sentences with *couldn't* and the phrases in the box.

he wasn't home   ~~I was ill~~   I wasn't tired
we weren't hungry   it was dark   it was wet
the water was very cold   they weren't 17 years old

1 I / go to school because …
  I couldn't go to school because I was ill.
2 I / read my book because …
3 She / swim because …
4 We / eat our dinner because …
5 I / speak to Kevin because …
6 They / play tennis because …
7 I / sleep because …
8 They / drive because …

4 Write questions and true answers.

1 read / four   *Could you read when you were four?*
2 write your name / two
3 walk / one
4 count to 10 / three
5 speak English / nine
6 ride a bike / ten
7 swim / four

5 Ask your partner the questions in exercise 4. Tell the class.

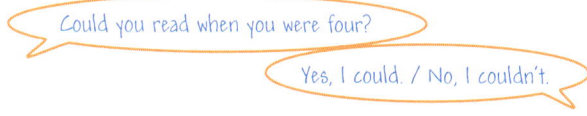

Could you read when you were four?

Yes, I could. / No, I couldn't.

● ● ● ○ ○ Grammar Builder: page 105

● ● ● ○ ○ Workbook: page 46

In town
VOCABULARY

1 Match the places on the map with the words in the box.

1 park

> **Places in town**   art gallery   bank   bus station   car park
> cinema   department store   library   museum   ~~park~~
> police station   post office   railway station   theatre
> tourist information office   town hall

2 🎧 (2.04) Listen, repeat and check your answers.

3 Complete the sentences with words from exercise 1.

1 You can catch a train at the railway station.
2 You can borrow a book from the _____.
3 You can buy stamps at the _____.
4 You can get information about interesting places at the _____.
5 You can go for a walk with your dog in the _____.
6 You can catch a bus at the _____.
7 You can park your car in the _____.
8 You can watch a film at the _____.
9 You can see a play at the _____.
10 You can look at paintings at the _____.

●●○○○ Workbook: page 47

LISTEN

🎧 (2.05) Listen and identify the places. Choose from the list in exercise 1.

1 _____	4 _____	7 _____
2 _____	5 _____	8 _____
3 _____	6 _____	

SPEAK

1 Work in pairs. Ask and answer about the places on the map. Use the prepositions below.

> Where's the park?

> It's next to the cinema.

between   near   next to   opposite

2 Write six sentences about your town or city.

There's a cinema opposite the bank.
The town hall is next to the museum.

3 Talk about a place in your town. Don't say the name of the place. Can the class say which place it is?

Past simple: affirmative (regular verbs)
EXPLORE

1 Read Joe's story and look at the verbs in blue. How do we form the past simple of regular verbs?

Last Saturday my friend Lee and I decided to go to the cinema. We agreed to meet at six at the café because we wanted to have a coffee before the film. I was late so I jogged to the café and arrived at ten past six. Lee wasn't there. I waited for a few minutes and then I phoned him on his mobile. 'Where are you?' I asked. Lee answered, 'I'm at the cinema. When I arrived at the café, you weren't there, so I walked to the cinema. Be quick, the film starts in five minutes!' So I hurried to the cinema. But Lee wasn't there! I phoned him again. 'I'm at the ABC cinema. Where are you?!' 'The ABC!? I'm at the Odeon Cinema!'

2 Read the spelling rules in the *Learn this!* box. Then put the blue verbs from exercise 1 into the correct groups (1–4).

LEARN THIS!

> **Past simple: affirmative (regular verbs)**
> **Endings**
> The form is the same for all persons: *I watched, you watched, she watched,* etc.
> **1** We add *-ed* to most verbs.
> watch→watch**ed**
> **2** We add *-d* to verbs that end in *-e*.
> phone→phone**d**
> **3** If the verb ends in a consonant and *-y* we change the *-y* to *-ied*.
> study→stud**ied**
> **4** If the verb ends in a short vowel and a consonant, we double the consonant and add *-ed.*
> chat→chat**ted**

3 🎧 (2.06) Listen and repeat. Pay attention to the endings.

1	/d/	phoned	arrived	agreed
2	/t/	asked	watched	walked
3	/ɪd/	waited	wanted	chatted

4 Put the time expressions in the box in the correct order. Start with the most recent.

1 – last night, 2 – …

> **Time expressions** the day before yesterday
> three months ago   two years ago   ~~last night~~
> yesterday afternoon   yesterday evening   last week
> last month   last year

●●○○ Grammar Reference: page 104

EXPLOIT

1 Complete the sentences with the verbs in the box. Use the past simple.

> arrive   ask   decide   hurry   park   stop   ~~visit~~   watch

1 Three days ago I visited an art gallery.
2 We _____ TV last night.
3 Last Tuesday I was late so I _____ to school.
4 The day before yesterday we _____ the car in a car park in the town centre.
5 Yesterday evening we_____ to have a pizza for dinner.
6 'What time is it?' I _____ her.
7 The bus _____ opposite the library five minutes ago.
8 I _____ at the railway station at ten to seven.

2 Complete the text. Use the past simple form of the verbs in brackets.

> One day a man [1] walked (walk) into a bank in the centre of London. He [2]_____ (want) to borrow £5,000 to pay for a trip to America. 'OK,' [3]_____ (reply) the cashier. 'We can lend you £5,000, but you have to leave your car here.' The man [4]_____ (agree) and [5]_____ (park) his expensive Ferrari in the car park at the bank. A week later he [6]_____ (return) to the bank.
> 'Can I have my car, please?' he [7]_____ (ask) the cashier.
> 'Of course. That's £5,000 and £10 interest. Can I ask you something?' [8]_____ (continue) the cashier. 'You've got an expensive Ferrari. Why do you need £5,000?'
> 'I don't need £5,000,' [9]_____ (answer) the man, 'but last week I was in America. Your car park is very cheap – only £10 for a week in the centre of London!'

3 Play a memory game with the class. Repeat what the last person said and add another action. You don't have to tell the truth. Use the verbs in the box to help you.

> chat   cycle   decide   listen   phone   play   stay
> study   talk   walk   want   watch   work

Student A: Yesterday morning, I watched TV.
Student B: Yesterday morning, I watched TV and I phoned my friend.
Student C: Yesterday morning, I watched TV, I phoned my friend and I …

●●●○ Grammar Builder: page 105

●●●○ Workbook: page 48

A phone message
READ

1 Read the notes (1–4) below. Where were the people when they phoned and left messages?

Caller	Where were they?
1 Uncle Jack	police station
2 Harry	
3 Jenny	
4 Dave Adams	

①

Mum,
Uncle Jack phoned from the police station. He wants to talk to you. It's urgent. Can you call him back?
The number is 01548 652265.
Tom

②

Sam,
Harry phoned at 10. He was at the park. He waited for you for ages. Haven't you got a football match this morning?
I don't think he's very happy. You can phone him on his mobile – 0797 56875.
Dad

③

Lisa,
Jenny phoned from London. She missed the train and arrived late. She wanted to speak to you, but you weren't here. Can you phone her tomorrow at Mary's house?
Sally

④

Dad,
The mechanic Dave Adams phoned from the garage. He tried to repair your car, but there's a problem. Please phone him on 674533. The garage closes at five.
Penny

2 Complete these sentences.

1 You _____ phone him _____ his mobile.
2 _____ phone Dave Adams _____ 674533.
3 Can _____ phone her tomorrow _____ Mary's house?
4 Can you _____ him back?

PREPARE

🎧 **2.07** Listen and complete the phone messages.

Mandy,
¹_____ phoned. She's going to the ²_____ with Vicky this afternoon at ³_____ o'clock. She wants you to come along. Can you ring her on her mobile? Her number is ⁴_____.
Mum

Dad,
Mr Grey from the ⁵_____ phoned. He says your car is ⁶_____. You can pick it up this ⁷_____. Go before ⁸_____ - that's when the garage closes. His number is ⁹_____.
Sarah

WRITE

Write a phone message (30–50 words). Include this information:

- Who phoned?
- Where is he / she?
- What's the message?
- What's his / her phone number?

Check your work
Have you
☐ included all the information in exercise 7?
☐ used *can* for requests correctly?
☐ written 40–60 words?

●●●●○ Workbook: page 49

Out and about
LANGUAGE SKILLS

1 🎧 (2.08) Complete the dialogue with the words from the box. Then listen and check your answers.

> cooking off speak think wants about on phoned isn't are

Mike Hi, James. ¹_____ you going to dinner at Tom's house on Saturday?

James Is Tom ²_____ dinner?

Mike No, he ³_____. His mum is! She's cooking for all the football team!

James I'd like to go. Tom's mum is a great cook!

Mike I know. Tom ⁴_____ you last night.

James Ah, I was at the cinema last night and my phone was ⁵_____.

Mike Well, he wanted to ⁶_____ to you.

James ⁷_____ the meal?

Mike Yes. He ⁸_____ you to organize some games for after the dinner.

James Oh, great. We can play chess.

Mike Well, I ⁹_____ he wants you to organize a competition.

James You mean questions about sport and things like that?

Mike Yes, I think so. Can you phone him ¹⁰_____ his mobile?

James Yes. That's a good idea.

2 Read the dialogue again and complete the sentences with the names James, Mike, Tom or Tom's mum.

1 _____ is cooking a meal.
2 _____'s mobile phone wasn't on last night.
3 _____ talks about a meal and a phone call.
4 _____ asks James to make a phone call.
5 _____ wants a friend to organize a competition.
6 _____ mentions some subjects he can write questions about.

3 Write these sentences in the past simple.

1 We live in Oxford and we study engineering at the university.
2 His mobile phone isn't on so I can't speak to him.
3 She stays at home and watches TV.
4 We can't go to the party because we're at our grandparents' house.
5 I phone my sister at 6 o'clock and we chat about our friends.
6 I'm at home, so I can watch the film on TV.

4 Put the verbs in the correct columns.

> stay jog watch study chat jump arrive hurry love stop try decide

add -ed	finish in e + -d	y + -ied	double final consonant + -ed

---

In town

1 Check the meaning of the words in the box and complete the sentences.

> airmail box office cash machine frame franchises leaflets mayor ~~reference~~ return ticket stage

1 When I'm studying, I use the reference books in the library.
2 We were very close to the _____ at the theatre.
3 There wasn't any money in the _____ at the bank.
4 We picked up some _____ about the city at the tourist information office.
5 I want a _____ to Waterloo railway station, please.
6 The _____ isn't at the town hall today.
7 I always buy tickets for the cinema on the internet instead of at the _____.
8 I don't like the painting but the _____ is nice!
9 The designer shops all have _____ in that department store.
10 Can I send this letter to Egypt by _____?

Jobs: *-er* or *-or*?

2 We can make some nouns that describe jobs by adding the suffixes *-er* or *-or* to verbs. Check which suffix is used with these verbs.

verb	noun
act	actor
instruct	_____
interview	_____
inspect	_____
sail	_____
translate	_____
dive	_____

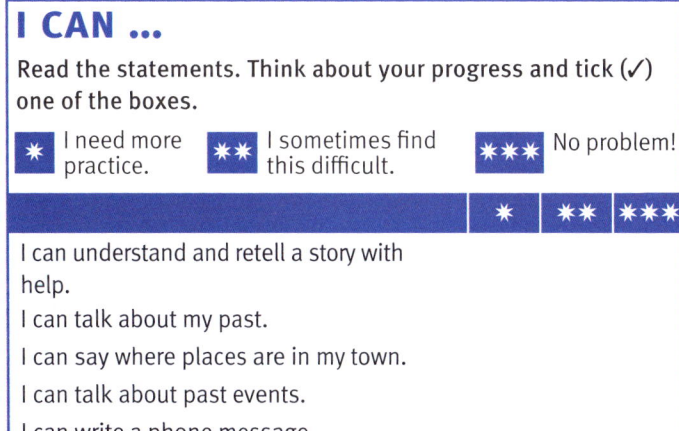

I CAN ...

Read the statements. Think about your progress and tick (✓) one of the boxes.

✳ I need more practice.	✳✳ I sometimes find this difficult.	✳✳✳ No problem!

	✳	✳✳	✳✳✳
I can understand and retell a story with help.			
I can talk about my past.			
I can say where places are in my town.			
I can talk about past events.			
I can write a phone message.			

●●●●● Workbook: Self check pages 50–51

VOCABULARY

1 Complete the sentences with the plural form of these words.

> beach desert island lake mountain ocean
> river sea

1 Everest, K2 and Rysy are _____.
2 The Nile, the Mississippi and the Vistula are _____.
3 Ireland, Hawaii and Cyprus are _____.
4 Copacabana, Waikiki and Bondi are _____.
5 The Sahara and the Gobi are _____.
6 The Caribbean and the Mediterranean are _____.
7 The Pacific and the Atlantic are _____.
8 Baikal, Michigan and Geneva are _____.

| Mark | /8 |

2 Complete the words for animals. Use *a, e, i, o* and *u*.

1 h _ p p _
2 g _ _ t
3 _ t _ p s
4 m _ s q _ _ t _
5 w h _ l _
6 r h _ n _ c _ r s
7 j _ l l y f _ s h
8 _ _ g l _
9 _ l _ p h _ n t

| Mark | /9 |

3 Answer the questions, using the places in the box.

> art gallery bus station car park cinema library
> park post office railway station theatre

Where can I …

1 see a film? _____
2 see a play? _____
3 catch a bus? _____
4 play football? _____
5 buy stamps? _____
6 see paintings? _____
7 borrow books? _____
8 leave my car? _____
9 catch a train? _____

| Mark | /9 |

4 Write the names of the places where you can read these sentences.

1 Phone 999 when you are in danger. _____
2 There are some Egyptian mummies in room 33. _____
3 Special prices on trainers in the sports section. _____
4 You can also take out money from the machine. _____
5 Visit the beautiful country park and waterfalls. _____
6 The mayor is in an important meeting. _____

| Mark | /6 |

GRAMMAR

1 Write sentences, using comparative adjectives and *than*.

1 Lake Superior / large / Lake Victoria
2 Stockholm / far north / London
3 the Mediterranean Sea / big / the Baltic Sea
4 Waikiki beach / long / Bondi beach
5 Mount Everest / famous / Mount Kenya
6 Africa / hot / Europe
7 the Amazon / wide / the Danube

| Mark | /7 |

2 Complete the superlative sentences using the adjectives in brackets and words from the box or your own ideas.

> free diamond my brother English
> Manchester United maths

1 (beautiful) _____ stone in the world is a _____.
2 (funny) _____ person in my family is _____.
3 (good) _____ football team in the world is _____.
4 (important) _____ things in life are _____.
5 (easy) _____ language to learn is _____.
6 (difficult) _____ subject at school is _____.

| Mark | /6 |

3 Complete the dialogue with the correct past simple form of *be* or *can*.

Girl You missed Jack's birthday celebration yesterday. Where [1]_____ you?
Boy I [2]_____ at home.
Girl Really? Why?
Boy I [3]_____ very well.
Girl Oh dear. What [4]_____ wrong with you?
Boy Nothing much, just a bad cold. But I [5]_____ go out.

| Mark | /5 |

4 Complete the email with the past simple form of the verbs in brackets.

We aren't having a great time in London. We [1]_____ (arrive) at the hotel on Friday evening. Our room wasn't ready, so we [2]_____ (wait) outside while they [3]_____ (clean) it. Then we [4]_____ (phone) Reception and [5]_____ (try) to book a table in the restaurant. The receptionist [6]_____ (reply) that the restaurant was closed. We [7]_____ (walk) to a café near the hotel and [8]_____ (ask) for four pizzas to take away. When we [9]_____ (return) to the hotel with our pizzas, they said we couldn't take the food to our room. My dad really [10]_____ (shout) at them. We're looking for another hotel.

| Mark | /10 |

| TOTAL | /60 |

National Parks
READ

1 Read the text. Match the questions (1–3) with the paragraphs (A–C).

1 What can people do there?
2 Where is it, and how big is it?
3 What is the scenery like?

2 Are the sentences true or false?

1 There are fifteen National Parks in the north of England.
2 The Lake District is forty-five kilometres wide.
3 There aren't any beaches in the Lake District.
4 There are more than sixteen lakes.
5 Forty thousand people visit the Lake District every year.
6 You can visit the homes of two famous English writers.

The Lake District

A The Lake District National Park is in the north of England. There are 15 National Parks in Britain, but the Lake District is bigger than the others. It is about 55 kilometres from east to west and 55 kilometres from north to south. There are mountains, lakes, woods, towns, villages and even some beaches.

B The Lake District is famous for its beautiful scenery. There are a lot of mountains and hundreds of hills. There are 16 large lakes, and many smaller ones. This area has also got a lot of different animals: for example, you can see rare animals like the red squirrel and the golden eagle.

Lake District National Park

C Over 40,000 people live and work in the Lake District. There are also many visitors every year. You can go walking and climbing in the hills, and go swimming and sailing on the lakes. You can also visit many pretty villages and towns, and the homes of two famous English writers: William Wordsworth (1770–1850) and Beatrix Potter (1866–1943). It is a very popular place for visitors because there is something for everyone!

3 Which of these outdoor activities are mentioned in the text?

> **Outdoor activities** birdwatching canoeing climbing cycling diving fishing horse riding mountain biking sailing snowboarding swimming skiing walking

4 Can you do these activities in your country?

LISTEN

1 🎧 (2.12) Listen to speakers 1–3. Match their descriptions of national parks with the photos (A–C) below.

Speaker 1: ☐   Speaker 2: ☐   Speaker 3: ☐

A Killarney National Park

B Banff National Park

C Great Barrier Reef National Park

2 🎧 (2.12) Listen again and complete the chart.

Great Barrier Reef National Park
Natural features: ¹_____ with beaches
Activities: swimming, ²_____, ³_____

Killarney National Park
Natural features: ⁴_____, ⁵_____, forests
Activities: sailing, ⁶_____, walking

Banff National Park
Natural features: ⁷_____, lakes
Activities: skiing, ⁸_____, ⁹_____, canoeing

WRITE AND SPEAK

Find out about one of the national parks in the box below or another national park you know. Use the reading text to help you write 80–100 words about it. Then read your information to the rest of the class.

> Yellowstone National Park
> Serengeti National Park

7 World famous

THIS UNIT INCLUDES ● ● ●

Vocabulary • countries • nationalities • university life • collocations with *do, give, go* and *take* • places of work • prepositions: biography • chemistry • stages in life
Grammar • past simple: affirmative (irregular verbs) • past simple: negative and interrogative
Skills • reading, listening and talking about famous people • describing your weekend • game: 20 questions
Writing • an email

Discoveries

BEFORE READING

Match these great scientists (1–4) with their work (a–d).

1 Nicolaus Copernicus (1473–1543) …
2 Alexander Fleming (1881–1955) …
3 Albert Einstein (1879–1955) …
4 Ada Lovelace (1815–1852) …

a discovered the formula $E=mc^2$.
b wrote the world's first computer program.
c said that the earth went round the sun.
d discovered penicillin.

READ

1 Look at the photo of the famous scientist on page 59. What is her name? Do you know why she is famous? Read the text quickly and check your answers.

A great scientist

Marie Curie was born in Warsaw, Poland, in 1867. Her father taught physics and her mother was the head teacher of a girls' school. Marie was a very intelligent student at secondary school, but she couldn't go to university because she was a woman. So she worked as a governess for the children of a wealthy family and studied secretly at a university in Warsaw. Marie was extremely hard-working and she sometimes stayed awake all night to study. Later she moved to France and studied science at the Sorbonne, a famous university in Paris. In 1906, she became the first woman to teach at the Sorbonne when she got the job of Professor of Physics.

At the university laboratory at the Sorbonne she met another scientist, Pierre Curie. They got married in 1895 and had two children. Pierre thought that Marie was a genius and he was happy to help her. Together they did a lot of important work on radioactivity and discovered radium and polonium. In 1903 they won the Nobel Prize for Physics and they used the prize money they collected to help needy students. Sadly, three years later Pierre died in a road accident, but Marie didn't stop working. In fact, she won the Nobel Prize for Chemistry in 1911. She is the only woman to win two Nobel Prizes.

Marie Curie stayed in France for the rest of her life. She tried to use her discoveries to help people who were ill in hospital. At that time people didn't know that it was dangerous to work with radium. Marie became ill because of the radioactivity and died of cancer in 1934. In 1995 the French government moved the remains of Marie and her husband Pierre to the Panthéon, the building in Paris where people can visit the tombs of the most famous people in French history.

Reading tip

When you are looking for information in a biographical text, remember that this type of text usually follows a logical order. For example, information about the person's birth and childhood is usually near the beginning.

2 🎧 **2.13** Read the *Reading tip*. Are the sentences true or false? Correct the false sentences.

1 Marie Curie was born in Warsaw.
2 Her mother taught physics.
3 She couldn't go to university because she was a governess.
4 She met Pierre Curie at a university in Paris.
5 Marie and Pierre discovered radioactivity.
6 She died because of her work.

3 Read the text again. Then choose the best answers.

1 Marie Curie was
  a from a rich family.
  b a secondary school teacher.
  c a university professor
2 Pierre Curie
  a won a Nobel Prize for Chemistry.
  b kept the prize money.
  c enjoyed working with his wife.

3 After Pierre Curie died Marie Curie
  a won two more Nobel Prizes.
  b continued her work.
  c became poor.
4 Marie Curie
  a tried to help ill people with her work.
  b worked in a hospital.
  c went back to Poland.
5 At the Panthéon you can visit the tombs of
  a lots of famous scientists.
  b well-known people.
  c people from the French government.

4 Answer the questions.

1 What did Marie Curie's father teach?
2 What did Marie Curie study at the Sorbonne?
3 When did Marie and Pierre Curie get married?
4 How many Nobel Prizes did she win?
5 How did Pierre Curie die?

UNDERSTANDING IDEAS

Answer the questions. Look at the text, and use your own words and ideas.

1 Which adjectives do you think describe Marie Curie?
2 How did Marie Curie help people?
3 Why did the French government move the remains of Marie and Pierre?

VOCABULARY

A great scientist

1 Match the highlighted words in the text with these definitions.

1 The part of something that is left.
2 The body of a dead person.
3 Not well.
4 Places where they put important dead people.
5 Found or learned something that people didn't know before.
6 The group of people who control a country.
7 A woman who teaches children in their home.
8 Having a lot of money.
9 A person who is much more intelligent than other people.
10 Very.
11 Went and got something from a place.
12 Something that a person or team wins in a game or competition.
13 Not having enough money, food or clothes.
14 Not sleeping.
15 A room where scientists do research and experiments.

2 Do you know these words?

cancer   Nobel Prize   polonium   professor
radioactivity   radium   road accident   secretly

●●● ○   Workbook: page 52

A great scientist
ACTIVATE

Complete these sentences with the words from the box.

> awake collected discovered extremely genius governess government ill laboratory needy prize remains rest tomb wealthy

1 The _____ put the dead king's _____ in a _____ in the centre of the city so that people could visit it.
2 I was _____ tired last night but I stayed _____ to watch the football match between Liverpool and Milan.
3 Jack won first _____ in the school chess competition. He _____ it from the head teacher's office on Friday.
4 I studied at school but the _____ of my brothers and sisters studied with our _____.
5 After the earthquake there were a lot of _____ people, who were hungry and _____. Many _____ people gave money to help them.
6 He spent all his time in the university _____ and his teachers thought he was a _____ when he _____ a new chemical formula.

EXTEND

University life

1 Match the words with the definitions.

1	research	a	a class at university
2	undergraduate	b	a university qualification
3	lecturer	c	a very important teacher at a university
4	notes	d	a university student
5	lecture	e	a teacher at a university
6	graduate	f	information from class that you write on a piece of paper
7	degree	g	someone who has a university qualification
8	professor	h	a careful study of something

Collocations with *do, give, go* and *take*

2 Complete the sentences with the verbs *do*, *give*, *go* and *take*.
1 I always take lots of notes when I'm in a lecture.
2 Professor Roberts and Professor Williams _____ lectures on nuclear physics.
3 Did you _____ to the lecture on Roman cities?
4 We want to _____ research into chemicals in food.
5 My brother is planning to _____ to university and _____ a degree in biology. But first he is going to _____ a break and go travelling.
6 The careers office at school can _____ advice about jobs or further education.
7 I'd like to _____ a course on accounting, but maths is my worst subject!

Places of work

3 Complete the sentences with the words in the box.

> court studio surgery operating theatre ~~laboratory~~ stock exchange

1 A scientist works in a / an laboratory.
2 A surgeon works in a / an _____.
3 A broker works in a / an _____.
4 A judge works in a / an _____.
5 An artist works in a / an _____.
6 A doctor works in a / an _____.

Prepositions: biography

4 Complete the biography of Sameera Moussa with the prepositions.

> in with in at for in to of for ~~on~~ into after in

Sameera Moussa was born [1] on March 3, 1917 [2] _____ Egypt. Her mother died [3] _____ cancer when she was young. She moved [4] _____ Cairo [5] _____ her father [6] _____ her mother's death. [7] _____ Cairo she studied science [8] _____ Cairo University. She did research [9] _____ atomic radiation at the university. She wanted to use nuclear energy to help people and she organized the Atomic Energy [10] _____ Peace Conference. The American government wanted her to become an American but she said, 'Egypt is waiting [11] _____ me.' Sadly, she died [12] _____ 1952 in an accident in the USA.

(●●●●○ Workbook: page 53)

Past simple: affirmative (irregular verbs)

EXPLORE

1 Complete the text with the past simple forms of the irregular verbs in brackets.

Doctor Sir Magdi Habib Yacoub [1]_____ (be) born on 16th November 1935 in Belbis, Egypt. Sir Magdi studied at Cairo University and he [2]_____ (become) a doctor in 1957. He [3]_____ (spend) some time in the USA and then he [4]_____ (go) to Britain in 1962 and he worked with heart patients at the famous Harefield Hospital. At the hospital Sir Magdi [5]_____ (begin) a special programme that [6]_____ (give) hundreds of patients new hearts. Then he [7]_____ (teach) medicine at the Imperial College School of Medicine. Because of his fantastic work as a doctor, the Queen of England [8]_____ (make) him Sir Magdi Habib Yacoub in 1992 and today he is a hero in Britain and Egypt.

2 Write the past simple forms of these irregular verbs. Use the irregular verb list on page 124.

1 get _____
2 come _____
3 do _____
4 have _____
5 write _____
6 know _____
7 take _____
8 spend _____
9 become _____
10 win _____

●●●●● Grammar Reference: page 106

EXPLOIT

1 Complete the sentences about famous leaders. Use past simple forms from Explore exercises 1 and 2.

1 Nelson Mandela spent 27 years in prison. In 1994, he _____ president of South Africa. When Rolihlala Mandela was a schoolboy, his teacher _____ him the English name Nelson. Mandela _____ the Nobel Peace Prize in 1993.

2 Mahatma Gandhi _____ born in India. At the age of 18, he _____ to University in London and then _____ a job in South Africa.

3 The Chinese leader Mao Zedong _____ 'The Little Red Book' in the 1950s.

There aren't any rules for irregular past simple forms so you have to learn them! Use the list on page 124.

2 Read the *Look out!* box. Then complete the first halves of the sentences (1–6) with irregular past simple forms and match them with the second halves (a–f).

1 The Spanish brought (bring) [c]
2 Before Copernicus, people _____ (think) ☐
3 Marie Curie _____ (teach) ☐
4 In 1626 Peter Minuit _____ (buy) ☐
5 Rosa Parks _____ (fight) ☐
6 King Henry VIII _____ (catch) ☐

a physics at the Sorbonne University.
b for the rights of black Americans.
c potatoes to Europe from South America.
d malaria when he was 35.
e Manhattan Island for $24 from Native Americans.
f the sun went round the earth.

3 🎧 (2.14) What are the past simple forms of these verbs? Put them into pairs that rhyme. Then listen and check your answers.

~~begin~~ break go make pay read ~~run~~ say see sell send speak tell wear

began – ran

4 When did you last do these things? Write true sentences, using the time expressions in the box.

Time expressions the day before yesterday   last night yesterday afternoon   yesterday evening   last week last month   last year   two days (weeks, months, years) ago

1 do some housework
  I did some housework last week.
2 buy some chocolate
3 read a book
4 make a phone call
5 make a new friend
6 tell a lie
7 see a film
8 send an email
9 take an exam
10 write a letter

5 Tell the class some of the things you did last weekend.

I went shopping …   I played computer games…

●●●●● Grammar Builder: page 107

●●●●● Workbook: page 54

On the map
VOCABULARY

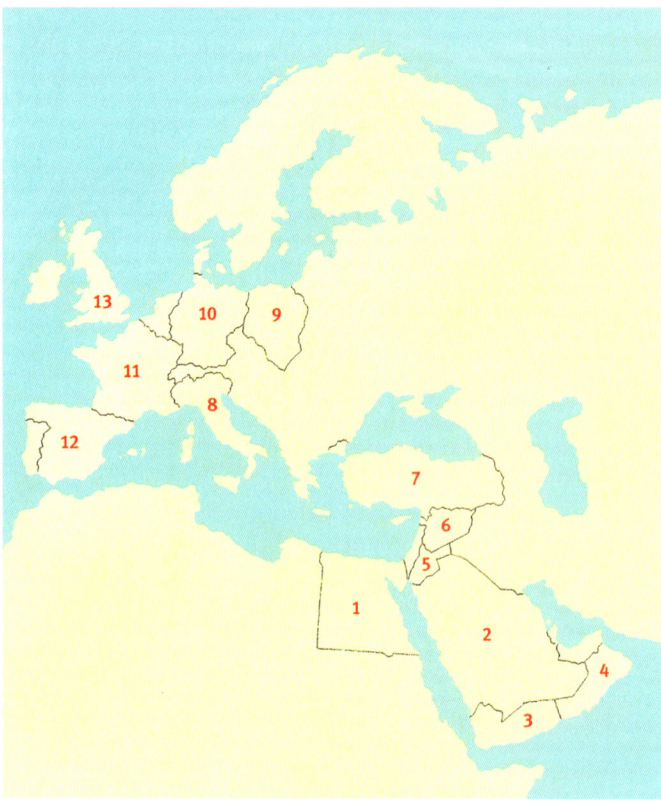

1 Look at the map. Where do you live? Put a cross (✓).

2 Look at the list of countries in the box. Which are neighbours of your country?

> **Countries** Australia Brazil Britain China Egypt France Germany Italy Japan Jordan Kuwait Oman Poland Russia Saudi Arabia Spain Sweden Syria Turkey the UAE the USA Yemen

3 🎧 (2.15) Write the nationalities of the countries in exercise 2. Then listen, repeat and check your answers.

1 Australia – Australian
2 Brazil –

4 Label the countries 1–13 on the map.

●●●●○ Workbook: page 55

LISTEN

1 Look at the photos. Do you know these people? Where were they born?

2 🎧 (2.16) Listen and check your answers to exercise 1.

3 🎧 (2.16) Listen again. Are the sentences true or false?
1 Picasso lived all of his life in France.
2 Picasso died in 1937.
3 Mohamed Al Fayed's father was a professor of Arabic.
4 Mohamed Al Fayed arrived in Britain in 1985.
5 Queen Rania went to university in Jordan.
6 Queen Rania married the Prince of Jordan in 1993.
7 Pelé played for four football clubs.
8 Pelé scored 92 goals in 77 matches for Brazil.

SPEAK

Play 20 questions. Think of a famous person who is alive today. Your classmates have 20 questions to guess their name. They must be yes / no questions. Use the ideas in the box to help you.

> **Are you …**
> a man? a woman?
> Turkish? Syrian?
> a sportsperson? an actor / actress? an artist?
> a writer? a scientist? a businessman?
> **Do you …**
> live in …? work in …? study …? play a sport?
> appear in films / on TV? invent things?
> write books? own a company?

Are you a man?   Yes, I am.

Are you Turkish?   No, I'm not.

Is your name …?

Past simple: negative and interrogative

EXPLORE

1 🎧 (2.17) Complete the dialogue with the words in the box. Then listen and check your answers.

> Africa   acts   documentaries   London   photo   speech

Helen   This is a good ¹_____. Where did you take it?

Suzie   I didn't take it. My friend Molly took it at the Live 9 event in ²_____.

Helen   Live 9?

Suzie   It was a charity event for ³_____. I didn't go, but I watched it on TV. It was amazing. Did you see it?

Helen   No, I didn't. Did a lot of ⁴_____ perform?

Suzie   Yes, they did. In between the music, there were ⁵_____ about Africa. And Bill Gates was there, too.

Helen   Really? Can he sing? I didn't know that.

Suzie   He didn't sing! He made a ⁶_____ about Africa.

2 Look at the table below. Then find more examples of past simple negative and interrogative in the dialogue.

Past simple
negative He didn't sing.
interrogative Where did you take it?
interrogative and short answers Did you see it? Yes, I did. / No, I didn't.

3 Read the *Learn this!* box and complete the rules.

1 We form the negative of the past simple with
   ¹_____ + base form

2 We form the interrogative of the past simple with
   ²_____ + *he / you / they*, etc. + base form

● ○ ○ ○ ○   Grammar Reference: page 106

EXPLOIT

1 Write questions and short answers about the dialogue in Explore exercise 1. Use the past simple.

1 Suzie / take / the photo?
   Did Suzie take the photo? No, she didn't.

2 Molly / take / the photo?

3 Molly / go / to the Live 9 event?

4 Suzie / go / to the Live 9 event?

5 Suzie / watch / the event on TV?

6 Helen / watch / the event on TV?

7 Bill Gates / make / a speech at the event?

2 Make these sentences negative.

1 I watched Live 9 on television.
   I didn't watch Live 9 on television.

2 We went on holiday last year.

3 It rained last weekend.

4 I had breakfast this morning.

5 My sister broke my mobile phone.

6 England won the World Cup in 2006.

3 What did you do last weekend? Tick the activities.

	You	Your partner
1 go shopping		
2 tidy your bedroom		
3 go to the cinema		
4 have a bad dream		
5 eat in a restaurant		
6 get an email		
7 listen to music		
8 meet your friends		

4 Work in pairs. Ask and answer about the activities in exercise 3. Tick the activities your partner did.

Did you go shopping?   *No, I didn't.*

5 Tell the class about your partner's weekend. Use the past simple affirmative and negative.

Laila didn't go shopping, but she tidied her bedroom. She didn't ...

● ● ○ ○ ○   Grammar Builder: page 107

● ● ○ ○ ○   Workbook: page 56

WRITING

An email message
READ

1 Read the emails. Who had a better weekend, Gail or Lauren?

Dear Lauren,
I hope you're well. How was your weekend? My weekend was great. I finished all my homework on Saturday morning. Then I went into town and met some friends. We had lunch in a café and then we went shopping. I bought two new T-shirts. In the evening, I went to a basketball match with my brother and his friends. It was really exciting!
I didn't get up until midday on Sunday. I had lunch at home with my family and then I went to the park and played tennis with some friends. I didn't go out in the evening. I watched a DVD at home.
Say hi to Ann.
Love,
Gail

Hi Gail,
Great to hear from you! Ann sends her love. I'm fine, but my weekend wasn't very good. I played volleyball for the school team on Saturday morning, but we lost. I didn't play very well. In the evening, I went to the cinema with my parents. The film was really boring.
On Sunday, it was my dad's birthday. We had a barbecue in the garden, but it rained, so it wasn't much fun. In the evening, I didn't feel well, so I went to bed early. Oh, well.
Speak to you soon.
Best wishes,
Lauren

2 Look at the list of activities. Tick the ones that Gail or Lauren did.

Activity	Gail	Lauren
do homework	✓	
go to bed early		
go to the cinema		
go shopping		
have a barbecue		
have lunch in a café		
play tennis		
play volleyball		
watch a basketball match		
watch a DVD		

3 Read the emails again and answer the questions.
1 What did Gail buy in town?
2 Did Gail enjoy the basketball match?
3 Did Gail go out on Sunday evening?
4 Did Lauren's team win the volleyball match?
5 What did Lauren think of the film?
6 Why did Lauren go to bed early on Sunday?

PREPARE

Writing tip: useful phrases for emails

We often use these phrases in emails to friends and family:
Great to hear from you!   *How was your weekend?*
I hope you're well.   *(Ann) sends her love.*
Say hi to (Ann).   *Speak to you soon.*

1 Read the *Writing tip*. Who uses the phrases in the emails in exercise 1, Gail or Lauren? Write *G* or *L*.

2 Choose four activities that you did at the weekend – two on Saturday, two on Sunday. Make notes in the table.

	Morning	Afternoon
Saturday		
Sunday		

WRITE

Write an email to a friend. Use the writing plan below, your notes and the useful phrases for emails.

- Begin with *Hi …* or *Dear …*

Paragraph 1
- Start the paragraph with a useful phrase.
- Describe what you did on Saturday.

Paragraph 2
- Describe what you did on Sunday.
- Add a useful phrase.
- Finish with *Love* or *Best wishes* and your name.

Check your work
Have you
☐ used some of the phrases from the *Writing tip* box?
☐ divided your email into two paragraphs?
☐ written 90–110 words?
☐ checked your spelling and grammar?

●●●○○ Workbook: page 57

World famous
LANGUAGE SKILLS

1 🎧 2.18 Complete the dialogue with the words from the box. Then listen and check your answers.

> didn't had see was on did went about bought how

Pete   Hi, Tony. How are you?
Tony   Hi, Pete. I'm fine!
Pete   ¹ _____ was your weekend?
Tony   It was great. We ² _____ shopping.
Pete   Shopping? Shopping is boring!
Tony   I agree, but last weekend ³_____ different. It was my birthday and my mum and dad ⁴_____ me an MP4 player.
Pete   I ⁵_____ know it was your birthday. Happy Birthday!
Tony   Thanks. So I enjoyed shopping this time.
Pete   Of course you did! ⁶_____ you celebrate?
Tony   Yes. ⁷_____ Saturday evening we went to a restaurant.
Pete   That's nice.
Tony   Yes, it was. How ⁸_____ you? What did you do?
Pete   I didn't go out because my grandparents came for the weekend. We ⁹_____ a good time.
Tony   Well, it's time for class.
Pete   Yes.¹⁰_____ you at football training.

2 Read the dialogue again. Are the sentences true or false? Change the false sentences to true ones.

1 Tony had a boring weekend.
2 Tony doesn't usually like shopping.
3 Tony bought his parents a present.
4 Pete knew it was Tony's birthday.
5 Tony ate in a restaurant on Sunday evening.
6 Pete didn't stay at home.
7 Pete's grandparents stayed with Pete and his family at the weekend.
8 Pete and Tony play football.

3 Write the past simple form of the verbs.

1 become _____
2 bring _____
3 catch _____
4 fight _____
5 meet _____
6 sing _____
7 teach _____
8 think _____

4 Write the negative (✗) or interrogative (?) forms of the sentences.

1 Simon saw the film last night. (?)
2 They went to Turkey. (✗)
3 My dad won the tennis club final. (✗)
4 They spent all their money. (?)
5 Kate visited her sister in Oxford. (?)
6 We ate at a Lebanese restaurant. (✗)
7 Tom travelled to Paris. (?)
8 He gave me an interesting book. (✗)

Stages in life

1 Look up the words in bold and read the examples. Then complete the sentences, using the correct form of the verb where necessary.

1 He was **born** in 1983.
2 He **graduated** _____ chemistry _____ Oxford University.
3 He met his wife at Oxford and they _____ **married** two years ago.
4 They are _____ a **baby** next year so they are going to **move** _____ a bigger house.
5 I _____ my end-of-year **exams** last week. They were hard so I'm not sure if I _____ or _____ .

2 What's the difference between the verbs *grow up* and *bring sb up*? Write two example sentences to show how they are different.

Chemistry

3 Match the names of the metals with the definitions.

> aluminium brass copper iron lead magnesium ~~radium~~ uranium

1 A white radioactive metal, used to treat some serious diseases. radium
2 A reddish-brown metal.
3 A silver-coloured metal, used for making cooking equipment.
4 A hard metal, used for making steel.
5 A silver metal that burns with a bright white flame.
6 A hard yellow metal that is a mixture of copper and zinc.
7 A metal that can be used to produce nuclear energy.
8 A heavy metal used for pipes and roofs.

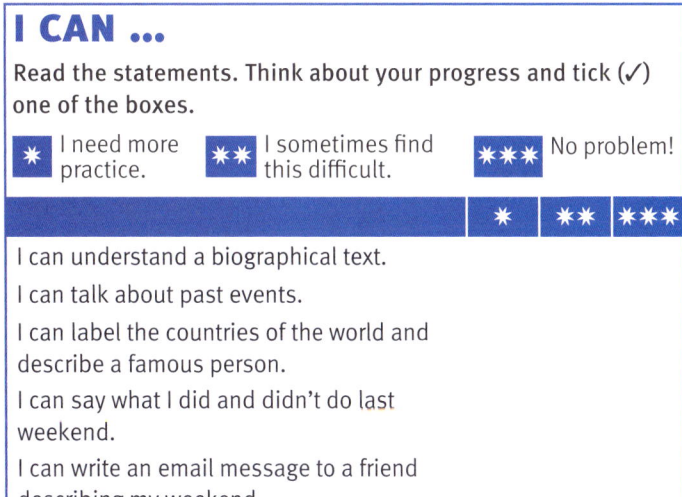

I CAN ...

Read the statements. Think about your progress and tick (✓) one of the boxes.

| ✴ | I need more practice. | ✴✴ | I sometimes find this difficult. | ✴✴✴ | No problem! |

	✴	✴✴	✴✴✴
I can understand a biographical text.			
I can talk about past events.			
I can label the countries of the world and describe a famous person.			
I can say what I did and didn't do last weekend.			
I can write an email message to a friend describing my weekend.			

●●●● Workbook: Self check pages 58–59

8 On the menu

THIS UNIT INCLUDES ●●●

Vocabulary • food and drink • countable and uncountable nouns •
ways of cooking • describing food • phrasal verb synonyms •
word building • food and cooking words • compound nouns: food
Grammar • Quantity: *some* and *any*, *How much / many?* • Articles (definite
and indefinite)
Skills • reading and listening to an interview about eating competitions •
talking about traditional food • discussing what you have for breakfast
Writing • a formal letter

Healthy eating

BEFORE READING

Read the *Reading tip*. Look at the photo and the title of the
text. What do you think the text is about?

a Food in restaurants.
b Working in a restaurant.
c Writing about food.
d Eating food quickly.

> **Reading tip**
>
> Before you start reading, think about the title of a text and
> any photos. They often give you an idea about the content.

READ

1 Read the text quickly. What does Sonya Thomas do?

2 🎧 (2.22) Read the text again. Are the sentences true or
false? Correct the false sentences.

1 Sonya only eats vegetables once or twice a month.
2 A lot of people in the USA know Sonya Thomas.
3 Sonya was a child when she became interested in eating
competitions.
4 Sonya says it's not good to eat a lot of food in a short
time.
5 Sonya has eating competitions once or twice a week.
6 Sonya does sport every day.

Can eating be a sport?

Sonya Thomas is not a big woman. She's 165 cm tall and
she only weighs about 45 kilos. She usually eats healthy food
– rice, vegetables, fruit, fish and chicken. But once or twice
a month she has a big meal – an enormous meal – and she
eats it very quickly. Why? Because she participates in eating
competitions. They are very popular in the USA. One of the
most famous, a meat sandwich eating competition in New
York, started in 1916 and is now a tradition. And thanks to
TV coverage, some competitive eaters like Sonya Thomas are
celebrities. In fact, she's one of the best competitive eaters in
the world. For example, she can eat:

🍴 65 boiled eggs in six minutes 40 seconds

🍴 5 kilograms of cheesecake in nine minutes

🍴 3.8 kilograms of baked beans in two minutes 47 seconds

🍴 2.3 kilograms of chicken in 12 minutes

In this interview, Sonya tells us about her life and her work.

Q: Why did you first take part in eating competitions?

A: When I was a child I saw an eating competition on TV.
A man ate 50 meat sandwiches in 12 minutes. I wanted to
be like him.

**Q: Your nickname in competitions is 'the Black Widow'.
Why did you choose that name?**

A: Because in competitions I'm small but very dangerous –
like the black widow spider!

Q: How do you prepare for a competition?

A: I often don't prepare at all. It's unhealthy to eat a lot of
food quickly. And the night before a competition I fast so
that I have a good appetite the next day.

Q: Do you do a lot of exercise?

A: Yes, I do. I exercise for about two hours a day, five days a
week.

**Q: How can you stay thin when you eat so much in
competitions?**

A: There are only one or two competitions a month. The rest
of the time, I eat healthy food.

Q: Do you believe eating competitions are real sport?

A: Yes, of course! It's the most natural sport in the world.
You need a strong body and a strong mind for eating
competitions – just like other sports.

3 Choose the best answers.

1 Sonya Thomas is
  a tall.
  b heavy.
  c thin.

2 She became interested in eating competitions when
  a she ate 50 meat sandwiches in 12 minutes.
  b she appeared on TV.
  c she saw an eating competition on TV.

3 Her nickname is 'the Black Widow' because
  a she's dangerous in competitions.
  b she looks like a spider.
  c she takes part in competitions.

4 Sonya is thin because
  a she usually eats healthy food.
  b she doesn't like fat or sugar.
  c she takes part in eating competitions.

5 In Sonya's opinion, why are eating competitions real sport?
  a Because you can eat and stay thin.
  b Because everybody eats and eating is natural.
  c Because there are only one or two competitions a month.

UNDERSTANDING IDEAS

Answer the questions. Look at the text, and use your own words and ideas.

1 How does TV coverage make people like Sonya Thomas into celebrities?
2 What things does Sonya Thomas do that other sportsmen and women usually do?
3 Would you like to take part in an eating competition? Why? Why not?

VOCABULARY

Can eating be a sport?

1 Match the highlighted words in the text with these definitions.

1 Food cooked in a hot oven.
2 A small animal with eight legs that eats insects.
3 Something that people started in the past and continue to do now.
4 A name your friends or family give you that isn't your real name.
5 To have a certain number of kilos.
6 The feeling of wanting to eat.
7 To take part.
8 A woman whose husband is dead.
9 Not made by people.
10 Helping to produce a condition of being well and free from illness.
11 Famous people.
12 To eat no food for a period of time.
13 The part of our body that thinks, remembers and knows things.
14 The time something appears on TV, the radio or in newspapers.
15 Food cooked in very hot water.

Food and eating

2 Look at the diagram. What food and drink can you see?

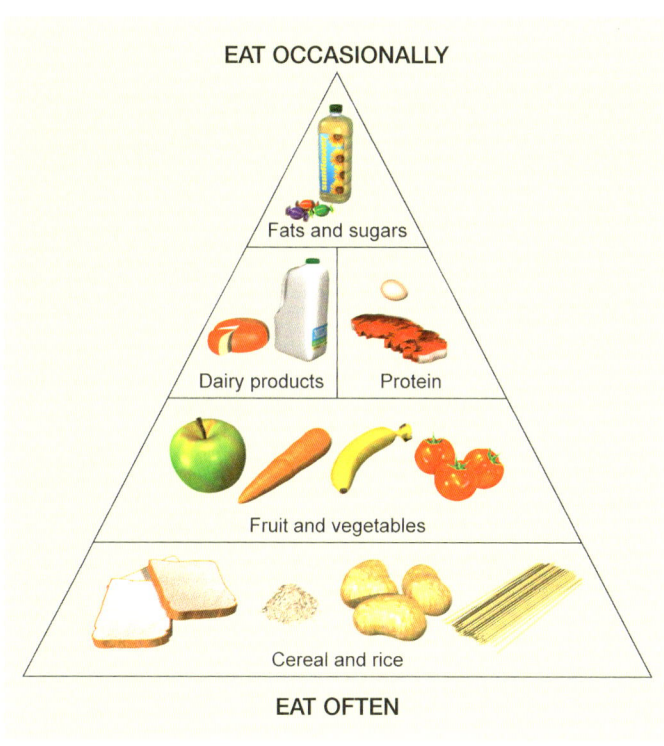

EAT OCCASIONALLY

Fats and sugars

Dairy products   Protein

Fruit and vegetables

Cereal and rice

EAT OFTEN

3 Work in pairs. Look at the food in the photos. Match each food with two or more groups in the diagram above.

1 chicken curry: protein and cereal and rice

① chicken curry
② strawberries and cream
③ blackcurrant cheesecake
cheeseburger
④ baked beans on toast
⑤

(●●●○   Workbook: page 60)

Can eating be a sport?

ACTIVATE

Complete these sentences with the words from the box.

> appetite baked boiled celebrities coverage fast
> healthy mind natural nickname participate spider
> tradition weighs widow

1 Einstein was a genius. He had a fantastic _____.
2 My name is Eduardo Ronaldo but my friends call me by my _____, Ronnie.
3 I didn't take part in the last game but I want to _____ in the next one.
4 He's got a very good _____ but his favourite food is pizza.
5 This _____ is 100 years old. They do it every year on 31st August.
6 He always eats a _____ egg for breakfast.
7 My grandmother is very _____. She walks for two hours every day.
8 We always _____ in my house during Ramadan. We only eat at night.
9 Oh no! There's a big _____ on my bed!
10 I hate sport and I think there's too much _____ of it on TV.
11 I love the smell of freshly _____ bread!
12 My aunt became a _____ last year. My uncle died in a car accident.
13 He eats a lot of hamburgers and fast food. He _____ 120 kilos!
14 All our meals are made with _____ food. All the vegetables come from our own garden.
15 Most TV _____ are only famous for a short time.

EXTEND

Phrasal verb synonyms

1 Complete the sentences with the synonyms for the words in **bold**.

> discover continue stretch complete stop collect
> ~~participate~~ return

1 We didn't **take part** in training last week but we want to participate in tomorrow's race.
2 I can **pick up** the children on Friday but can you _____ them tomorrow?
3 He doesn't want to **carry on** with the work but I want to _____ until 6 o'clock.
4 We always **go back** to the office at two o'clock but today we didn't _____ until 3 o'clock!
5 In this exercise you **push out** your arms and _____ your legs at the same time.
6 You **find out** his phone number and we can _____ where he lives.
7 Anne **gave up** smoking but Peter can't _____.
8 **Fill in** this form for the gymnasium and then _____ this form for the tennis club, please.

Word building

2 Complete the table.

verb	noun	adjective
bore	[1] boredom	boring
[2] _____	competition	competitive
defend	defence	[3] _____
[4] _____	difference	different
excite	[5] _____	exciting
imagine	imagination	[6] _____
[7] _____	isolation	isolated
prepare	[8] _____	prepared

Describing food

3 Match the words in **bold** with the definitions.

1 I think pasta is **bland**.
2 She likes very **sweet** tea.
3 This meat is very **tender**.
4 The bread here is always **fresh**.
5 The food he cooks is always **salty**.
6 He prefers **lean** meat.

a It is easy to cut.
b They made it a very short time ago.
c There is a lot of salt.
d Without fat.
e It doesn't have a strong taste.
f With a lot of sugar.

Ways of cooking

4 These verbs are used for different kinds of cooking. Can you match them with the pictures?

> fry grill bake boil roast

5 How do you usually cook the food in the pictures in your country?

(●●●○○ Workbook: page 61)

some / any, How much / many?
EXPLORE

1 🎧 (2.23) Read and listen to the dialogue. Find all the examples of *some* and *any*.

Oliver	Let's have some lunch.
Toby	Good idea. Are there any pizzas in the fridge?
Oliver	No, there aren't.
Toby	What have we got?
Oliver	There's some cheese. And there's some lettuce.
Toby	Is there any butter?
Oliver	Yes, there is.
Toby	OK. Let's have lettuce and cheese sandwiches.
Oliver	Ah. There's a problem.
Toby	What is it?
Oliver	We haven't got any bread.

2 Circle the correct words in the rules.

> 1 We use **some** / **any** in affirmative sentences.
> 2 We use **some** / **any** in negative sentences.
> 3 We use **some** / **any** in questions.

3 Read the advertisement quickly. Find the name of the pizza and how much it costs.

The biggest pizza in the world!

**Come and order The Big One at
Mama Lena's Pizza House in Pittsburgh, USA**
Only $99!!
150 slices of delicious pizza
There are **NINE KILOS** of pizza dough,
FOUR LITRES of tomato sauce
and **SEVEN KILOS** of cheese
in The Big One!!
It takes 40 minutes to cook! Come in and
chat with your friends while you are waiting.
We sell 300 Big Ones every year!

4 Read the information in the *Learn this!* box. Then order the words to make questions about the advertisement.

> 1 We use *How much ...?* with uncountable nouns.
> *How much time have you got?*
> *How much water is there?*
> 2 We use *How many ...?* with plural countable nouns.
> *How many tomatoes are there?*
> *How many books did you buy?*

1 money / does The Big One cost / how much
   How much money does the Big One cost?
2 is there in the pizza / pizza dough / how much
3 slices / how many / are there / in the pizza
4 in the pizza / how much / is there / cheese
5 to cook / does it take / how many / minutes
6 Big Ones / how many / do they sell a year

● ● ● ● **Grammar Reference: page 108**

EXPLOIT

1 Complete the second part of the dialogue between Toby and Oliver with *some* and *any*.

Toby	Is there ¹ any pasta?
Oliver	Yes, there is.
Toby	Let's make ² _____ tomato sauce for the pasta.
Oliver	We haven't got ³ _____ tomatoes.
Toby	Are there ⁴ _____ mushrooms?
Oliver	No, there aren't. But there's ⁵ _____ money on the table.
Toby	What for?
Oliver	Let's go out and buy ⁶ _____ chips!

2 🎧 (2.24) Listen and check your answers to exercise 1.

3 Complete the questions with *How much?* or *How many?*

1 How much homework do you do a day?
2 _____ sleep do you get a night?
3 _____ text messages do you send a day?
4 _____ money have you got in your pocket?
5 _____ cousins have you got?
6 _____ pizzas do you eat a week?
7 _____ people are in this room?
8 _____ time is there to the end of the lesson?

● ● ● ● **Grammar Builder: page 109**

● ● ● ● **Workbook: page 62**

Talking about food
VOCABULARY

LISTEN

1 Match the food and drink in the picture with the words in the box.

1 toast

> **Food** apples yoghurt bananas bread cereal cheese eggs mushrooms jam beans ~~toast~~ tomatoes olives
> **Drink** coffee hot chocolate milk orange juice tea water

2 Read the information in the *Look out!* box. Then divide the food and drink in exercise 1 into two groups, countable and uncountable nouns.

LOOK OUT!

> 1 **Countable nouns** are things that you can count. They have a singular and a plural form.
> *an apple two apples*
> 2 **Uncountable nouns** are things that you can't count. They only have a singular form.
> *toast ~~toasts~~ milk ~~milks~~*

Countable nouns	Uncountable nouns
apples	bread

3 🎧 (2.25) Listen, repeat and check your answers.

4 Cover the words in exercise 1 and say what food is on the table. Use *There are* for plural nouns and *There's* for singular (uncountable) nouns.

> There are some apples.   There's some toast.

●●●●○ Workbook: page 63

1 🎧 (2.26) Listen to three orders for room service. Write the room number and tick the food and drink that they order.

	Room 101	Room ___	Room ___
bread			
tomatoes			
cereal	✓		
cheese			
eggs			
a banana			
toast			
jam			
water			
orange juice			
tea			
coffee			
hot chocolate			

2 🎧 (2.26) Match the two halves of these expressions from the dialogues. Then listen again and check your answers.

1 a bowl of …   a orange juice
2 two slices of …   b cereal
3 a glass of …   c hot chocolate / tea / coffee
4 a cup of …   d toast
5 a bottle of …   e water

SPEAK

Work in pairs. Find out what your partner has for breakfast.

> What do you have for breakfast?

> I always / usually / sometimes have a bowl of cereal and …

> What do you drink?

> I always / usually / sometimes drink a cup / glass of …

GRAMMAR

Articles
EXPLORE

1 Read the text. Find examples of *the*, *a* and *an*.

' There are three restaurants near my house. On the High Street, there's a Chinese restaurant and an Italian restaurant. The Chinese restaurant is good, but it's expensive. The Italian restaurant is cheaper and the pizzas there are brilliant. There's an Indian restaurant on Mill Lane. I don't go to the Indian restaurant because the food isn't very good. '

Jack

2 Look at the examples of *the*, *a* and *an* in the text. What kinds of noun do they go with? Tick or cross the boxes in the chart.

	a / an	the
singular countable nouns		
plural countable nouns		
uncountable nouns		

3 Write *a* or *an*. What is the rule?

1 _____ banana
2 _____ English book
3 _____ egg
4 _____ Indian restaurant
5 _____ Spanish orange
6 _____ enormous tomato
7 _____ uncle
8 _____ young American

4 Study the text in exercise 1 again. Then circle the correct word in the rules below and complete the examples.

1 We use *a* or *an* / *the* when we mention something for the first time.
  There's _____ supermarket in my street.

2 We use *a* or *an* / *the* when we mention something again.
  The food at _____ supermarket is expensive.

●●●●   Grammar Reference: page 108

EXPLOIT

1 Circle the correct words in the text.

In 2001, Richard Evans went to [1]**a** / **the** pizza parlour near his house and bought [2]**a** / **the** large, vegetarian pizza. When he got home, he opened [3]**a** / **the** box and saw that it was [4]**a** / **the** meat pizza. He went back to [5]**a** / **the** shop and complained. [6]**A** / **The** waiter apologized but Richard was still angry, so he phoned his local newspaper. [7]**A** / **The** reporter said that lots of people complained about getting [8]**a** / **the** wrong pizza from the same pizza parlour. [9]**A** / **The** newspaper wrote [10]**an** / **the** article about [11]**a** / **the** pizza parlour. Now [12]**a** / **the** pizza parlour is very careful when it takes orders.

2 Read the information in the *Learn this!* box. Then complete the sentences with *a*, *an* or *the*, or tick them if they are correct without an article.

Some common expressions include an article and others do not. There are no rules – you have to learn them!

no article	article
• *play football, tennis, etc.*	• *listen to the radio; see a film*
• *watch television*	• *have a snack, a drink, a sandwich, etc.*
• *have breakfast, lunch, dinner*	• *go to the theatre, the cinema, the doctor's*
• *go to school, work, hospital, university*	• *during the day; in the morning, afternoon, evening*
• *at night*	

1 He goes to _____ work by train. ✔
2 I went to *the* cinema last night.
3 He never eats anything before he goes to _____ school.
4 My sister is a nurse and often works at _____ night.
5 He usually does his homework in _____ morning.
6 Let's have _____ snack before we go out.
7 What time do you usually have _____ dinner?
8 I sometimes listen to _____ radio on the bus.
9 I want to go to _____ university when I leave school.
10 I never watch _____ TV before breakfast.

●●●●   Grammar Builder: page 109

●●●●   Workbook: page 64

A formal letter
READ

1 Read the advertisement and the letter. Find the three requests for information in the letter that match with the numbered notes.

1 Vegetarian dishes?

Taj Mahal Restaurant
Traditional Indian food.
Set menu available.   Great value.
46 Market Street.

2 How much?   3 Table for 10 - Friday 14th?

Dear Sir or Madam,

I am organizing a meal for a group of friends to celebrate the end of the school year. We would like to book a table for 10 on Friday 14 July for seven o'clock. Could you please let me know if that is possible?

I have two further questions. First, could you please let me know how much the set menu costs? Secondly, could you please tell me if there is a good choice of vegetarian dishes on the menu, as two of my friends do not eat meat or fish?

I look forward to hearing from you.

Yours faithfully,

Jonathan Harwood

Jonathan Harwood

2 Complete the sentences with information from the advertisement and the letter.

1 The restaurant serves _____ food.
2 There are _____ people in Jonathan's group.
3 They plan to arrive at the restaurant at _____ o'clock.
4 Two of Jonathan's friends only eat _____ food.

PREPARE

1 Complete these phrases for requesting information from the letter.

1 Could you please _____ me _____ if … ?
2 _____ you please _____ me if … ?

2 Use the phrases in exercise 1 to request the following information.

1 Do you serve fish?
2 Are you open on Sunday evenings?
3 Do you have a table for 5 people?
4 Do you have a set menu?
5 Is the restaurant in the town centre?

3 Read the *Writing tip*. How is the beginning and ending of a formal letter different from an informal letter?

> ### Writing tip: starting and ending a formal letter
>
> - Start the letter: *Dear (Mr Jones)* if you know the name of the person you are writing to, or *Dear Sir or Madam* if you don't.
> - If you want a reply to your letter, write *I look forward to hearing from you* after the final paragraph.
> - Finish the letter with *Yours sincerely* if you used the person's name at the start, or *Yours faithfully* if you didn't.

WRITE

Imagine you want to organize a meal out for yourself and a group of friends. Look at the advertisement for a restaurant and the notes you have made. Write a letter (90–110 words) to the restaurant following the writing plan.

Set menu?   Open from?

Stefano's
Italian restaurant
Large choice of dishes!
Great atmosphere
22 High Street

> **Paragraph 1**
> - Say how many people, what the occasion is, the date and the time. Check the availability.
>
> **Paragraph 2**
> - Request the two pieces of information in the notes.

> ### Check your work
> **Have you**
> ☐ started and ended the letter correctly?
> ☐ followed the writing plan?
> ☐ written 90–110 words?
> ☐ checked your spelling and grammar?

●●●○○   Workbook: page 65

On the menu
LANGUAGE SKILLS

1 (2.27) **Complete the dialogue with the words from the box. Then listen and check your answers.**

> any forward many can much choice how would
> book about

Manager	Good afternoon. The Tower Bridge restaurant. How ¹_____ I help you?
Diane	Hello. I'm phoning to ²_____ a table for next Friday evening.
Manager	Certainly, madam. How ³_____ people?
Diane	It's for twelve.
Manager	A table for twelve on Friday 5th of May. And what time ⁴_____ you like the table for?
Diane	Er, we'd like to eat at ⁵_____ six thirty.
Manager	Six thirty. Can I have your name, please?
Diane	Yes. It's Diane Shelton.
Manager	Diane Shelton. Thanks.
Diane	Is there a set menu?
Manager	Yes, we have a set menu for groups.
Diane	Oh, good! How ⁶_____ is it?
Manager	It's £22.
Diane	Fine. We'd like the set menu. And, er, do you serve ⁷_____ dishes for vegetarians?
Manager	Yes, we do. We have a good ⁸_____ of vegetarian dishes. ⁹_____ many vegetarians are in your group?
Diane	There are four.
Manager	Four vegetarians. Well, Miss Shelton, I look ¹⁰_____ to seeing you on Friday.

2 **Read the dialogue again. Complete the booking form.**

> Date: ¹_____ Time: ²_____
> Name: ³_____
> Number of people: ⁴_____
> Set menu: ⁵Yes ☐ No ☐
> Number of vegetarians: ⁶_____

3 **Complete the sentences with *many*, *much*, *any* and *some*.**

1 How _____ children have they got?
2 There weren't _____ emails for you.
3 We've bought _____ fish for lunch.
4 How _____ milk do you drink every day?
5 Is there _____ lamb in the fridge?
6 We've got _____ good films to watch this weekend.

Food and cooking words

1 **Check the meaning of the words in the box and complete the sentences.**

> toaster saucepan ~~kettle~~ oven frying pan

1 In Britain people boil water for tea in a *kettle*.
2 Put the rice in a _____ full of boiling water.
3 Are those fried eggs in the _____ for me?
4 I'm baking some bread in the _____.
5 Put the bread in the _____. The butter and jam are in the fridge.

Odd word out

2 **Check the definitions and circle the wrong word in each group. Say why it is wrong.**

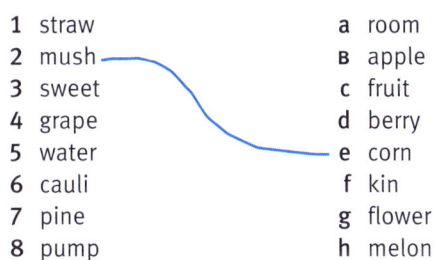

1	cooker	oven	cook	microwave

A cook is a person. The other words are machines.

2	fried	baked	raw	grilled
3	milk	yoghurt	cheese	pasta
4	peas	pear	pineapple	peach
5	can	piece	jug	bottle
6	mussels	prawns	grapes	lobster

Compound nouns: food

3 **Match the words to make the names of fruit and vegetables.**

1	straw	a	room
2	mush	b	apple
3	sweet	c	fruit
4	grape	d	berry
5	water	e	corn
6	cauli	f	kin
7	pine	g	flower
8	pump	h	melon

I CAN ...

Read the statements. Think about your progress and tick (✓) one of the boxes.

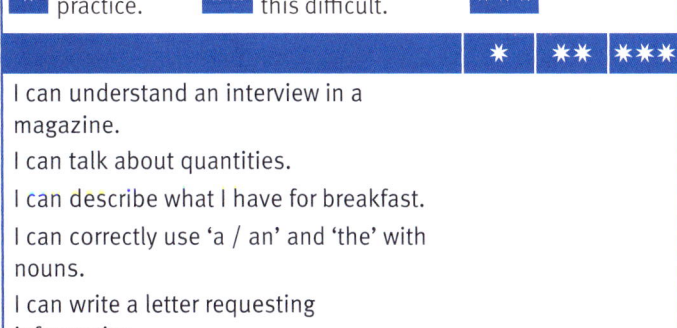

✳	I need more practice.	✳✳	I sometimes find this difficult.	✳✳✳	No problem!

	✳	✳✳	✳✳✳
I can understand an interview in a magazine.			
I can talk about quantities.			
I can describe what I have for breakfast.			
I can correctly use 'a / an' and 'the' with nouns.			
I can write a letter requesting information.			

⬤⬤◯◯ **Workbook: Self check pages 66–67**

VOCABULARY

1 Complete the sentences with the correct countries and nationalities.

1 She's from Italy. She's _____.
2 She's from _____. She's Emirati.
3 He's from Jordan. He's _____.
4 She's _____. She's from Russia.
5 He's _____. He's from China.
6 She's from Turkey. She's _____.
7 He's from _____. He's Swedish.
8 She's Egyptian. She's from _____.
9 He's from Britain. He's _____.
10 They're from the USA. They're _____.

Mark ☐ **/10**

2 Complete the text with the correct countries and nationalities.

I'm studying in London and the students in the class are from all over the world. Ashwaq is ¹_____ . She comes from Alexandria. Fatimah is ²_____ and lives in Damascus. Montse and María are ³_____ and they live in Madrid and Tarragona. Glykeria was born in Athens, in ⁴_____, and Gül is ⁵_____ , from the capital city, Ankara. Bianca and Giulia are from ⁶_____ and they live in the beautiful city of Venice. Karin lives in Stockholm, the capital of ⁷_____. Oh, and of course, the teacher is ⁸_____ ! She's called Abby and she's from Manchester.

Mark ☐ **/8**

3 Complete the words for food and drink. Use *a, e, i, o* and *u*.

1 _ r _ ng _ j _ _ c _
2 t _ _ st
3 t _ _
4 ch _ _ s _
5 t _ m _ t _ _ s
6 h _ t ch _ c _ l _ t _
7 b _ _ ns
8 c _ ff _ _

Mark ☐ **/8**

4 Write the plural form of the countable nouns. Write U next to the uncountable nouns.

1 banana _____
2 bread _____
3 cereal _____
4 jam _____
5 orange juice _____
6 water _____
7 apple _____
8 yoghurt _____
9 mushroom _____
10 rice _____

Mark ☐ **/10**

5 Complete the sentence.

For breakfast, he usually has a bowl of ¹_____, two slices of ²_____, a glass of ³_____, and a cup of ⁴_____.

Mark ☐ **/4**

GRAMMAR

1 Complete the sentences with the past simple of the verbs in the box.

| be   be   become   give   go   spend   win   write |

Nicholas Harris ¹_____ born in 1934. He ²_____ to school in London. His parents ³_____ poor. His uncle ⁴_____ him a violin. He ⁵_____ two years at a music school in Paris. He ⁶_____ a prize for his performances. He ⁷_____ a professional musician. Famous composers ⁸_____ music for him.

Mark ☐ **/8**

2 Look at the chart. Then complete affirmative and negative sentences about Liam's weekend.

Liam's weekend	
1 go out with friends ✓	4 write a letter ✗
2 watch TV ✗	5 see a film ✗
3 play computer games ✓	6 buy a book ✓

1 _____ with friends.
2 _____ TV.
3 _____ computer games.
4 _____ a letter.
5 _____ a film.
6 _____ a book.

Mark ☐ **/6**

3 Complete the dialogue with the words in the box.

| a   any   many   much   some   the |

Lisa We need to make some pizzas for the party. Have we got ¹_____ mushrooms?
Hana No, we haven't. But we've got ²_____ tomatoes.
Lisa Really? How ³_____ tomatoes have we got?
Hana About five. Is that enough?
Lisa Not really. Is there ⁴_____ supermarket near here?
Hana Yes, there is. It's on West Street. And it's open in ⁵_____ evening.
Lisa Great! How ⁶_____ money have you got?
Hana I've only got £2. Oh dear!

Mark ☐ **/6**   **TOTAL** ☐ **/60**

Heroes
READ

1 Look at the photo of Martin Luther King. Do you know what he fought for? Choose the correct answer.

1 women's rights
2 the rights of black Americans
3 workers' rights

2 Read the text and check your answer to exercise 1.

I have a dream

'I have a dream that my four children will one day live in a nation where they will not be judged by the colour of their skin but by the content of their character.'

The third Monday of January each year is a national holiday in the USA. It is called Martin Luther King Day.

Martin Luther King was born in 1929 in Georgia, in the south of the USA. He studied at college and got a job in Alabama.

At that time, black and white people in the USA were not considered equal. For example, in Alabama, a black person had to stand up on a bus if a white person wanted to sit down. One day, a brave black woman called Rosa Parks refused to do this. Parks and King decided to work together to change the law. In the end they won, and in 1956 Alabama changed the law.

King continued to fight for the rights of black Americans. He made some famous speeches, won the Nobel Peace Prize in 1964, and was a hero for millions of Americans. But some

white people hated him. On 3rd April 1968, he made a speech to a big crowd in Memphis, Tennessee. He talked about his enemies and his own death. The next day, James Earl Ray shot Martin Luther King.

King had four children: two boys and two girls. They all decided to continue his work and to fight for the rights of black Americans.

3 Are these sentences true or false? Correct the false sentences.

1 Martin Luther King Day is a British national holiday.
2 Martin Luther King was born in Alabama.
3 King went to college.
4 Rosa Parks and King wanted the same thing.
5 King and Parks weren't successful.
6 King won the Nobel Peace Prize in 1968.
7 King died in 1968.
8 Only two of King's children continued King's work.

LISTEN

1 How much do you know about these famous people? Choose the correct answers.

1 Lance Armstrong won the Tour de France
   a 5 times.
   b 7 times.

2 Now Lance Armstrong has a charity which
   a helps people be better cyclists.
   b helps people who have cancer.

3 Nelson Mandela fought for the rights of
   a black Americans.
   b black Africans.

4 Nelson Mandela
   a worked in a prison.
   b spent a long time in prison.

5 Mahatma Gandhi died in
   a 1948.
   b 1969.

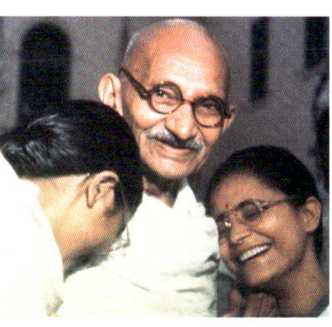

6 Mahatma Gandhi wanted the British to
   a stay in India.
   b leave India.

2 🎧 (2.31) Listen and check your answers.

WRITE AND SPEAK

1 Write three sentences about a famous person from the past that you admire. Use the words and phrases in the box to help you.

> was born … lived … studied … worked as … helped …
> fought for / against …
> brave   honest   intelligent   kind

2 Read your sentences out to the class. Can they guess the name of your hero?

9 Journeys

Alone on the water

BEFORE READING

Answer the questions.

1 Have you ever been on a boat?
2 How do sailors usually control a boat?
3 Do you notice anything unusual about the sailor in the picture?

READ

Reading tip

Newspaper and magazine articles often start with a summary of the story in the first paragraph. The other paragraphs give more details.

THIS UNIT INCLUDES ●●●●

Vocabulary • transport • transport collocations • weather • boats • expressions with *come*
Grammar • present perfect (affirmative) • present perfect (negative and interrogative) • *just, already, yet*
Skills • talking about how you get around • reading and listening to an article about an amazing achievement • talking about sightseeing
Writing • a holiday email

1 Read the *Reading tip*. Then read the first paragraph of the text and answer the questions.

1 What has Hilary Lister just done?
2 Why was it a great achievement?

2 Read the article and put the events in the correct order.

- [ ] She couldn't use her arms or hands any more.
- [ ] She started to design her own boat.
- [ ] She couldn't walk any more.
- [ ] She sailed alone across the English Channel.
- [1] She played a lot of sports.
- [ ] A friend took her sailing for the first time.
- [ ] She had sailing lessons.
- [ ] Her legs started to hurt.

Living again!

Hilary Lister, 33, can't move her limbs or her head – she is completely paralysed. However, she has just sailed alone across the English Channel! How did she do it? Sam Wollaston finds out.

'Where do you want to go?' laughs Hilary Lister. We are on a boat going out of Portsmouth Harbour, and Hilary is sailing it. Suddenly, she's happy and free. Sailing does that to her. 'It's given me my life again,' she says.

Hilary is paralysed because of an unusual disease, but she hasn't always been like this. When she was a child she was always active, and she played a lot of sports. But when she was 11, her legs started to hurt. By the time she was 15, she couldn't walk any more.

About six years ago the disease spread to her arms and hands and she can't use them any more. She thought her life was over. Then, two years ago, a friend took her sailing for the first time. She loved it! But she didn't want to be a passenger. She wanted to sail a boat herself. So she took up sailing as a way to become more confident. 'I had this mad dream to sail across the English Channel,' she said.

Hilary didn't know anything about boats or sailing. But she started to design her own boat. Then she found a boat and some people to help her. The controls of her boat come from her wheelchair and she can steer the boat with her mouth. She sucks a tube to make the boat go left and blows into another tube to make it go right. She has had some lessons, and she is now a very good sailor.

Last month Hilary's dream came true. She left Dover alone in her boat. It was sunny but quite windy. Six hours later she arrived in Calais, France. She was exhausted, but very happy. It was the longest journey made by a completely paralysed person. And she has become the first disabled person to sail across the Channel. Hilary says the experience has really changed her life. 'Next I want to sail around Britain,' she says.

3 🎧 (2.32) **Read the text again. Choose the best answers.**

1 Hilary feels happy and free when she is
   a in Portsmouth.
   b alone.
   c sailing.
2 By the time Hilary was 15 she
   a was completely paralysed.
   b couldn't use her legs.
   c couldn't use any of her limbs.
3 The first time Hilary went sailing she
   a was a passenger.
   b wasn't paralysed.
   c had a dream.
4 She controls her boat
   a with somebody's help.
   b with her mouth.
   c by blowing into the sail.
5 No other disabled person has
   a sailed a boat.
   b been to Calais.
   c sailed from England to France.

UNDERSTANDING IDEAS

Answer the questions. Look at the text, and use your own words and ideas.

1 How do you think sailing has changed Hilary Lister's life?
2 Why do you think Hilary thought her life was over?
3 Do you think Hilary Lister is a good example for all people, disabled and able-bodied? Give reasons.

VOCABULARY

Living again!

1 Match the highlighted words in the text with these definitions.

1 A chair with big wheels that someone who can't walk uses.
2 Finished.
3 Started doing something as a hobby.
4 Something that happens in your mind when you are sleeping.
5 An illness.
6 To decide how you will make something.
7 To pull air or liquid into your mouth.
8 Extremely tired.
9 To push out air from your mouth.
10 To be certain that you can do something and not nervous about it.
11 To control the direction that a vehicle moves.
12 The arms and legs of a person.
13 When you can't move your body or part of your body.
14 To gradually affect a bigger area.
15 When you can't use part of your body or brain normally.

2 Do you know these words?

> by the time   completely   controls   experience
> harbour   sailor   the Channel   tube

3 Match the weather adjectives in the box with the pictures.

> cloudy   cold   foggy   freezing   hot   icy   rainy
> snowy   stormy   sunny   warm   windy

● ● ○   Workbook: page 68

Living again!
ACTIVATE

Complete these sentences with the words from the box.

> blew confident design disabled disease dream
> exhausted limbs over paralysed spread steer
> suck taken up wheelchair

1 Some people suffer from a _____ which leaves them _____ and in need of help.
2 It's sunny in the south at the moment and the good weather is going to _____ to the rest of the country this afternoon.
3 My granddad was 80 last week. We made a cake for him with 80 candles on it and he _____ them all out!
4 I've _____ Kung Fu. I started three months ago and I go three times a week. At first, after every class my _____ hurt! I couldn't move my arms or legs!
5 My brother is _____ because of a motorcycle accident. He can't move his legs at all and he has to use a _____.
6 When I finish university, I want to work for a car company. I want to _____ sports cars – the kind of sports cars that people _____ about when they go to bed!
7 We are not allowed to eat in the classroom, but the teacher lets us _____ sweets when we need to concentrate.
8 At first, I found it difficult to _____ my car into small parking spaces. But now I've got more driving experience and I'm more _____, so I don't usually have any problems.
9 Our grandfather is very old. When I take him shopping he gets _____ quickly and he has to sit down. The shopping trip is usually _____ in five minutes and he wants to go home again!

EXTEND

The weather

1 Match the words with the definitions.

1	chilly	**a**	weather that changes a lot and that often becomes rainy
2	showery	**b**	warm and pleasant weather
3	unsettled	**c**	very bad weather
4	humid	**d**	weather with frequent short periods of rain
5	mild	**e**	hot and wet weather
6	severe	**f**	quite cold weather

2 Circle the correct weather adjectives.

1 They say we're going to have **chilly** / **severe** weather this weekend. They're expecting very strong winds.
2 Take your umbrella. It's been **mild** / **showery** all day.
3 Well, it was sunny for a few days, but since then the weather has been quite **mild** / **unsettled**.
4 You'll need to put a blanket on your bed tonight. It's really **chilly** / **humid**.
5 We're having a **showery** / **mild** autumn. It's not cold at all.
6 I like hot weather, but I hate it when it's **humid** / **severe**. I want to shower all the time!

Boats

3 Match the words with the correct parts of the boat.

> bow hull mast port rudder ~~sail~~ starboard stern

1 sail

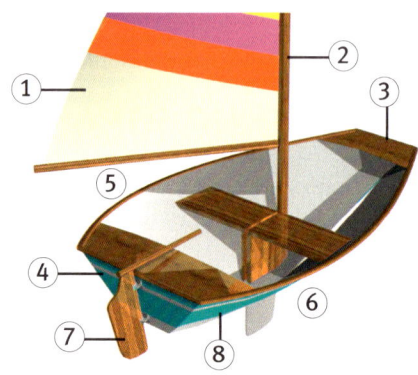

Expressions with *come*

4 Match the expressions with *come* with the definitions.

1	come true	**a**	when a new book, CD or film becomes available
2	come and go	**b**	when someone visits you at home
3	come apart	**c**	when something breaks into pieces
4	come on	**d**	when something you hope for becomes reality
5	come out	**e**	when you tell someone to hurry up
6	come round	**f**	when something is present for a short time and then goes

5 Complete the sentences.

1 Things only come **true** if you work hard!
2 Why don't you come _____ to my house and we can watch a DVD?
3 The pain in my stomach is only there sometimes. It comes and _____.
4 Come _____! We're late and the train leaves in five minutes.
5 Oh no! I dropped the radio and it's come _____!
6 I want to see that new film next week. It comes _____ on Friday.

> ●●●○○ Workbook: page 69

Present perfect: affirmative
EXPLORE

1 Look at the picture. Complete the sentences with the names.

Sam   Julie   Simon   Lucy

1 _____ has lost his passport.
2 _____ and _____ have missed their plane.
3 _____ has dropped her bag.

2 Read the information in the table and complete the examples.

Present perfect: affirmative

- We form the present perfect affirmative with *have* or *has* + the past participle

  I / We / You / They ¹_____ arrived.

  He / She / It ²_____ arrived.

- The short forms of *have* and *has* are *'ve* and *'s*.

  I ³_____ finished my homework.

  She ⁴_____ finished her homework.

- The past participle of regular verbs are the same as the past simple form.

base form	past simple	past participle
drop	⁵_____	⁶_____
miss	⁷_____	⁸_____

- You need to learn the past participle of irregular verbs. Use the Irregular verb list on page 124.

base form	past simple	past participle
eat	⁹_____	¹⁰_____
hear	¹¹_____	¹²_____

Use

- We use the present perfect to talk about recent events that have a result in the present.

  He ¹³_____ _____ (lose) his ticket. Now he can't get on the plane.

  They ¹⁴_____ _____ (eat) a pizza. Now they aren't hungry.

LEARN THIS!

just
We often use *just* with the present perfect for very recent events. We put it between *have / has* and the past participle.
'Do you want a biscuit?'
'No, thanks. I've just had lunch.'

Grammar Reference: page 110

EXPLOIT

1 Write the past participles of these verbs. Check the irregular verbs in the list on page 124.

write   have   cook   walk   drink   do   stop   go

2 Complete the sentences with the present perfect affirmative of verbs from exercise 1. Use the short forms *'ve* and *'s*.

1 They've walked 20 kilometres. They're really tired.
2 I _____ a song. Do you want to hear it?
3 Look. The rain _____. We can go out now.
4 I'm not feeling very well. I _____ six cups of coffee!
5 Mum _____ dinner. Come and sit down at the table!
6 John _____ an accident. He's in hospital.
7 'Where's Chris?' 'He _____ to London for the day.'
8 I _____ my homework, so I can go out now.

3 Complete answers (a–f) with *just* and the present perfect.

a 'I've just heard a really funny story.' (hear)
b 'Sorry. I _____ _____ _____ them all.' (eat)
c 'I don't know. I _____ _____ _____.' (arrive)
d 'They _____ _____ _____ football.' (play)
e 'No. She _____ _____ _____ out.' (go)
f 'Yes. He _____ _____ _____ it.' (buy)

4 Match the answers (a–f) in exercise 3 with the questions (1–6).

1 'What happened here?' ☐
2 'Why are you laughing?' [a]
3 'Is your brother wearing a new jacket?' ☐
4 'Can I have a biscuit?' ☐
5 'Is Suzie at home?' ☐
6 'Why are they tired?' ☐

Grammar Builder: page 111

Workbook: page 70

Transport
VOCABULARY

1 Match the photos with eight of the words from the box.

1 scooter

> **Transport** bicycle (bike) boat bus car coach
> helicopter lorry motorbike plane ~~scooter~~ ship
> taxi train tram underground van

2 🎧 (2.33) Listen, repeat and check your answers.

3 Put the means of transport into the correct groups.

Land	Air	Sea
bicycle		

> ●●●○○ Workbook: page 71

LISTEN

1 🎧 (2.34) Listen to five teenagers talking about their journeys to school. How do they answer the questions? Complete the table.

1 How far do you live from the school?
2 How long does it take?

		Distance	Time
1	Danny	_____ km	_____ mins
2	Charlotte	_____ km	_____ mins
3	Craig	_____ km	_____ mins
4	Ann	_____ km	_____ mins
5	Joe	_____ km	_____ mins

2 🎧 (2.34) Read the information in the *Look out!* box. Then listen again and complete the sentences about how they get to school.

LOOK OUT!

> **We can say**
>
> | go **by** bike | or | cycle |
> |---|---|---|
> | go **on** foot | or | walk |
> | go **by** car | or | drive |
> | go **by** bus, train, taxi | or | take / catch a bus, train, taxi |
> | give somebody a lift to … | or | drive somebody to … |

1 _____ walks or goes by bike.
2 _____ takes the tram.
3 _____ usually goes on foot.
4 _____ walks to the station and goes by underground.
5 _____ goes with her dad in the morning and goes home by bus.

SPEAK

Work in pairs. Ask and answer.

How far do you live from the school?

About …

How do you get to school?

I …

How long does it take?

It …

GRAMMAR

Present perfect: negative and interrogative
EXPLORE

Things to do
- book tickets ☐
- find passports ☐
- change money ☐
- buy guidebook ☐
- pack suitcase ☐

1 🎧 (2.35) Emily and Sarah are getting ready to go to Cairo. Read and listen to the dialogue. Tick the things on the list that they have done.

Emily OK, we've booked the tickets. Have you found the passports?

Sarah Yes, they're here. Have you changed the money?

Emily No, I haven't. We can do that at the airport.

Sarah OK. Have you bought a guidebook?

Emily Yes, I have.

Sarah Good. Now, we haven't packed the suitcase. Let's do that now.

2 Complete the table with the correct form of *have*.

Present perfect
negative
I / You / We / They _____ packed the suitcases.
He / She / It hasn't packed the suitcases.
interrogative and short answers
_____ I / you / we / they bought a guidebook?
Has he / she / it bought a guidebook?
Yes, I have. / No, I _____.
Yes, she has. / No, she hasn't.

●●●○○ Grammar Reference: page 110

EXPLOIT

1 Write sentences about the list in Explore exercise 1. Use the present perfect affirmative and negative.

They've booked the tickets. They haven't ...

2 Complete the questions about the list using the present perfect interrogative. Then write short answers.

1 Have they booked the tickets? Yes, they have.
2 _____ Sarah _____ the passports?
3 _____ Emily _____ the money?
4 _____ Emily _____ a guidebook?
5 _____ they _____ the suitcase?

3 🎧 (2.36) Sarah is in Cairo. She is phoning her friend Tania in London. Listen and tick (✓) the things Sarah and Emily have done.

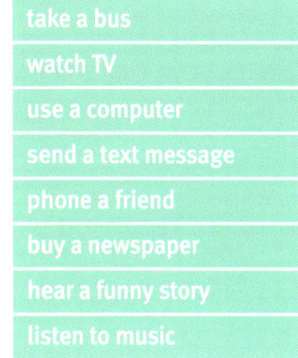

Six things to do in Cairo
- visit the Citadel ✓
- explore the Pyramids of Giza
- visit the Egyptian Museum and see the mummies
- take a boat trip on the River Nile
- walk around Heliopolis
- go shopping at Khan Al-Khalili

4 Write sentences about Emily and Sarah. Say what they have and haven't done.

They've ...
They haven't ....

5 What have you done today? Tick or cross the activities in the list.

take a bus
watch TV
use a computer
send a text message
phone a friend
buy a newspaper
hear a funny story
listen to music

6 Write full sentences about the activities in your list.

I've taken a bus. / I haven't taken a bus.

7 Swap sentences with your partner. Tell the class what your partner has and hasn't done today.

My partner has taken a bus today. She hasn't ...

●●●○○ Grammar Builder: page 111

●●●○○ Workbook: page 72

A holiday email

READ

Read the emails. Are the sentences true or false?

1 The weather isn't very good in Sydney.
2 Debbie enjoyed the boat trip.
3 Debbie hasn't bought any souvenirs yet.
4 Debbie has already seen some kangaroos.
5 Chris likes cold weather.
6 Chris did two things yesterday.
7 Chris hasn't seen a ballet yet.
8 Chris is coming home tomorrow.

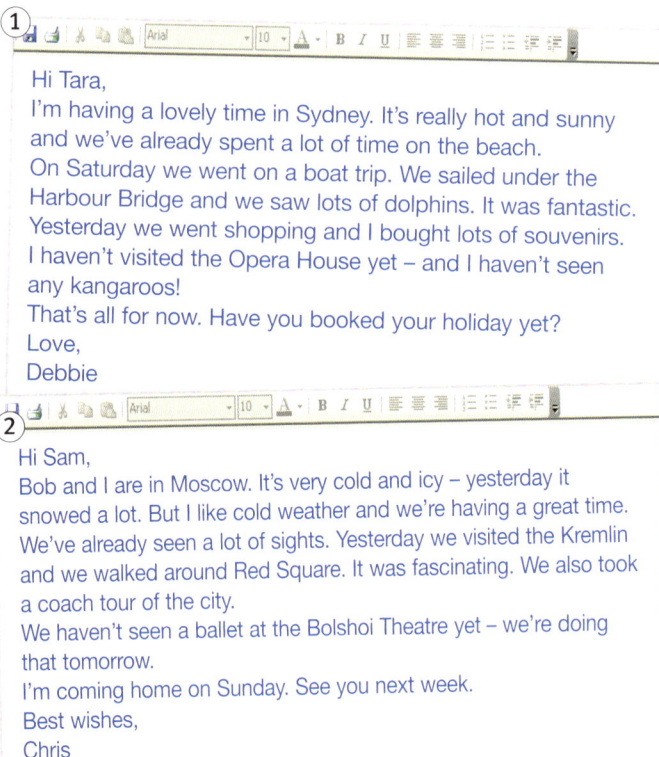

1

Hi Tara,
I'm having a lovely time in Sydney. It's really hot and sunny and we've already spent a lot of time on the beach.
On Saturday we went on a boat trip. We sailed under the Harbour Bridge and we saw lots of dolphins. It was fantastic.
Yesterday we went shopping and I bought lots of souvenirs. I haven't visited the Opera House yet – and I haven't seen any kangaroos!
That's all for now. Have you booked your holiday yet?
Love,
Debbie

2

Hi Sam,
Bob and I are in Moscow. It's very cold and icy – yesterday it snowed a lot. But I like cold weather and we're having a great time. We've already seen a lot of sights. Yesterday we visited the Kremlin and we walked around Red Square. It was fascinating. We also took a coach tour of the city.
We haven't seen a ballet at the Bolshoi Theatre yet – we're doing that tomorrow.
I'm coming home on Sunday. See you next week.
Best wishes,
Chris

PREPARE

1 Read the information and find examples of *yet* and *already* in the emails.

already and yet

1 We use **already** with the present perfect affirmative to say that something has happened earlier than expected.
'Do your homework!' 'I've already done it.'

2 We use **yet** with the present perfect interrogative to ask if something expected has happened.
Have you found the passports yet?

3 We use **yet** with the present perfect negative to say that something expected hasn't happened.
It's 9 p.m. but Dad hasn't come home yet.

2 Read the *Writing tip*. Which endings do the writers use in the emails?

Writing tip: ending an email

You can use one of these phrases:
See you soon.   *Hope to see you soon.*
See you next (week).   *Look forward to seeing you.*
That's all for now.   *Write soon.*

... followed by one of these phrases and your name:
Love   Lots of love   Best wishes   Regards

WRITE

1 Look at the list of things to do in London. Imagine you are on holiday there. Choose three things that you have already done (✓), and two that you haven't done yet (✗).

- visit the Tower of London ☐
- see the Queen ☐
- buy lots of souvenirs ☐
- take a ride on the London Eye ☐
- visit the British Museum ☐
- take a coach tour of the city ☐

2 Write an email to a friend. Use the writing plan below.

- Begin with *Hi...* or *Dear...*
Paragraph 1
- Say where you are.
- Describe the weather.
Paragraph 2
- Describe three things you did. (Use the past simple and time expressions, e.g. *Yesterday we visited...*)
Paragraph 3
- Say two things that you haven't done yet. (Use the present perfect negative.)
Paragraph 4
- Say when you're coming home.
- Finish with phrases from the *Writing tip* box and your name.

Check your work

Have you
☐ used some of the phrases from the *Writing tip* box?
☐ followed the writing plan?
☐ written 70–90 words?
☐ checked your spelling and grammar?

●●●●○ Workbook: page 73

Journeys
LANGUAGE SKILLS

1 🎧 (2.37) Complete the dialogue with the words from the box. Then listen and check your answers.

> fascinating been bought thanks yet home like already tour time

John Hi Steve, is that you?

Steve Yes. Hi, John. Are you phoning from New York?

John Yes, I am. We're sitting on a tourist bus. We're taking a ¹_____ of the city.

Steve Lucky you! Are you having a good ²_____?

John Yes! We're having a great time! We've ³_____ seen lots of sights.

Steve Where have you ⁴_____?

John Yesterday we went to Fifth Avenue and visited the Metropolitan Museum of Art.

Steve Was it interesting?

John It was ⁵_____!

Steve Have you been to the Statue of Liberty ⁶_____?

John No. We're going there now. And then we're going to Central Park.

Steve Great. What's the weather ⁷_____?

John It's really sunny. Good weather for seeing the city.

Steve And have you ⁸_____ any souvenirs?

John Yes, I have. I bought a New York Mets shirt.

Steve Wow!

John And I got one for you!

Steve Fantastic! ⁹_____ a lot! I can't wait to see it.

John Well, I'm coming ¹⁰_____ on Friday. See you at the weekend.

Steve See you then. Bye.

2 Read the dialogue again, and then answer the questions.

1 Where is John sitting?
2 What is he doing now?
3 What has John seen lots of?
4 Where did John go yesterday?
5 Where is John going now?
6 What's the weather like?
7 How many shirts has John bought?
8 When is John coming home?

3 Circle the correct words and short forms.

1 He's **just arrived** / **arrived just** from Rio Janeiro.
2 Sara has **gone** / **went** to the shopping centre.
3 We **'s** / **'ve** seen the new Disney film.
4 I've **wrote** / **written** three emails today.
5 You **'s** / **'ve** eaten a lot of pasta.
6 My parents have **drank** / **drunk** all the coffee.
7 Andrew **'s** / **'ve** phoned his parents.
8 I've **yet** / **already** done my homework.

Transport

1 Check the meaning of the words in the box and match them with the pictures.

> dinghy ~~ferry~~ freighter kayak lifeboat yacht

1 ferry

2 Look up the words in **bold**. Answer the questions.

1 Which form of transport travels on **rails**?
  train
2 Which form of transport do the Americans call a **truck**?
  _____
3 Which forms of transport do you need a **boarding card** for? _____ and _____
4 Which form of transport has **pedals**? _____
5 Which form of transport has a **rotor**? _____

I CAN ...

Read the statements. Think about your progress and tick (✓) one of the boxes.

| ✳ | I need more practice. | ✳✳ | I sometimes find this difficult. | ✳✳✳ | No problem! |

	✳	✳✳	✳✳✳
I can read a magazine article in detail.			
I can say what I have just done.			
I can explain how I get to school.			
I can talk about recent events.			
I can write an email about my holiday.			

●●●○○ Workbook: Self check pages 74–75

A year abroad

BEFORE READING

Look at the photos. Answer the questions.

1 Where do you think the people are?
2 What are the people doing?
3 What do you think a gap year is?

READ

1 Read the *Reading tip*. Then look through the text quickly. Match the photos with paragraphs A–C.

Reading tip

Use the photos to help you understand difficult vocabulary in the text: for example, one of these photos will help you understand the word *castle*.

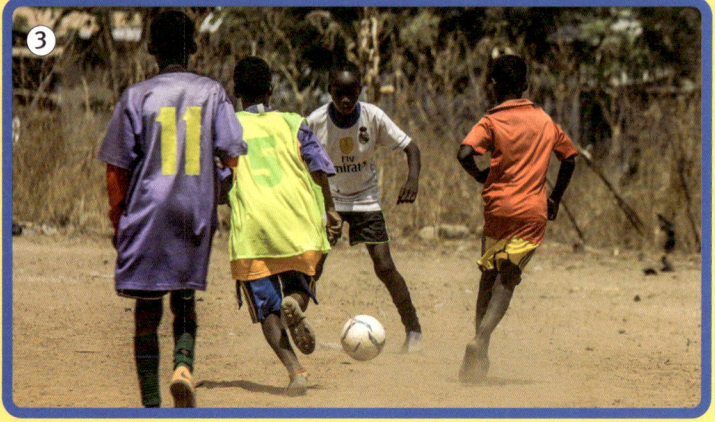

Gap Years

This year, about 150,000 young people in the UK will take a 'gap year'. A gap year is a break between school and university, or between school and starting work in a profession. For most young people, it will be a chance to travel and to have interesting experiences.

So how do young people spend their time? A lot of students finance their gap years by working in the countries they visit and some do voluntary work. Here are three young people who are going to do very different things.

A 'Next year, I'm going to study physics at university. Before then, I want to spend some time abroad and do something completely different. I've got a student work visa for Thailand and I'm going to work at an animal rescue centre for nine months. It will be a demanding job. My responsibilities will be to help to look after the animals and I'll also show visitors around the centre. It will be a great experience.'
Jacqui

2 🎧 (2.41) **Read the text again. Choose the best answers.**

1 A gap year is
   a a chance to start a new profession.
   b a year away from work or study, usually spent in another country.
   c the first year at university.
2 Jacqui is going to
   a study in Thailand.
   b take animals to a rescue centre.
   c do different things at an animal rescue centre.
3 Oliver's job in Ghana
   a will possibly give him the chance to teach different things.
   b is completely different to the job he'll have at the sports centre.
   c can't be found on the internet.
4 Darren doesn't want
   a to work in an office in six months' time.
   b to speak English all the time.
   c to work outside in France.
5 Darren is
   a not going to receive any money for his bank job.
   b going to travel to lots of countries.
   c going to work on an old building.

B 'Next summer, I'm going to start a job at a sports centre – it'll be my first full-time job. But before that, I want to take a break and live abroad and I've found the ideal job for me with Gap Sports. I'm going to live in Ghana, in Africa, for six months and work as a school basketball coach. It will be a really rewarding experience. As the company's website says, I won't just teach sport. I'll probably help with other lessons in school too.'
Oliver

C 'I'm going to start work next October. It's an office job – a post in a bank. Before that, I want to spend a few months working with my hands outdoors. So I've volunteered to work with a charity called Concordia. I'm going to help to restore an old castle in the west of France. There will be 16 other young people from other countries, so it will be a great way to make friends and learn about other cultures. And it'll be a great opportunity to practise my French too!'
Darren

UNDERSTANDING IDEAS

Answer the questions. Look at the text. Use your own words and ideas.

1 Which of the three gap year experiences do you think is the most interesting? Why?
2 Who will probably have experiences that will be useful for his / her future job?
3 What do you think the students on gap years learn from their experiences?

VOCABULARY

Gap years

1 **Match the highlighted words in the text with these definitions.**

1 To provide the money for an event or activity.
2 An official document that lets you enter or leave a country.
3 Working the number of hours that people normally work every week.
4 To clean and repair something that is old and dirty.
5 A chance to do something.
6 A person that trains someone in a sport.
7 Not in a building.
8 Work that is done for no pay.
9 A job that needs special training and education.
10 Giving pleasure or satisfaction.
11 A job.
12 Needing a lot of work, time and energy.
13 The things you have to do in your job.
14 An organization that gives money and helps people.
15 The best for a person or situation.

2 **Match verbs (1–7) with words (a–g). Then find the phrases in the text.**

1 have   a time
2 spend   b abroad
3 take   c a break
4 show   d an interesting experience
5 live   e about other cultures
6 make   f friends
7 learn   g a visitor around

3 **Do you know these words?**

abroad   animal rescue centre   chance   culture
gap year   probably   show around   volunteer

●●○   Workbook: page 76

Gap years
ACTIVATE

Complete these sentences with the words from the box.

charity coach demanding finance full-time ideal
opportunity outdoors post profession responsibilities
restore rewarding visa voluntary

1 I work for a _____ that looks after children without parents.
2 My dad has bought an old sports car but he says he's going to _____ it so that it looks new again.
3 My mother has got a good teaching _____ at the university. She really likes it.
4 When we were at the seaside we had the _____ to go sailing. We really enjoyed it.
5 When I leave university I don't want to work in an office. I want to work _____.
6 It isn't a _____ job. He only works 15 hours a week.
7 I really had a good time on the course and I learnt a lot. It was very _____.
8 They don't pay him to train the school football team. It's a _____ job.
9 You need a passport and a _____ to go to China.
10 The internet is an _____ place to find information about jobs. All the information is there.
11 My brother's a doctor and he's been in the medical _____ for three years.
12 He hurt his leg five years ago and he can't play any more, so now he's the team _____.
13 Your _____ in the job will be to meet visitors and show them the museum.
14 Sam likes his job but he works 12 hours a day and he's always exhausted. It's very _____.
15 We want to travel around the world, so we're working for six months to _____ the trip.

EXTEND

Synonyms: work

1 Match the words with their synonyms.

1 ideal   a trainer
2 outdoors   b repair
3 post   c chance
4 opportunity   d perfect
5 restore   e duties
6 coach   f job
7 responsibilities   g hard
8 demanding   h outside

The world of work

2 Match the work expressions with the definitions.

1 to apply for a job g
2 to offer someone a job
3 to resign from a job
4 to be in charge of a department
5 to have an interview
6 to give someone the sack
7 to go on a training course
8 to work part-time

A to work fewer hours than people normally work
b to go to a meeting about a possible job
c to have a position of responsibility
d to tell someone they can't work for a company any more
e to attend a series of lessons to learn about a job
f to tell a person he / she can work in your company
g to ask to work for a company
h to leave a company

3 Complete the text with the correct form of expressions from exercise 2.

I saw an advertisement for a job on the internet and I ¹applied for it. I had three ²_____ and finally the company ³_____ me the job. At first, I really enjoyed the work and I went on a few ⁴_____ courses. After six months I was in ⁵_____ of the sales department. However, I was exhausted because I worked 50 hours a week, so I decided to only work ⁶_____. Then things started to go badly at the company and I wanted to ⁷_____ and find a new job. I started looking for a job but before I found one, the company closed and they gave me the ⁸_____!

job or work

4 Complete the sentences with job, jobs or work.

1 My brother's got a new job in an office.
2 They're doing voluntary _____ with young people.
3 I want to leave _____ early today.
4 She likes her _____ but the pay isn't very good.
5 There are lots of good _____ on the internet.
6 The people at _____ bought me a birthday present.

●●●●● ○ Workbook: page 77

GRAMMAR

going to
EXPLORE

1 Read about Oliver's plans for the summer. Find examples of *going to*.

After my exams, I'm going to backpack around Europe with my friend, Jeremy. We're going to start in France. Then we're going to visit Italy. We aren't going to stay in hotels. We're going to camp. Where are we going to go after Italy? We don't know. We're going to see how we feel.

2 Read the information in the *Learn this!* box. Complete the table with the examples from the text in exercise 1.

We use **going to** to talk about plans for the future. We form the structure with: *be + going to +* the base form of the verb.

affirmative
I'm going to buy some new trainers.
We ¹_____ in France.

negative
She isn't going to take the exam.
We ²_____ in hotels.

interrogative
Are you going to phone your parents?
Yes, I am. / No, I'm not.
Where ³_____ after Italy?

Grammar Reference: page 112

EXPLOIT

1 Complete the texts about three teenagers' plans for the summer holiday. Use the *going to* future of the verbs in brackets.

> Ella ¹ is going to travel (travel) around Spain with some friends. They ²_____ (not work). They ³_____ (stay) at campsites.

> Tony ⁴_____ (work) in a shop. He ⁵_____ (not have) a holiday. He ⁶_____ (save) his money.

> Victoria ⁷_____ (have) lessons at a summer school. She ⁸_____ (not see) her friends. She ⁹_____ (study) music and drama.

2 Write questions with *going to* about Ella, Tony and Victoria.

1 where / Ella / go / with her friends?
   Where is Ella going to go with her friends?
2 they / work?
3 where / they / stay?
4 where / Tony / work?
5 Tony / have / a holiday?
6 what / he / do / with his money?
7 where / Victoria / have / lessons?
8 Victoria / see / her friends?
9 what / she / study?

3 What are your plans for this evening? Tick or cross the activities in the list.

Activities			
do homework	☐	read a book	☐
go out with friends	☐	send emails	☐
go to bed early	☐	stay up late	☐
phone a friend	☐	surf the internet	☐
play computer games	☐	watch TV	☐

4 Write sentences about your plans for this evening, using the chart in exercise 3.

I'm going to do homework. / I'm not going to do homework.

5 Tell the class about your plans.

> I'm going to do homework and watch TV.

Grammar Builder: page 113

Workbook: page 78

Jobs and work
VOCABULARY

1 Match the photos of the jobs with six of the words from the box.

1 chef

| Jobs | actor artist builder bus driver ~~chef~~ cleaner computer programmer doctor engineer factory worker farmer hairdresser inspector mechanic nurse photographer politician scientist secretary shop assistant translator waiter |

2 🎧 (2.42) Listen, repeat and check your answers.

3 Read the *Look out!* box. Then write three sentences about your friends and family.

LOOK OUT!

> We use *a* or *an* when we say what somebody's job is.
> *She's a doctor. He's an actor.*

My cousin Eric is a bus driver.

●●●○○ Workbook: page 79

LISTEN

Listening tip

Before you do a matching task, read the task and decide what the topic is, e.g. jobs. Then think about some key words that you might hear. For example, a nurse might use these words:
hospital   doctors   patients

1 Read the *Listening tip*. What key words might these people say? Choose from the words in the box. Add your own ideas.

1 a chef   2 a shop assistant   3 a farmer

| animals clothes countryside customers department store dish kitchen outside weather |

2 🎧 (2.43) Listen to four people talking about their jobs. Match the speakers (1–4) with the jobs. Use the words from exercise 1 to help you.

a chef ☐   a farmer ☐
a nurse ☐   a shop assistant ☐

3 🎧 (2.43) Listen again and complete the sentences.

1 I like working _____.
2 I don't earn a lot of _____.
3 I work as part of a _____.
4 I have to work with the general _____.
5 I enjoy working with my _____.
6 I'm on my _____ all day.
7 I don't like using a _____.
8 I have to work with _____.

SPEAK

1 Decide which is the best job in Vocabulary exercise 1, in your opinion, and which is the worst. Write down some reasons.

The best job is computer programmer.
Computer programmers earn a lot of money.
They don't have to deal with the general public.

2 Work in pairs. Ask and answer questions about the best and worst jobs and your reasons.

What's the best job, in your opinion?

Computer programmer. They earn a lot of money and they don't have to deal with the general public.

I agree with you. / I don't agree with you. I think the best job is …

will
EXPLORE

1 Read the text quickly. How many examples of *will / won't* can you find?

Million Dollar Idea

How can I become a millionaire? That's what Alex Tew, a British student, wrote on a piece of paper. A few minutes later, he had an idea: 'I'll invent a new kind of webpage!' So he invented the 'million dollar homepage'. Companies pay Alex for very small advertisements on his webpage – $1 for one pixel. Alex is going to university next year. He'll need money to pay for his studies – but he won't need a million dollars. What will he do with all the extra money? 'I'll save some and I'll spend some,' he says.

2 Read the information in the *Learn this!* box. Then find an affirmative, negative and interrogative example of *will* in the text.

LEARN THIS!

We use *will* to talk about the future and make predictions. We form the structure with: *will* + the base form of the verb.

affirmative

My grandmother will be 80 on her next birthday.

I'll be home before midnight.

(*'ll* is the short form of *will*)

negative

They won't be at school next week.

(*won't* is the short form of *will not*)

interrogative

Will she be home soon?

Yes, she will. / No, she won't.

When will you get your exam results?

●●●○○ Grammar Reference: page 112

EXPLOIT

1 Complete the text. Use the *will* future (affirmative, negative or interrogative) of the verbs in brackets.

Up, up and away!

Martin Halstead is only 19, but he already owns an airline company. Alpha One Airways [1]will make (make) its first flight on 14 December this year. The plane [2]_____ (fly) from the Isle of Man (an island between Britain and Ireland) to Edinburgh, the capital of Scotland. It [3]_____ (not carry) a lot of passengers because it is a small plane. The journey [4]_____ (take) about 45 minutes. Tickets [5]_____ (be) cheap and passengers [6]_____ (not get) any food or drink on the flight. [7]_____ the company _____ (make) money? Nobody knows – but most people think that Martin Halstead [8]_____ (be) successful one day.

2 Complete the questions for these answers about Alpha One Airways. Use *will* and the verbs in the box.

carry   fly   fly   get   ~~make~~   take

1 When will Alpha One Airways make its first flight?
   On 14th December this year.
2 Where _____ the plane _____ from?
   The Isle of Man.
3 Where _____ it _____ to?
   Edinburgh.
4 _____ it _____ a lot of passengers?
   No, it won't.
5 How long _____ the journey _____?
   About 45 minutes.
6 _____ the passengers _____ any food or drink?
   No, they won't.

3 Make predictions about your future. Complete the sentences with *will* or *won't*.

1 I will / won't make a lot of money.
2 I _____ have children.
3 I _____ live in this town.
4 I _____ work with my hands.
5 I _____ have an expensive car.
6 I _____ visit the USA.
7 I _____ be famous.
8 I _____ have the same friends when I'm 30.

●●●○○ Grammar Builder: page 113

●●●○○ Workbook: page 80

A letter of application
READ

Look at the letter. Why did Emily write it?

Dear Sir or Madam,

I am writing to apply for a summer job at Westlake Shopping Centre. I saw the advertisement in the Coventry Daily News.

I have experience of working in a shop. Last summer, I worked for six weeks as a shop assistant in a local book shop.

I am honest, reliable and hard-working. I can send you a reference from the manager of the book shop and also from a teacher at my school. I can start work on 2nd July.

I look forward to hearing from you.

Yours faithfully,

EBlunt

Emily Blunt

PREPARE

1 In which paragraphs does Emily give this information?

when she can start work	who can give references
her work experience	her personal qualities
where she saw the advert	the job she is applying for

Paragraph 1 mentions:
- _____
- _____

Paragraph 2 mentions:
- _____

Paragraph 3 mentions:
- _____
- _____
- _____

2 Match the beginnings and endings of the sentences. Then find similar sentences in the letter.

1 I am writing to apply for
2 I saw the advertisement in
3 I have experience of
4 I worked for a month as
5 I can send you a reference from

a the newspaper.
b the manager of the cinema.
c a job in your shop.
d a waiter.
e working with computers.

3 Read the *Writing tip*. Find phrases in the letter where the writer has avoided using a short form.

> **Writing tip: language in formal letters**
> We don't use short forms (*I'm, he's,* etc.) in formal letters.

WRITE

1 Read the job advert. Imagine you worked at a sports centre last summer. How is that experience useful for this job?

Summer camp helper

We need a reliable, hard-working person to work at our summer camp in Oxford for children aged 5 to 12 from around the world. Your job will include teaching sports and taking the children on trips.

Please apply in writing to:

Happy Days Summer Camps
8 Lincoln Drive
Oxford OX4 7UH

2 Use the writing plan to make notes for your letter of application.

> Paragraph 1:
> - what job you're applying for
> - where you saw the job advertised
>
> Paragraph 2:
> - what experience you have
>
> Paragraph 3:
> - what your personal qualities are
> - when you can start work
> - a reference

3 Write a formal letter applying for the job. Include the information in Prepare exercises 1 and 3.

> **Check your work**
> **Have you**
> ☐ used some of the phrases from Prepare exercise 2?
> ☐ started and ended the letter correctly?
> ☐ divided the letter into paragraphs?
> ☐ written 90–110 words?
> ☐ checked your spelling and grammar?

●●●○○ Workbook: page 81

Just the job
LANGUAGE SKILLS

1 🎧 (2.44) Complete the dialogue with the words from the box. Then listen and check your answers.

> reliable experience reference manager advertisement between forward application interview taught

Mr Adams	Good morning, Simon. Thank you for coming to the ¹_____.
Simon	Er, good morning.
Mr Adams	Now, where did you see the ²_____?
Simon	I saw it on the sport centre's website.
Mr Adams	How old are you?
Simon	17, but I'll be 18 next month.
Mr Adams	And what ³_____ do you have of teaching swimming?
Simon	Well, last year I ⁴_____ swimming classes to children at a swimming club two evenings a week.
Mr Adams	I see. And how old were the children?
Simon	They were ⁵_____ 7 and 14.
Mr Adams	Perfect. Now Simon, are you a good coach?
Simon	I think so! All of the children in my group learnt to swim at the swimming club. And I'm hard-working and ⁶_____.
Mr Adams	Good. Can I ask for a ⁷_____ from the swimming club?
Simon	Of course. In fact I've got a letter here from the club ⁸_____.
Mr Adams	Ah, thank you. We're very interested in your ⁹_____. I'll phone you on Friday and tell you our decision.
Simon	I look ¹⁰_____ to hearing from you then.

2 Complete Mr Adams' notes about the interview.

> ¹Simon taught children between ²_____ and ³_____.
> Personal qualities: He says he's ⁴_____ and reliable.
> Reference: ⁵_____ from the swimming club ⁶_____.
> Contact: ⁷_____ on Friday.

3 Write affirmative, negative and interrogative sentences using *going to* about Kate, Sarah and Ann.

	Kate	Sarah	Ann
do homework	✓	✓	✗
cook lunch	✓	?	?
travel abroad	✗	✗	?

DICTIONARY CORNER

Jobs

1 Check the meaning of the words and match the jobs with the definitions.

> accountant architect ~~barrister~~ bricklayer plumber vet

1 A / An barrister is a lawyer who works in the high courts.
2 A / An _____ builds walls.
3 A / An _____ installs and repairs water pipes, kitchens and bathrooms.
4 A / An _____ looks after sick animals.
5 A / An _____ designs buildings.
6 A / An _____ examines the financial situation of a company.

The world of work

2 Check the meaning of the words in **bold**. Match the questions with the answers.

1 Why did they **promote** him? e
2 Why didn't they give him a **pay rise**?
3 Why did they **dismiss** him?
4 Why did he **retire**?
5 Why did he **attend** the meeting?
6 Why did he do **overtime**?

a Because he was 65 years old.
b Because he wanted to tell everybody about his idea.
c Because he wanted to earn more money.
d Because he always arrived at the office late.
e Because he was very good at his job.
f Because the company had money problems.

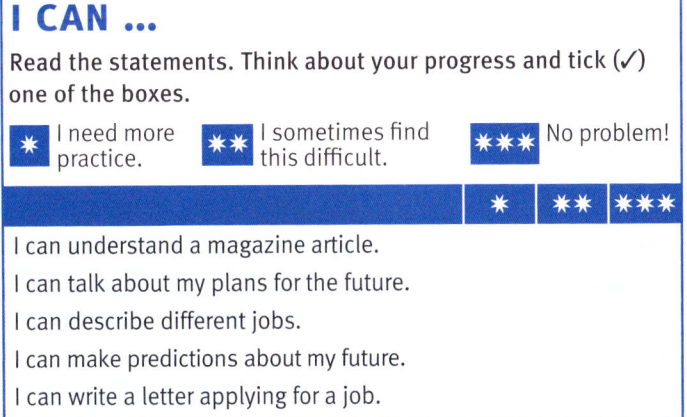

> **I CAN ...**
>
> Read the statements. Think about your progress and tick (✓) one of the boxes.
>
> ✳ I need more practice.   ✳✳ I sometimes find this difficult.   ✳✳✳ No problem!
>
> | | ✳ | ✳✳ | ✳✳✳ |
> |---|---|---|---|
> | I can understand a magazine article. | | | |
> | I can talk about my plans for the future. | | | |
> | I can describe different jobs. | | | |
> | I can make predictions about my future. | | | |
> | I can write a letter applying for a job. | | | |

> ●●○○○ Workbook: Self check pages 82–83

VOCABULARY

1 Complete the second sentence so that it means the same as the first.

1 He drives to work. He goes to work by _____.
2 She sailed across the Atlantic. She crossed the Atlantic by _____.
3 They cycled home. They went home by _____.
4 She walks to school. She goes to school on _____.

Mark /4

2 Complete the words for transport. Use *a, e, i, o* and *u*.

1 b _ _ t
2 sc _ _ t _ r
3 tr _ _ n
4 h _ l _ c _ pt _ r
5 _ nd _ rgr _ _ nd
6 m _ t _ rb _ k _
7 c _ _ ch
8 pl _ n _

Mark /8

3 Complete the sentences with *A* or *An* and the correct job.

1 _____ helps people when they are not well.
2 _____ builds houses.
3 _____ cuts people's hair.
4 _____ takes part in plays or films.
5 _____ mends cars and motorbikes.
6 _____ draws and paints pictures.
7 _____ cooks food in a restaurant or hotel.
8 _____ serves customers in a shop.

Mark /8

4 Complete the words in the text.

I work [1] o _____ and I like it. I spend all my time at the beach. I don't think I would like to work all day in an office sitting in front of a [2] c _____. We work in a [3] t _____ and we also work with the general [4] p _____ although I don't think I can call them [5] c _____! If there is a problem, we help them. I'm on my [6] f _____ all day, except for when I'm in the water, but I also work with my [7] h _____, sometimes pulling people out of the sea! I don't earn a lot of [8] m _____ but I like working as a lifeguard.

Mark /8

GRAMMAR

1 Write replies using the present perfect affirmative.

1 Do your homework!
2 Clean your room!
3 Eat your dinner!
4 Have a shower!

Mark /4

2 Write sentences in the present perfect affirmative with *just*.

1 we / finish / our dinner
2 my friend / go / home
3 the rain / stop
4 I / see / a terrible film
5 I / hear / a great joke
6 he / book / a holiday

Mark /6

3 Make these sentences negative.

1 I've bought a ticket.
2 The play has started.
3 You've finished your lunch.
4 He's gone for a walk.
5 She's cooked dinner for everybody.

Mark /5

4 What have Rosie and Louise done today? Write questions and short answers.

1 Rosie / have breakfast? ✓
2 Louise / phone / her mum? ✗
3 Rosie and Louise / play / tennis? ✗
4 Rosie / do / the housework? ✓
5 Rosie and Louise / eat / all the bread? ✓

Mark /5

5 Complete the dialogue with the correct form of *going to* and the verbs in brackets.

Paul [1]_____ (you / be) at the cinema tomorrow night?
Andy No, I'm not. I [2]_____ (stay) at home.
Paul Really? Why [3]_____ (you / do) that?
Andy Because we've got an exam the next day!
Paul But it isn't an important exam.
Andy [4]_____ (you / miss) it?
Paul No, I'm not. But I [5]_____ (not revise) for it!

Mark /5

6 Complete the text with the correct form of *will* and the verbs in brackets.

The Space Hotel [1]_____ (open) in 2020. It [2]_____ (have) 350 rooms, each with a view of planet Earth from the window. Guests [3]_____ (arrive) by spaceship, and during their stay, they [4]_____ (enjoy) a wide variety of activities. They certainly [5]_____ (not get bored). But holidays at the Space Hotel [6]_____ (not be) cheap. How much [7]_____ (they / cost)? About $500,000 for two weeks!

Mark /7   **TOTAL** /60

Jobs for teenagers
READ

1 Look at the photos. Answer the questions.

1 What are the people doing? Use the words in the box to help you.

> **Verbs** check clean serve
> **Nouns** counter customer fast-food restaurant shop till

2 Are they enjoying their work? How can you tell?
3 Which jobs are popular in your country for people your age?

About half of 16- and 17-year-olds in the UK have got jobs, and three quarters of this age group also go to school. They do part-time jobs before or after school and at weekends. The most common jobs are babysitting (very popular with girls) and paper rounds (popular with boys). Cleaning and working in a shop are also popular jobs.

In the UK, school students are not allowed to work more than two hours on a school day, or more than twelve hours in total during a school week. They are not allowed to work before 7 a.m. or after 7 p.m. (but babysitters can work later). They must have at least two weeks' holiday from school each year when they don't work at all.

Teenagers do part-time jobs because they want to earn some money. However, they don't usually earn very much. In the UK, there is a minimum wage for adults: £5.52 an hour. For 16- and 17-year-olds, it is £3.40 an hour. For children under 16, there is no minimum wage, so many teenagers work for £2 or £3 an hour.

2 Read the text. Answer the questions.

1 How many young people aged 16 and 17 have jobs in the UK?
2 What is the most common job for teenage girls?
3 What is the most common job for teenage boys?
4 How many hours in total can young people work during a school week?
5 Can babysitters work after 7 p.m.?
6 Why do teenagers get part-time jobs?
7 What is the minimum wage for a 16-year-old?
8 What is the minimum wage for a 15-year-old?

LISTEN

1 🎧 2.47 Listen to Jack, Ryan and Lauren talking about part-time jobs. Match the speakers with three of the opinions.

a It is a good idea for teenagers to work.
b It is a bad idea for teenagers to work.
c It is a good idea, but only if they earn a lot of money.
d There are good things and bad things about it.

1 Jack ☐   2 Ryan ☐   3 Lauren ☐

2 🎧 2.47 Listen again and complete the opinions.

1 Part-time jobs give you good _____ of working.
2 The other _____ of a part-time job is that you can earn some money.
3 Part-time jobs are a good way of _____ people.
4 Sometimes part-time jobs make teenagers too _____ to study!
5 The most important thing for teenagers is to get a good _____.
6 Teenagers can only get part-time jobs that are badly _____.

WRITE AND SPEAK

Work in pairs. What do you think about part-time jobs? Make notes. Student A: Express an opinion from Listen exercise 2 or your own idea. Student B: Use the phrases in the box to say if you agree or disagree.
Take turns to be A and B.

> I agree (with you).   I don't agree (with you).
> That's a good point.   That's true.   I don't think that's true.

> Part-time jobs give you good experience of working.

> That's a good point./I don't think that's true.

GRAMMAR REFERENCE 1

be

Affirmative	Negative
I am	I am not
you are	you are not
he / she / it is	he / she / it is not
we are	we are not
you are	you are not
they are	they are not

Interrogative	Short answers
Am I?	Yes, I am. / No, I am not.
Are you?	Yes, you are. / No, you are not.
Is he / she / it?	Yes, she is. / No, it is not.
Are we?	Yes, we are. / No, we are not.
Are you?	
Are they?	Yes, they are. / No, they are not.

Contracted forms

I am → I'm you are → you're we are → we're they are → they're
I am not → I'm not   is not → isn't   are not → aren't

We don't use contracted forms in affirmative short answers.
Yes, I am. ~~Yes, I'm.~~ ✗

have got

Affirmative	Negative
I have got	I haven't got
you have got	you haven't got
he / she / it has got	he / she / it hasn't got
we have got	we haven't got
you have got	you haven't got
they have got	they haven't got

Interrogative	Short answers
Have I got ...?	Yes, I have. / No, I haven't.
Have you got ...?	Yes, you have. / No, you haven't.
Has he / she / it got ...?	Yes, she has. / No, he hasn't.
Have we got ...?	Yes, we have. / No, we haven't.
Have you got ...?	Yes, you have. / No, you haven't.
Have they got ...?	Yes, they have. / No, they haven't.

We use *have got* to talk about possession, and for describing people.
Have you got a brother?   We haven't got any homework.
Kate has got brown eyes and black hair.

Demonstrative pronouns

Singular	this that	Plural	these those

We use *this* and *these* with objects that are near to us.
This is a bag. These are my books.
We use *that* and *those* with objects that are further away from us
That's my PC. Those are tall trees.
We use *this* to introduce people.
This is Sarah.
We use *that* to talk about something that somebody has just said.
'Are you Harry?' 'That's right.'

Present simple: affirmative

Affirmative	
I work.	We work.
You work.	You work.
He / She / It works.	They work.

Spelling rules for 3rd person singular (*he / she / it*)
Most verbs: add -s.
play + -s → *play**s***
Verbs ending in -ch / -ss / -sh / -o: add -es
watch + -es → *watch**es***   *go* + -es → *go**es***
Verbs ending in consonant + -y, ~~-y~~ → ies
study ~~-y~~ → ies → *stud**ies***

We use the present simple:
• for something that happens always or regularly.
  I watch TV every day.   I get up at 7.30.   My brother plays basketball.
• for a fact, or something that is always true.
  Russell comes from New Zealand.
  I live in Oxford.

Present simple: negative

Negative
I / You / We / They don't play. He / She / It doesn't play.

Full forms
I don't play. = I do not play.
He doesn't play. = He does not play.

We form the negative with *don't* or *doesn't* + the base form.
(The base form of the verb is the infinitive without *to*, e.g. *go, have, work*.)

Present simple: affirmative

1 Write the third person singular forms.

1 study   he studies
2 watch   she _____
3 go   it _____
4 fly   he _____
5 do   she _____
6 like   it _____
7 finish   he _____
8 play   she _____

2 Complete the sentences with the verbs in exercise 1.

1 She _____ TV every evening.
2 Tom _____ his homework on the bus.
3 School _____ at four o'clock.
4 Madeleine _____ to school by bus.
5 Eva _____ maths at university.
6 Pete _____ football every Saturday.
7 My mum _____ travelling.
8 John _____ to New York once a month.

3 Order the words to make sentences.

1 uncle / in a shop / works / my
My uncle works in a shop.
2 pizza / brother / loves / my
3 to school / go / we / by bike
4 me / my / like / classmates
5 grandmother / french / his / speaks
6 my cousins / I / football / play / and
7 lives / New York / in / my friend's aunt

4 Complete the sentences with the verbs in the box.

cook   drive   get up   live   read   speak   teach   work

1 My dad _____ the newspaper every morning.
2 I _____ French and English.
3 We _____ in a small house.
4 Paul and Kate _____ in London.
5 You _____ to work.
6 My mum is a teacher. She _____ English at my school.
7 My sister sometimes _____ dinner.
8 I _____ at six o'clock every morning.

Present simple: negative

5 Complete the sentences with *don't* or *doesn't*.

1 School _____ finish at three o'clock. It finishes at half past three.
2 We _____ speak German.
3 My mum _____ drive.
4 I _____ go to school by bus. I walk.
5 Fiona and Sally _____ like coffee. They like tea.
6 Mark _____ read books. He reads newspapers.
7 Tom and I _____ come from Manchester. We're from London.
8 I'm sorry. I _____ understand this word.
9 My sister _____ watch TV in the evening. She reads.
10 I _____ play basketball but I play tennis.

6 Complete the sentences. Use the present simple affirmative or negative.

1 'Where's Kate?' 'I'm sorry. I _____.' (know)
2 Dave and Sue haven't got bikes – they _____ (walk) to school.
3 Jason _____ (like) maths. He thinks it's difficult.
4 I _____ (stay) at home on Saturdays. I don't go to school.
5 Tina likes English, but she _____ (hate) French.
6 We _____ (love) computer games. They're great!
7 My aunt is a teacher. She _____ (work) in an office.
8 John hasn't got a brother. He _____ (play) football with his cousin.

7 Look at the pictures and write two sentences, one affirmative and one negative.

1 she / play tennis
   she / play football
   She plays tennis.
   She doesn't play football.

2 he / walk to school
   he / go to school by bike

3 she / read books / in her bedroom
   she / watch TV / in her bedroom

4 he / get up early / on Sundays
   he / stay in bed / on Sundays

5 she / teach maths
   she / teach English

Present simple: interrogative

Interrogative
Do I work?
Do you work?
Does he / she / it work?
Do we work?
Do you work?
Do they work?

Short answers
Yes, I do. / No, I don't.
Yes, she does. / No, he doesn't.
Yes, they do. / No, you don't.

We form present questions with *do* or *does* + the base form of the verb. (The base form of the verb is the infinitive without *to*.)

Do you play football?

Does he play football?

Note: we don't use the third person singular form.

Does he ~~plays~~ football? ✗
Does he play football? ✓

Wh- questions

We use question words (*who, what, where, when,* etc.) to ask for information. The question word comes at the beginning of the question.

Where do you live?
When do you go to bed?

What is sometimes followed by a noun.

What books do you like?
What subjects do you study at school?

If the question includes a preposition, the preposition usually goes at the end.

Who do you work for?
Who do you live with?

Adverbs of frequency

We use adverbs of frequency to say how often we do something.

0%	➡	➡	➡	➡	100%
never	hardly ever	sometimes	often	usually	always

The normal position for an adverb of frequency is:
– immediately after the verb *be*

He's always late for school.
She isn't always happy to see me.

– immediately before most other verbs.

They often play tennis at the weekend.
You never phone me.

Imperatives

We often use imperatives in announcements.
We form the imperative by using the base form of the verb, with or without *don't*.

Join our reading group!
Don't forget – we meet every Monday.

EVERYDAY ENGLISH

Object pronouns

Subject pronoun	Object pronoun
I	me
you	you
he	him
she	her
it	it
we	us
you	you
they	them

We use *me, him, her, us* and *them* for people.

There's Ann. Do you know her?

We use *it* and *them* for things.

This is your pen. Do you want it?
I never eat apples. I hate them.

We use object pronouns after prepositions.

Listen to me!
Do you want to come with us?

Present simple: interrogative

1 Complete the questions and short answers.

1 *Do* you like football?
No, I *don't*.
2 _____ your brother walk to school?
Yes, he _____.
3 _____ they live in London?
No, they _____.
4 _____ your parents watch TV in the evenings?
Yes, they _____.
5 _____ Kate read a lot?
No, she _____.
6 _____ it rain a lot in Scotland?
Yes, it _____.
7 _____ you get up early?
Yes, I _____.
8 _____ you and your friends go swimming on Saturdays?
No, we _____.

2 Put the words in the correct order to make questions.

1 you / do / swimming / like?
2 work / does / your mum?
3 chess / your best friend / play / does?
4 do / speak / you / Russian?
5 go / you and your friends / do / to the cinema?
6 play / computer games / do / you?

3 SPEAKING Ask and answer the questions in exercise 2.

Wh- questions

4 Read the answers and choose the correct question words.

1 **How** / **When** do you get to school?
By bike.
2 **Where** / **Who** do you sit next to in class?
I sit next to Ahmed.
3 **When** / **Where** do you do your homework?
After dinner.
4 **What** / **How** sports do you like?
I like football and tennis.
5 **Who** / **Where** does your best friend live?
Next door to my house.

5 Complete the questionnaire with the question words in the box.

How	What	When	Where	Who

1 _____ do you live?
2 _____ do you live with?
3 _____ do you get up on Sunday mornings?
4 _____ do you relax?
5 _____ programmes do you watch on TV?

6 SPEAKING Work in pairs. Ask and answer the questions in exercise 2.

Adverbs of frequency

7 Rewrite the sentences. Use the adverb of frequency in brackets.

1 I get up early on Sundays. (often)
I often get up early on Sundays.
2 I'm late for school. (never)
3 I speak English in English classes. (always)
4 I do my homework before dinner. (often)
5 I read a book in English. (hardly ever)
6 I help my friends with their homework. (sometimes)
7 I'm happy with my exam results. (usually)

8 Which of your answers to exercise 7 are true for you? Rewrite the others and change the adverbs of frequency so that they are true for you.

Imperatives

9 Match the sentence halves.

1 Come   a this number for more information.
2 Don't be   b new people and make friends.
3 Learn   c healthy – and have fun!
4 Be   d how to make films.
5 Meet   e late.
6 Phone   f and see what it's like.

EVERYDAY ENGLISH

Object pronouns

10 Work in pairs. Student A: Say a subject pronoun. Student B: Say the object pronoun.

11 Put the words in the correct order. Don't forget to add punctuation.

1 know / them / we / don't
2 her / can't / I / find
3 like / don't / him / I
4 me / hardly ever / phones / she
5 never / listen to / us / they
6 do / like / it / you

there is / there are

Singular	Plural
Affirmative	
There's a book.	**There are** some books.
Negative	
There isn't a book.	**There aren't** any books.
Interrogative	
Is there a book?	**Are there** any books?
Short answers	
Yes, there is. / No, there isn't.	Yes, there are. / No, there aren't.

We usually use the short form of *there is: there's*. However, we use the full form in affirmative short answers.

Is there a TV? Yes. there is. (NOT Yes, ~~there's~~.)

there are does not have a short form.

We use *Is there a...?* to ask about singular nouns.

Is there a bin in the classroom?

We use *Are there any...?* to ask about plural nouns.

Are there any pens on the desk?

We use *There isn't a...* with singular nouns.

There isn't a noticeboard in our classroom.

We use *There aren't any...* with plural nouns.

There aren't any books in my schoolbag.

See Grammar Reference 8 for more information on *some* and *any*.

have to

Affirmative	
I have to	
You have to	
He has to	
She has to	
It has to	be here before ten o'clock.
We have to	
You have to	
They have to	

Negative	
I don't have to	
You don't have to	
He doesn't have to	
She doesn't have to	
It doesn't have to	be here before ten o'clock.
We don't have to	
You don't have to	
They don't have to	

Interrogative	
Do I have to	
Do you have to	
Does he have to	
Does she have to	
Does it have to	be here before ten o'clock?
Do we have to	
Do you have to	
Do they have to	

Short answers
Yes, I / we / you / they do.
No, I / we / you / they don't.
Yes, he / she / it does.
No, he / she / it doesn't.

We use *have to* to say that something is necessary or compulsory.

She has to be at school before 8:30.

We use *don't have to* to say that something is not necessary (but it isn't against the rules).

We don't have to have lunch at school. Some people go home for lunch.

there is / there are

1 Complete the sentences with *There's* or *There are*.

1 _____ 14 classrooms in our school.
2 _____ a TV in this classroom.
3 _____ eight boys in this class.
4 _____ a book on my desk.
5 _____ three pens in my bag.
6 _____ seven lessons in one school day.
7 _____ a clock on the wall.
8 _____ a bin near the teacher's desk.

2 Make these sentences negative.

1 There's a computer in the room.
_____

2 There are 650 students in the school.
_____

3 There are two possible answers.
_____

4 There's a teacher in the classroom.
_____

5 There's a table next to the door.
_____

6 There are three plants near the window.
_____

7 There are five shelves near the board.
_____

8 There's a bin under the desk.
_____

3 Write questions and answers. Use *Is there?* / *There is* or *Are there?* / *There aren't*.

1 Is there a computer? Yes, there is.
2 Are there any plants? No, there aren't.

1 a computer ✓
2 any plants ✗
3 a noticeboard ✗
4 any students? ✓
5 a clock? ✓
6 a table? ✗
7 any CDs? ✗
8 any blinds? ✓

have to

4 Match the jobs in the chart with the pictures. Write the numbers (1–6) in the boxes.

Jobs	Mark	Suzie
tidy his / her bedroom	yes	no
clean the house	yes	no
cook dinner	no	no
do the washing	yes	yes
make breakfast	yes	yes
go to the supermarket	no	yes

5 Look at the chart. Then write sentences, using the prompts and *have to*, affirmative or negative.

1 Mark / tidy his bedroom
Mark has to tidy his bedroom.

2 Suzie / tidy her bedroom
3 Mark / clean the house
4 Suzie / clean the house
5 Mark and Suzie / cook dinner
6 Mark and Suzie / do the washing
7 Mark and Suzie / make breakfast
8 Suzie / go to the supermarket
9 Mark / go to the supermarket

6 Ask and answer questions, using the prompts in exercise 5.

Does Mark have to tidy his bedroom?   Yes, he does.

7 Find out what your partner has to do at home. Ask and answer about the activities in exercise 4.

Do you have to tidy your bedroom?   Yes, I do. / No, I don't.

Present continuous

Affirmative	Negative
I'm eating.	I'm not eating.
You're eating.	You're not eating.
He's / She's / It's eating.	He / She / It isn't eating.
We're / You're / They're eating.	We / You / They aren't eating.

Interrogative	
Am I	
Are you	
Is he / she / it	eating?
Are we / you / they	

Short answers
Yes, I am. / No, I'm not.
Yes, she is. / No, she isn't.
Yes, we are. / No, we aren't.

We form the present continuous with the correct form of *be* + the *-ing* form of the main verb.

drink   She is drinking.
work   They aren't working.
listen   Are you listening?

Spelling: *-ing* forms

We add *-ing* to the end of most verbs

play + -ing → *play**ing***

If the verb ends in a consonant + *-e*, we usually drop the *-e*, and add *-ing*.

wave -e + -ing → *wav**ing***

If the verb ends in a short vowel + consonant, we double the consonant and add *-ing*.

swim + m + -ing → *swim**ming***

We use the present continuous:
- for something that is happening now.
  Mum's in the kitchen. She's cooking dinner.
- for arrangements in the future.
  We're going to the cinema this evening.

can

Affirmative
I / You / We / They / He / She / It can swim.
Negative
I / You / We / They / He / She / It can't swim.

The full form of *can't* is *cannot*.

Interrogative
Can I / you / we / they / he / she / it swim?
Short answers
Yes, I can. / No, they can't.

We use the short form *can't* in short answers.

We use *can* to:
- talk about ability.
  I can swim. Pete can't cook. Can you play football? Yes, I can.
- make requests.
  Can you come to the barbecue?

Adverbs

We form most adverbs by adding *-ly* to the adjective.

slow → slowly   careful → carefully   easy → easily

Some adjectives don't change when we form adverbs.

fast   high   late   low   early   hard

The adverb form of *good* is *well*.

We use adverbs with verbs to say how something happens.

It's raining hard.   He sings badly.

EVERYDAY ENGLISH

Present continuous for future

We can use the present continuous to talk about arrangements in the future. We include a future time reference: *this evening*, *tomorrow afternoon*, *next Sunday* etc.

Pete is going to the library on Saturday morning.
We're meeting at six o'clock this evening.

Sometimes there isn't a time expression when it's clear we are talking about the future.

'What are you doing this evening?' 'I'm staying in and watching TV.'
What time are you going out?

Present continuous

1 Complete the sentences with the correct form of *be*.

1 Pete _____ eating a pizza.
2 I _____ wearing a jacket.
3 Neil and I _____ watching a film.
4 Sarah _____ checking her emails.
5 It _____ raining.
6 You _____ smiling.

2 Write the *-ing* forms.

1 study _____
2 do _____
3 write _____
4 swim _____
5 read _____
6 have _____

3 Complete the sentences with the correct form of *be* and the *-ing* forms in exercise 2.

1 Jake and Andy _____ in the pool.
2 My sister's at university. She _____ Spanish.
3 We _____ gymnastics.
4 I _____ a magazine.
5 You _____ a good time.
6 John _____ a letter to his uncle.

4 Make the sentences negative.

1 I'm working.
2 Tom and I are reading.
3 Kate is sitting next to Paul.
4 David and Lucy are watching TV.
5 Martin is wearing brown shoes.
6 I'm walking to town.
7 The sun is shining.
8 We're chatting to Robert.

5 Write questions. Put the words in the correct order and add the correct form of *be*.

1 wearing / a skirt / Maria?
   Is Maria wearing a skirt?

2 playing / Fred and Sue / computer games?
3 gymnastics / doing / Sarah?
4 you / phone / your friend?
5 to Oxford / he / drive?

6 Write questions and affirmative (✓) or negative (✗) short answers.

1 he / speak / Arabic? ✗
   Is he speaking Arabic? No, he isn't.

2 Wendy and Pam / go cycling? ✓
3 you / use / that computer? ✗
4 Pam / get up? ✓
5 Cathy and Steve / cook? ✗
6 Harry / do / the washing up? ✓

can and adverbs

7 Write sentences with *can*, affirmative or negative.

1 I / swim ✗
2 we / speak English ✓
3 Jenny and Mary / rollerblade ✓
4 Anne / sing ✗
5 Charles and Jeff / use a computer ✗
6 Philip and I / cook ✓
7 Edward / do gymnastics ✗
8 you / play table tennis ✓

8 Look at the chart and write questions and answers.

	Rob	Clare and Beth
ride a bike	✓	✓
play volleyball	✗	✓
speak Italian	✓	✗

Can Rob ride a bike?   Yes, he can.

9 Draw lines to match the opposites.

1 early   a badly
2 fast   b late
3 quietly   c loudly
4 well   d slowly

10 Complete the sentences with adverbs from exercise 9.

1 'Is he still in bed?' 'Yes. He always gets up _____ on Sundays.'
2 'You're talking very _____. I can't hear you.'
3 'He's very good at sport. He plays football and rugby very _____.'
4 I always arrive _____ at school. I do my homework in the classroom before lessons start.
5 'Wait for me! I can't walk very _____ in these boots!'
6 'Why are you writing _____?'
   'Because I don't want to make mistakes.'

EVERYDAY ENGLISH

Present continuous for future

11 Complete the conversation. Use the present continuous.

Helen What [1]_____ you _____ (do) this evening, Shelly?
Shelly Nothing really. I [2]_____ (stay) at home.
Helen Well, Pam and I [3]_____ (go) bowling. Do you want to come?
Shelly Yes, please. What time [4]_____ you _____ (go)?
Helen Pam [5]_____ (work) at the café this afternoon, so I [6]_____ (meet) her when she finishes work at six o'clock.
Shelly OK, see you at the café at six.

Comparative adjectives

Short adjectives: spelling rules
We add -er to short adjectives to make the comparative form.

old → old**er**

If the adjective ends in -e, we add -r.

large → larg**er**

If the adjective ends in a vowel and a consonant, we double the consonant and add -er.

wet → wett**er**

If the adjective ends in -y, we change the -y into -ier.

dry → dr**ier**

Irregular adjectives
Some adjectives have irregular comparative forms.

good → better

bad → worse

far → further

Long adjectives
We use *more* for most long adjectives (adjectives with more than one syllable).

intelligent → more intelligent

than
We use *than* when we compare two things.

Africa is hotter than Europe.

We usually use the object pronoun after *than*. The subject pronoun sounds very formal.

She's shorter than me. ✓

She's shorter than I. ✗

but She's shorter than I am. ✓

Superlative adjectives

Short adjectives: spelling rules
We add -est to short adjectives to make the superlative form.

old → old**est**

If the adjectives ends in -e, we add -st.

large → larg**est**

If the adjective ends in a vowel and a consonant, we double the consonant and add -est.

wet → wett**est**

If the adjective ends in -y, we change the -y into -iest.

DRY → dr**iest**

Irregular adjectives
Some adjectives have irregular superlative forms.

good → the best

bad → the worst

far → the furthest

Long adjectives
We use *the most* for most long adjectives (adjectives with more than one syllable).

intelligent → the most intelligent

EVERYDAY ENGLISH

would like

I'd like is a polite way of saying *I want*.
(*I'd like = I would like*)

I'd like the soup, please, then the chicken.

We'd like to buy tickets for the show, please.

We use *Would you like ...?* to make offers and invitations.

'Would you like a sandwich?' 'Yes, please.'

'Would you like to come to the cinema?' 'No, thank you.'

Comparative adjectives

1 Write the comparative form of the adjectives.

1 high _____
2 easy _____
3 big _____
4 wet _____
5 friendly _____
6 nice _____
7 tall _____
8 late _____

2 Complete the sentences. Use the comparative forms of the adjectives in brackets.

1 Are motorbikes _____ than cars? (noisy)
2 Sue is _____ than Tina. (short)
3 The Sahara Desert is _____ than the Gobi Desert. (wide)
4 Is Paris _____ from Cairo than London? (far)
5 Rome is _____ than Oxford. (hot)
6 John is _____ at maths than me. (good)
7 Is Tom _____ than Michael? (heavy)
8 France is _____ than Germany. (large)

3 Write your opinions. Use comparative forms of the adjectives.

1 science / history / difficult
   Science is more difficult than history. or
   History is more difficult than science.
2 books / TV / interesting
3 Wayne Rooney / Ronaldinho / famous
4 lions / elephants / dangerous
5 girls / boys / intelligent
6 money / love / important
7 baseball / football / exciting

Superlative adjectives

4 Complete the sentences with the superlative form of the adjectives.

1 Tom's very quiet. He's *the quietest* boy in the class.
2 Mount Everest is very high. It's _____ mountain in the world.
3 I think Geography is easy. It's _____ subject in school.
4 It's very wet today. It's _____ day of the year.
5 Rachel is very nice. She's _____ girl I know.
6 Fred's exam results are bad. They're _____ results in the school.
7 My friend Jake is very funny. He's _____ boy in the class.
8 Neptune is very far away. It's _____ planet from the sun.

5 Write questions. Use the superlative form of the adjectives. Then give your opinion.

1 What / beautiful / place in the world?
   What's the most beautiful place in the world?
   I think … is the most beautiful place in the world.
2 Who / intelligent / person in your family?
3 What / popular / food in your country?
4 Who / famous / person in the world?
5 What / important / school subject?
6 What / boring / sport?

6 Write sentences, using comparative and superlative forms of the adjectives.

1 Natalie / old / Mary, but Sarah …
   Natalie is older than Mary, but Sarah is the oldest.
2 France / hot / Britain, but Spain …
3 Harry / intelligent / Dave, but Robert …
4 Magazines / cheap / books, but newspapers …
5 History / interesting / science, but music …
6 Kate / friendly / Steve, but Wendy …
7 New York / large / London, but Tokyo …
8 Rugby / good / tennis, but football …

EVERYDAY ENGLISH

would like

7 Choose the correct verbs.

1 'Do you like / Would you like a coffee?' 'Yes, please.'
2 'Do you like / Would you like pizza?' 'No, I hate it.'
3 'Do you like / Would you like to come on a picnic?' 'Yes, I'd love to.'
4 I'm thirsty. I like / I'd like a glass of water.
5 'I like / I'd like something to eat.' 'OK. Here's an apple.'
6 'Do you like / Would you like to come shopping with me?' 'No, thanks. I'm doing my homework.'

8 Work with a partner. Student A: Make offers and invitations with *would like*. Student B: Reply politely.

1 a cola
2 come to the park
3 a cake
4 go to the football match
5 a banana
6 go for a walk
7 a cup of tea
8 borrow my bike

Would you like a cola? — Yes, please.

Would you like to come to the park? — No, thank you.

Past simple: *be* and *can*

The past simple of *be* is *was* or *were*.
wasn't = was not

Affirmative	Negative
I was ill.	I wasn't ill.
You were ill.	You weren't ill.
He / She / It was ill.	He / She / It wasn't ill.
We were ill.	We weren't ill.
You were ill.	You weren't ill.
They were ill.	They weren't ill.

Interrogative	Short answers
Was I ill?	
Were you ill?	Yes, I / he / she / it was.
Was he / she / it ill?	No, I / he / she / it wasn't.
Were we ill?	Yes, you / we / they were.
Were you ill?	No, you / we / they weren't.
Were they ill?	

The past simple of *can* is *could*.
The forms of *could* are the same for all persons.
couldn't = could not

We use the base form after *could*.

Affirmative	Negative
I could read.	I couldn't read.
You could read.	You couldn't read.
He / She / It could read.	He / She / It couldn't read.
We could read.	We couldn't read.
You could read.	You couldn't read.
They could read.	They couldn't read.

Interrogative	Short answers
Could I read?	
Could you read?	Yes, I / you / he / she / it / we / they could.
Could he / she / it read?	
Could we read?	No, I / you / he / she / it / we / they couldn't.
Could you read?	
Could they read?	

Past simple: affirmative (regular verbs)

The affirmative form of the past simple is the same for all persons.

Affirmative
I watched TV.
You watched TV.
He / She / It watched TV.
We watched TV.
You watched TV.
They watched TV.

Spelling: past simple form (affirmative) of regular verbs
Most verbs
play + -ed → played

Verbs ending in *-e*
wave + -d → waved

Verbs ending in a consonant and *-y*
hurry -y → -ied → hurried

Verbs ending in a short vowel and a consonant
double consonant + *-ed*
stop → stopped

We use the past simple for an action or event at a definite point in the past.
We played football yesterday afternoon.
I walked to school this morning.

EVERYDAY ENGLISH

I'll for offers

We use *I'll* + the base form to make an offer.
'My homework is very difficult. I can't do it.'
'I'll help you.'

'I haven't got any money.'
'I'll lend you some.'

Past simple: *be* and *can*

1 Look at the calendar and write sentences about Helen and Joe. Use *be*, past simple (affirmative or negative).

1 Helen / Manchester / Monday
   Helen was in Manchester on Monday.
2 Joe and Helen / Alexandria / Wednesday
3 Joe / Paris / Tuesday
4 Helen / Liverpool / Saturday
5 Joe / Qatar / Thursday
6 Joe and Helen / Liverpool / Friday
7 Helen / Istanbul / Monday

Day	Joe	Helen
Mon	London	Manchester
Tues	Berlin	Paris
Wed	Alexandria	Alexandria
Thurs	Qatar	Athens
Fri	Stockholm	Istanbul
Sat	Liverpool	Liverpool

2 Where were Joe and Helen last week? Complete the questions, then write answers. Use *be*, past simple.

1 *Was* Joe in London on Monday? *Yes, he was.*
2 Where _____ Helen on Tuesday?
3 _____ Helen in Istanbul on Wednesday?
4 _____ Joe in Stockholm on Saturday?
5 _____ Joe and Helen in Alexandria on Thursday?
6 Where _____ Helen and Joe on Wednesday?
7 Where _____ Joe on Thursday?
8 _____ Joe and Helen in Liverpool on Saturday?

3 Complete the sentences. Use *couldn't* and the verbs in the box.

find finish go hear play sleep understand ring

1 My dad _____ to work because he was ill.
2 John _____ his pen. It wasn't in his school bag.
3 Pam wasn't hungry – she _____ her lunch.
4 I _____ Jan because I don't speak German.
5 We _____ the teacher because the students were very noisy.
6 Ian _____ ring Paul because the phone was broken.
7 I was very tired but I _____ .
8 We _____ tennis because the weather was bad.

Past simple: affirmative (regular verbs)

4 Write the past simple forms.

1 phone _____
2 answer _____
3 watch _____
4 hurry _____
5 study _____
6 miss _____
7 stop _____
8 visit _____
9 travel _____
10 spot _____

5 Complete the sentences with verbs from exercise 4.

1 I was late, so I _____ to school.
2 My mum and dad _____ German at school.
3 Dave and Neil _____ TV last night.
4 'Where are you?' she asked. 'In the post office,' he _____ .
5 Last summer we _____ Paris.
6 The train _____ at the railway station.
7 Robert _____ the bus, so he walked to school.
8 Joe _____ Sue, but she wasn't at home.

6 Rewrite the sentences using the past simple.

1 I walk to school every day.
2 They agree to meet at six o'clock.
3 Kevin jogs in the park before breakfast.
4 Sue studies maths at school.
5 The bus stops near the school.
6 We arrive at school at quarter to nine.
7 Jim watches television after dinner.
8 Sally phones her friend on her mobile.
9 Fred helps his mum with the washing up.
10 The football match starts at seven o'clock.
11 We live in London.
12 My dad works in Manchester.

EVERYDAY ENGLISH

I'll for offers

7 Complete the sentences. Use *I'll* and a verb from the box.

answer buy carry make open send

1 'I'm hot.' '_____ the window.'
2 'My bag is very heavy.' '_____ it for you.'
3 'We haven't got any milk.'
   'I'm going to the shops now. _____ some.'
4 'I'm hungry.' '_____ a sandwich for you.'
5 'Have a good holiday!' 'Thanks. _____ you a postcard.'
6 'The phone is ringing.' '_____ it.'

Past simple: affirmative (irregular verbs)

Some verbs have irregular past simple (positive) forms. There are no spelling rules for these forms; you need to learn them as vocabulary. See the list on page 124.

go → went   I went shopping yesterday.
spend → spent   I spent all my money.

The affirmative form of the past simple is the same for all persons, singular and plural (*I*, *you*, *he*, *she*, *it*, *we*, *they*).

I saw a friend last night.
She saw a film.
They saw the accident.

Irregular verbs behave in the same way as regular verbs in negative sentences and questions.

Remember that the past simple of *be* is *was* / *were*. It behaves differently from other verbs. (See Grammar Reference 6.)

Past simple: negative and interrogative

Negative	Interrogative
I didn't watch.	Did I watch?
He / She / It didn't watch.	Did he / she / it watch?
We / You / They didn't watch.	Did we / you / they watch?
Full forms	**Short answers**
didn't = did not	Yes, I did. / No, I didn't.

The forms are the same for all persons, singular and plural
(*I*, *you*, *he*, *she*, *it*, *we*, *they*).

In negative sentences, for both regular and irregular verbs, we use:
*I, you, she, it, we, they + **didn't** + base form*
(NOT the past simple form)

In questions, for regular *and* irregular verbs, we use:
***Did** + I, you, he, she, it, we, they + base form*
(NOT the past simple form)
Did he have breakfast?

If there are time expressions, they usually go at the end of the question.
Did he go to the swimming pool **after school**?
Did you catch a bus to school **this morning**?

We can put a question word before *did* to ask for information.
What did you do last night?
Where did they go for their holiday?

Past simple: affirmative (irregular verbs)

1 Are these verbs regular or irregular? Write R or I. Then write the past simple forms.

1 win _____
2 get _____
3 study _____
4 live _____
5 work _____
6 take _____
7 come _____
8 start _____

2 Draw lines to match the irregular past forms with their base forms.

1 become
2 read
3 hear
4 spend
5 wear
6 write
7 send
8 buy

a spent
b wrote
c sent
d bought
e became
f wore
g heard
h read

3 Complete the sentences with the past simple of the verbs in brackets.

1 He _____ to school this morning because he was late. (run)
2 I _____ my dad a book for his birthday. (give)
3 She _____ pizzas for dinner last night. (make)
4 We _____ to the cinema last weekend. (go)
5 They _____ their teacher in town yesterday. (see)
6 My parents _____ on holiday last week. (be)
7 I _____ hello to the girl next door when I left the house. (say)
8 I had to take my new mobile phone back to the shop, because it _____ after a week. (break)
9 This lesson _____ 10 minutes ago. (begin)
10 I _____ the bus to school this morning. (catch)

Past simple: negative and interrogative

4 Put the words in the correct order to make negative sentences.

1 last night / watch / didn't / TV / they
2 win / he / a Nobel Prize / didn't
3 you / see / I / didn't / at the party
4 Harry / yesterday evening / tidy / didn't / his room
5 forget / your birthday / didn't / I
6 didn't / we / to school / yesterday / go
7 study / at university / she / French / didn't
8 a new sweatshirt / you / buy / didn't

5 Write negative sentences using the verbs in brackets.

1 I didn't go to school yesterday. (go)
2 I _____ any photos. (take)
3 Dad _____ the washing this morning. (do)
4 My friend _____ me an email last week. (send)
5 They _____ the match yesterday afternoon. (win)
6 We _____ very hard last year. (work)
7 I _____ dinner at home. (have)
8 She _____ her name in the book. (write)
9 He _____ President three years ago. (become)
10 They _____ three months in England. (spend)
11 I _____ my homework before dinner. (finish)

6 Write the words in the correct order to make questions about yesterday.

1 did / after school? / what / you / do
   What did you do after school?

2 get up? / did / what / you / time
3 go / to / you / did / school?
4 rain / in the morning? / did / it
5 have / you / lunch? / where / did
6 watch / you / did / television?
7 go to bed? / time / what / you / did

7 Work in pairs. Ask and answer the questions in exercise 6.

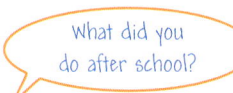

What did you do after school?

I went to the swimming pool.

8 Write the questions to match the answers. Start with the word in brackets.

1 I went to England. (Where)
   Where did you go last summer?

2 I went with my parents and some of our friends. (Who)
3 Oh, the weather was lovely – warm and sunny. (What)
4 Yes, we spent a week in London. (Did)
5 We went by plane from Cairo. (How)
6 We spent about three weeks in England. (How long)
7 The food was good. (What)
8 Yes, I did! I learnt quite a few English expressions! (Did)

some / any, How much / many?

Countable and uncountable nouns

- Countable nouns are things that you can count. They have a singular and a plural form:

an orange   two oranges

- Uncountable nouns are things that you can't count, you can only weigh or measure. They only have a singular form.

some bread   I like cheese

- We use words like *bowl, glass,* etc. with uncountable nouns when we want to talk about quantity.

a bottle of milk   a loaf of bread   a kilo of cheese
a glass of lemonade

some and any

- We usually use *some* in affirmative sentences. We use it with plural nouns and uncountable nouns.

There are some apples on the table.
There's some bread on the shelf.

- We usually use *any* in negative sentences and questions. We use it with plural nouns and uncountable nouns.

He doesn't want any food.
Are there any bananas?

How much / many ...?

We use *How much...?* with uncountable nouns.

'How much milk have we got?' 'Two litres.'

We use *How many...?* with plural nouns.

'How many eggs do you need?' 'Six.'

Articles

We use the indefinite article (*a* or *an*) with singular countable nouns only.

a restaurant   a computer

We can use the definite article (*the*) with singular and plural countable nouns:

the restaurant   the restaurants

and with uncountable nouns.

the cheese

We use *an* instead of *a* when the next word begins with a vowel sound. This means most words beginning with *a-,*

e-, i-, o- and *u-* and a few words that begin with silent *h-*.

an apple   an Italian restaurant   an hour

Note: some words that begin with the letter *u-* do not start with a vowel sound, they start with a /y/ sound. We do not use *an* with these words.

a university   a useful book   a username

We use *a* or *an* when we mention something for the first time.

There's a pizza in the fridge.

We use *the* when we mention it again.

We can have the pizza for dinner.

Some common expressions include an article and others do not. There are no rules – you have to learn them!

Expressions with no article
• play football, tennis, etc.
• watch television
• have breakfast, lunch, dinner
• go to bed, school, work, hospital, university
• at night

Expressions with an article
• play a game, etc.
• listen to the radio, see a film
• have a snack, a drink, a sandwich, etc.
• go to the cinema, the doctor's
• during the day, in the morning, afternoon, evening

some / any, How much / many?

1 Write the plural form of these nouns if they are countable. If they are uncountable, write U.

banana *bananas*   milk U

1 lettuce _____   5 onion _____
2 bread _____   6 water _____
3 apple _____   7 tomato _____
4 toast _____   8 carrot _____

2 Choose *some* or *any* with these uncountable nouns.

1 There's **some** / **any** toast on the table.
2 I didn't have **some** / **any** coffee for breakfast this morning.
3 Is there **some** / **any** milk?
4 We need **some** / **any** bread.
5 Have you got **some** / **any** money?
6 You didn't buy **any** / **some** lettuce.
7 Let's have **any** / **some** tea.
8 Is there **any** / **some** cheese?

3 Write *some* or *any* with these countable nouns.

1 There are _____ apples on the table.
2 Have we got _____ eggs?
3 John ate _____ chips.
4 We didn't buy _____ onions.
5 Did you cook _____ carrots?
6 We don't need _____ bananas.
7 Are there _____ tomatoes?
8 There aren't _____ sandwiches in my bag.

4 Complete the questions with *How much …?* and *How many …?*

1 _____ people live in your house?
2 _____ time is there until the end of the school day?
3 _____ lessons do you have a day?
4 _____ money do you spend a day on snacks?
5 _____ water do you usually drink in a day?
6 _____ pages are there in this book?

5 Ask and answer the questions in exercise 4.

Articles

6 Choose *a* or *an*.

1 **a** / **an** animal   5 **a** / **an** American man
2 **a** / **an** big onion   6 **a** / **an** young woman
3 **a** / **an** university   7 **a** / **an** uncle
4 **a** / **an** pizza   8 **a** / **an** hour

7 Write *a*, *an* or *the*.

1 I've got _____ cat and _____ dog. _____ cat's name is Lucky and _____ dog's name is Bouncer.
2 I've got _____ brother and _____ sister.
3 We've got _____ maths exam and _____ English exam tomorrow. _____ maths exam is in _____ morning and _____ English exam is in _____ afternoon.
4 I went into town this morning and bought _____ T-shirt and _____ jacket. _____ jacket was expensive but _____ T-shirt was cheap.
5 Where are _____ chocolates? I need _____ snack!
6 I had _____ chicken sandwich and _____ banana for lunch. _____ sandwich was delicious, but _____ banana was horrible. Tomorrow I'm going to have _____ apple.
7 'We need _____ egg.'
  '_____ eggs are in the fridge.'
8 There's _____ man and _____ woman at the door. _____ man wants to talk to you.

8 Write *a*, *an*, *the* or nothing.

1 I want to play _____ football.
2 Jack is listening to _____ radio.
3 Let's go to _____ cinema.
4 I'm thirsty. Can I have _____ drink, please?
5 'What time does your mum go to _____ work?'
  'At seven o'clock in _____ evening.'
6 My brother broke his leg and had to go to _____ hospital.
7 Dave eats _____ chicken and _____ tomatoes.
8 What time do you have _____ lunch?
9 If you're hungry, have _____ sandwich.
10 I went to _____ bed very late last night.

Present perfect: affirmative

Affirmative
I've finished. You've finished.
He / She / It's finished.
We've finished. You've finished. They've finished.

Full forms
I've = I have she's = she has

We form the present perfect with the auxiliary verb *have* and the past participle.

We use the present perfect to talk about past events that have a result in the present, for example, recent events and news.
Did you hear? Mandy has passed all her exams.

The past participle of regular verbs is the same as the past simple.
walked   cooked   studied   stopped

There aren't any rules for the past participles of irregular verbs. Sometimes they are same as the past simple form, sometimes they are different.
have → had → had
go → went → gone
For a list of irregular verbs, see page 124.

We use *just* with the present perfect affirmative to talk about very recent events.
I'm not hungry. I've just eaten.

We use *already* with the present perfect affirmative to say that something has happened earlier than expected.

I've already packed for the trip.

Present perfect: negative and interrogative

Negative
I haven't finished. You haven't finished.
He / She / It hasn't finished.
We haven't finished. You haven't finished. They haven't finished.

Full forms
haven't = have not hasn't = has not

Interrogative
Have I finished yet? Have you finished yet?
Has he / she / finished yet?
Have we finished yet? Have you finished yet? Have they finished yet?

Short answers
Yes, I have. / No, I haven't. Yes, she has. / No, she hasn't.

We form the negative with *haven't* or *hasn't* and the past participle.
We form the interrogative with *have* or *has* + subject + past participle.

We use *yet* with the present perfect interrogative to ask if something expected has happened.
Have you packed your suitcase yet?

We use *yet* with the present perfect negative to say that something expected hasn't happened.
Jim hasn't even started his revision yet.

Present perfect: affirmative

1 Complete the sentences with the verbs in the box. Use the present perfect. (All the verbs are regular.)

> cook   cycle   decide   land   phone   start   study

1 The lesson _____.
2 We _____ to go to France on holiday.
3 She _____ him three times, but he never answers.
4 I'm really tired. I _____ ten miles today.
5 We _____ nine units of this book.
6 Please stay for dinner. My mum _____ a lot of food!
7 The plane _____. Where are the passengers?

2 Add the verbs to the chart. Write the past simple and past participle forms.

> know   sell   sleep   think   write

	grow	– grew	– **grown** rhymes with
1	_____	– _____	– _____
	drive	– drove	– **driven** rhymes with
2	_____	– _____	– _____
	keep	– kept	– **kept** rhymes with
3	_____	– _____	– _____
	tell	– told	– **told** rhymes with
4	_____	– _____	– _____
	bring	– brought	– **brought** rhymes with
5	_____	– _____	– _____

3 Complete the sentences. Use the verbs in brackets. Check the past participle forms in the irregular verbs list in the Workbook.

1 I _____ (see) that film three times.
2 Matthew _____ (go) to the cinema for the evening.
3 We _____ (leave) our suitcases on the coach.
4 Italy _____ (win) the World Cup again.
5 Jake and Sally _____ (eat) all the chocolate.
6 Ann _____ (do) the shopping.
7 Phil can't play tennis. He _____ (break) his arm.

4 Complete the sentences. Use the present perfect affirmative.

1 'Is Dave still here?'
  'No, he *'s gone* home.' (go)
2 'Is it raining?'
  'No, it _____ (stop).'
3 'Are Oliver and Samantha here?'
  'Yes, they _____ (arrive).'
4 'Do you want a drink?'
  'No, thanks. I _____ (have) one.'
5 'Has Kate got her mobile with her?'
  'Yes, she has. I _____ (speak) to her.'
6 'Is Daniel watching TV?'
  'No, he _____ (finish).'
7 'Is that your bus over there?'
  'Yes, it is. I _____ (miss) it!'
8 'Are you hungry?'
  'No, I _____ (eat).'

5 Write replies with *just*. Use the present perfect affirmative.

1 Tidy your room!
  I've just tidied it.
2 Don't forget to phone Sam.
3 When is George leaving?
4 Let's watch this DVD.
5 Do you want to read this book after me?
6 Don't forget to write to your grandmother.
7 Can you pack your suitcase, please?
8 Don't forget to book the tickets.

Present perfect: negative and interrogative

6 Make the sentences negative.

1 Harry has had breakfast.
2 I've lost my mobile phone.
3 Rachel and I have spent all our money.
4 You've eaten the apple.
5 Vicky has taken the train to Leeds.
6 Luke and Emily have visited Spain.
7 I've done my homework.
8 He's gone to New York by ship.

7 Write questions and short answers. Use the present perfect.

1 Tim / go to bed? ✗
  Has Tim gone to bed? No, he hasn't.
2 you / decide what to do? ✓
3 Robert / pack his bags? ✗
4 Kate and David / write any postcards? ✗
5 you / buy any clothes? ✗
6 you and Tony / have lunch? ✓
7 Sarah / go to Edinburgh? ✓

8 Ask and answer questions using the present perfect. Use the words in brackets in the answer.

1 do your homework (Yes, just)

 Have you done your homework?

 Yes, I've just done it.

2 have breakfast? (No, yet)
3 phone Joanna? (Yes, just)
4 buy the sandwiches? (Yes, already)
5 find your keys? (No, yet)
6 write to Ian? (Yes, already)
7 change the holiday money? (Yes, already)
8 see my new scooter? (No, yet)

going to

We form *going to* with the present simple of *be* + *going to* + the base form of the verb.

Affirmative		
I'm		
You're		
He's / She's / It's	going to	sleep.
We're		
You're		
They're		

Full forms
I am, he / she / it is, we / you / they are

Negative		
I'm not		
You aren't		
He / She / It isn't	going to	sleep.
We aren't		
You aren't		
They aren't		

Full forms
I am not, he / she / it is not, we / you / they are not

Interrogative		
Am I		
Are you		
Is he / she / it	going to	sleep?
Are we		
Are you		
Are they		

We use *going to* to talk about plans for the future.
I'm going to get a job next year.
He isn't going to work in the holidays.
Are you going to play football on Saturday?
Yes, I am. / No, I'm not.

will

We form this tense with *will* + the base form of the verb. The form is the same for all persons.

Affirmative	
I'll / You'll / He'll / She'll / It'll	
We'll / You'll / They'll	go to Dubai.

Full forms
I / he / she / it / we / you / they will

Negative	
I / You / He / She / It won't	
We / You / They won't	go to Dubai.

Full forms
I / he / she / it / we / you / they will not

Interrogative	
Will I / you / he / she / it	
Will we / you / they	go to Dubai?

We use *will* to:
- talk about the future;
  I'll be at home at seven o'clock.
  I won't leave school until I'm 16.
  The sun will rise at 5.30 tomorrow morning.
- to make predictions.
  They won't get married.
  Will you live in this town all your life?

EVERYDAY ENGLISH

should

should is followed by the base form of the verb. The form of *should* is the same for all persons.

Affirmative	
I / You / He / She / It should	
We / You / They should	work now.

Negative	
I / You / He / She / It shouldn't	
We / You / They shouldn't	work now.

Interrogative	
Should I / you / he / she / it	
Should we / you / they	work now?

- We use *should* to give advice.
  It's cold. You should wear a coat.
  You shouldn't copy your friend's homework.

going to

1 Write sentences with *going to*, affirmative.

1 she / have lunch in town *She's going to have lunch in town.*
2 we / play tennis next Saturday
3 I / write an essay this evening
4 they / visit their grandparents next month
5 you / meet me at the café
6 we / see a film this evening
7 Pete and Sue / study maths at university
8 I / watch TV this evening

2 Make the sentences in exercise 1 negative.

She isn't going to have lunch in town.

3 Complete the conversation. Write questions with *going to*.

Dave What / you / do on Friday evening?
What are you going to do on Friday evening?

Sally I'm going to go to the cinema.
Dave What film / you / see?
1 _____

Sally The new French film.
Dave Who / you / go with?
2 _____

Sally Mark and Jane.
Dave How / you / get there?
3 _____

Sally By bus.
Dave What / you / do after the film?
4 _____

Sally We're going to go for a pizza.
Dave What time / you / arrive home?
5 _____

Sally At about 11 o'clock.

4 Work in pairs. Ask and answer questions.

1 What are you going to do this evening?
2 What are you going to do next weekend?
3 Where are you going to go in the summer holidays?

will

5 Complete the predictions about Robert's future. Use *will* or *won't*.

> ### Your future
> **Home:** London
> **Family:** wife, no children
> **Job:** computer programmer
> **Hobby:** skiing
> **Pets:** a cat

1 He _____ live in France.
2 He _____ live in Britain.
3 He _____ get married.
4 He _____ have children.
5 He _____ be a chef.
6 He _____ work with computers.
7 He _____ go skiing.
8 He _____ have a pet.

6 Work in pairs. Ask and answer questions about your future.

1 where / you / live when you're 25?
Where will you live when you're 25?
2 who / live with?
3 where / you / work?
4 what job / you / do?
5 how many children / you / have?
6 what car / you / drive?
7 you / have a house?

EVERYDAY ENGLISH

should

7 Look at the pictures. Complete the sentences with *should* or *shouldn't*.

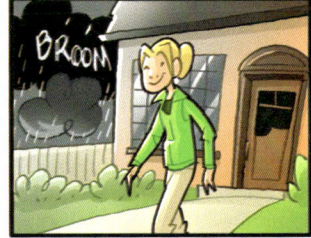

1 He _____ go in the sun today.

2 She _____ take an umbrella.

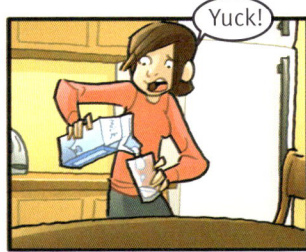

3 He _____ stand up.

4 She _____ drink it.

5 He _____ park there.

Nouns

airport 🔑 /ˈeəpɔːt/
aunt 🔑 /ɑːnt/
breakfast 🔑 /ˈbrekfəst/
brother 🔑 /ˈbrʌðə(r)/
chat show /ˈtʃæt ˌʃəʊ/
children 🔑 /ˈtʃɪldrən/
classmate /ˈklɑːsmeɪt/
cloth 🔑 /klɒθ/
clothes 🔑 /kləʊðz/
cousin 🔑 /ˈkʌzn/
daughter 🔑 /ˈdɔːtə(r)/
dinner 🔑 /ˈdɪnə(r)/
family 🔑 /ˈfæməli/
father 🔑 /ˈfɑːðə(r)/
flat 🔑 /flæt/
football 🔑 /ˈfʊtbɔːl/
granddaughter 🔑 /ˈɡrændɔːtə(r)/
grandfather 🔑 /ˈɡrænfɑːðə(r)/
grandmother 🔑 /ˈɡrænmʌðə(r)/
grandson 🔑 /ˈɡrænsʌn/
homework 🔑 /ˈhəʊmwɜːk/
housework /ˈhaʊswɜːk/
husband 🔑 /ˈhʌzbənd/
ice hockey /ˈaɪs ˌhɒki/
ice skater /ˈaɪs ˌskeɪtə(r)/
job 🔑 /dʒɒb/
litre 🔑 /ˈliːtə(r)/
lunch 🔑 /lʌntʃ/
minibus /ˈmɪnibʌs/
mother 🔑 /ˈmʌðə(r)/
nephew 🔑 /ˈnefjuː/
news programme 🔑 /ˈnjuːz ˌprəʊɡræm/
niece 🔑 /niːs/
office 🔑 /ˈɒfɪs/
parents 🔑 /ˈpeərənts/
penfriend /ˈpenfrend/
power station 🔑 /ˈpaʊə ˌsteɪʃn/
sister 🔑 /ˈsɪstə(r)/
son 🔑 /sʌn/
south 🔑 /saʊθ/
supermarket 🔑 /ˈsuːpəmɑːkɪt/
teacher 🔑 /ˈtiːtʃə(r)/
team 🔑 /tiːm/
uncle 🔑 /ˈʌŋkl/
volleyball /ˈvɒlibɔːl/
washing 🔑 /ˈwɒʃɪŋ/
washing-up /ˌwɒʃɪŋ ˈʌp/
weekday 🔑 /ˈwiːkdeɪ/
weekend /wiːkˈend/
wife 🔑 /waɪf/
work 🔑 /wɜːk/

Verbs

argue 🔑 /ˈɑːɡjuː/
collect 🔑 /kəˈlekt/
drive 🔑 /draɪv/
enjoy 🔑 /ɪnˈdʒɔɪ/
finish 🔑 /ˈfɪnɪʃ/
hate 🔑 /heɪt/
help 🔑 /help/
iron 🔑 /ˈaɪən/
learn 🔑 /lɜːn/
listen 🔑 /ˈlɪsn/
love 🔑 /lʌv/
need 🔑 /niːd/
play 🔑 /pleɪ/
speak 🔑 /spiːk/
spend 🔑 /spend/
stay 🔑 /steɪ/
study 🔑 /ˈstʌdi/
teach 🔑 /tiːtʃ/
tell 🔑 /tel/
think 🔑 /θɪŋk/
walk 🔑 /wɔːk/
want 🔑 /wɒnt/
wash 🔑 /wɒʃ/
watch 🔑 /wɒtʃ/
wear 🔑 /weə(r)/
work 🔑 /wɜːk/

Adjectives

annoying 🔑 /əˈnɔɪɪŋ/
athletic 🔑 /æθˈletɪk/
average 🔑 /ˈævərɪdʒ/
boring 🔑 /ˈbɔːrɪŋ/
colourful /ˈkʌləfl/
everyday /ˈevrideɪ/
fantastic /fænˈtæstɪk/
intelligent 🔑 /ɪnˈtelɪdʒənt/
lazy 🔑 /ˈleɪzi/
lively 🔑 /ˈlaɪvli/
noisy 🔑 /ˈnɔɪzi/
popular 🔑 /ˈpɒpjələ(r)/
professional 🔑 /prəˈfeʃənl/
quiet 🔑 /ˈkwaɪət/
unusual 🔑 /ʌnˈjuːʒuəl/

Adverbs

hard 🔑 /hɑːd/
late 🔑 /leɪt/
regularly 🔑 /ˈreɡjələli/
sometime /ˈsʌmtaɪm/
sometimes 🔑 /ˈsʌmtaɪmz/

Phrasal verbs

fill in 🔑 /ˌfɪl ˈɪn/
get on well 🔑 /ˌɡet ˌɒn ˈwel/
get up 🔑 /ˌɡet ˈʌp/
hang around 🔑 /ˌhæŋ əˈraʊnd/
look after 🔑 /ˌlʊk ˈɑːftə(r)/
look at 🔑 /ˈlʊk ˌæt/
look for 🔑 /ˈlʊk ˌfɔː(r), fə(r)/
look like 🔑 /ˈlʊk ˌlaɪk/
look out 🔑 /ˌlʊk ˈaʊt/
look round 🔑 /ˌlʊk ˈraʊnd/
pick up 🔑 /ˌpɪk ˈʌp/
put away 🔑 /ˌpʊt əˈweɪ/
put on 🔑 /ˌpʊt ˈɒn/
take after 🔑 /ˌteɪk ˈɑːftə(r)/
take off 🔑 /ˌteɪk ˈɒf/
try on 🔑 /ˌtraɪ ˈɒn/
turn down 🔑 /ˌtɜːn ˈdaʊn/

Expressions

clean the house 🔑 /ˌkliːn ðə ˈhaʊs/
come home 🔑 /ˌkʌm ˈhəʊm/
cook dinner 🔑 /ˌkʊk ˈdɪnə(r)/
do the shopping 🔑 /ˌduː ðə ˈʃɒpɪŋ/
do the washing 🔑 /ˌduː ðə ˈwɒʃɪŋ/
do your homework 🔑 /ˌduː jɔː ˈhəʊmwɜːk/
go shopping 🔑 /ˌɡəʊ ˈʃɒpɪŋ/
go to work 🔑 /ˌɡəʊ tə ˈwɜːk/
have a break 🔑 /ˌhæv ə ˈbreɪk/
have a celebration 🔑 /ˌhæv ə ˌselɪˈbreɪʃn/
have a shower 🔑 /ˌhæv ə ˈʃaʊə(r)/
iron clothes 🔑 /ˌaɪən ˈkləʊðz/
make a lot of noise 🔑 /ˌmeɪk ə ˌlɒt əv ˈnɔɪz/
make a phone call 🔑 /ˌmeɪk ə ˈfəʊn ˌkɔːl/
make breakfast 🔑 /ˌmeɪk ˈbrekfəst/
make your bed 🔑 /ˌmeɪk jɔː ˈbed/
spend ages 🔑 /ˌspend ˈeɪdʒɪz/

Idioms

drive someone crazy 🔑 /ˌdraɪv ˌsʌmwʌn ˈkreɪzi/
get a move on 🔑 /ˌɡet ə ˈmuːv ˌɒn/
give someone a hand 🔑 /ˌɡɪv ˌsʌmwʌn ə ˈhænd/

🔑 a keyword of the **Oxford 3000 list,** denoting words which should receive priority in vocabulary study because of their importance and usefulness.

/i/ happy	/æ/ flag	/ɜː/ her	/ʊ/ look	/ʌ/ mum	/ɔɪ/ noisy	/ɪə/ here
/ɪ/ it	/ɑː/ art	/ɒ/ not	/uː/ you	/eɪ/ day	/aʊ/ how	/eə/ wear
/iː/ he	/e/ egg	/ɔː/ four	/ə/ sugar	/aɪ/ why	/əʊ/ go	/ʊə/ tourist

Nouns

activity 🔑 /æk'tɪvəti/
appointment 🔑 /ə'pɔɪntmənt/
athletics /æθ'letɪks/
basketball /'bɑːskɪtbɔːl/
beach 🔑 /biːtʃ/
book 🔑 /bʊk/
bowling 🔑 /'bəʊlɪŋ/
break 🔑 /breɪk/
calendar /'kælɪndə(r)/
champion /'tʃæmpiən/
chat room /'tʃæt ˌruːm/
chess /tʃes/
competition 🔑 /ˌkɒmpə'tɪʃn/
computer games 🔑 /kəm'pjuːtə ˌɡeɪmz/
cricket /'krɪkɪt/
cycling 🔑 /'saɪklɪŋ/
excitement 🔑 /ɪk'saɪtmənt/
film 🔑 /fɪlm/
foot (feet) 🔑 /fʊt (fiːt)/
football 🔑 /'fʊtbɔːl/
gold medal /ˌɡəʊld 'medl/
gymnastics /dʒɪm'næstɪks/
hand 🔑 /hænd/
head 🔑 /hed/
hobby 🔑 /'hɒbi/
hockey /'hɒki/
holiday 🔑 /'hɒlədeɪ/
horse riding 🔑 /'hɔːs ˌraɪdɪŋ/
ice skating /'aɪs ˌskeɪtɪŋ/
interval 🔑 /'ɪntəvl/
interview 🔑 /'ɪntəvjuː/
jogging /'dʒɒɡɪŋ/
kung fu /ˌkʌŋ 'fuː/
martial arts /ˌmɑːʃl 'ɑːts/
medal /'medl/
midnight 🔑 /'mɪdnaɪt/
monthly /'mʌnθli/
music 🔑 /'mjuːzɪk/
(the) Olympic Games /ði əˌlɪmpɪk 'ɡeɪmz/
netball /'netbɔːl/
photography 🔑 /fə'tɒɡrəfi/
population 🔑 /ˌpɒpju'leɪʃn/
practice 🔑 /'præktɪs/
press-up /'pres ˌʌp/
relative 🔑 /'relətɪv/
rest 🔑 /rest/
rollerblading /'rəʊləbleɪdɪŋ/
routine 🔑 /ruː'tiːn/
rugby /'rʌɡbi/
skateboarding /'skeɪt ˌbɔːdɪŋ/
sport 🔑 /spɔːt/
sports club 🔑 /'spɔːts ˌklʌb/
step 🔑 /step/
stick 🔑 /stɪk/
swimming 🔑 /'swɪmɪŋ/
sword /sɔːd/
tennis player /'tenɪs ˌpleɪə(r)/
timetable 🔑 /'taɪmteɪbl/
weather 🔑 /'weðə(r)/
world record 🔑 /ˌwɜːld 'rekɔːd/

Verbs

appear in 🔑 /ə'pɪər ˌɪn/
attack 🔑 /ə'tæk/
catch 🔑 /kætʃ/
defend 🔑 /dɪ'fend/
fight 🔑 /faɪt/
hike /haɪk/
hit 🔑 /hɪt/
jog /dʒɒɡ/
jump 🔑 /dʒʌmp/
kick 🔑 /kɪk/
knock 🔑 /nɒk/
march 🔑 /mɑːtʃ/
practise 🔑 /'præktɪs/
protect 🔑 /prə'tekt/
relax 🔑 /rɪ'læks/
run 🔑 /rʌn/
rush 🔑 /rʌʃ/
score 🔑 /skɔː(r)/
shake 🔑 /ʃeɪk/
sprint /sprɪnt/
squeeze 🔑 /skwiːz/
start 🔑 /stɑːt/
stretch 🔑 /stretʃ/
stroll /strəʊl/
train 🔑 /treɪn/
wave 🔑 /weɪv/

Adjectives

active 🔑 /'æktɪv/
dangerous 🔑 /'deɪndʒərəs/
easy 🔑 /'iːzi/
hard 🔑 /hɑːd/
perfect 🔑 /'pɜːfɪkt/
popular 🔑 /'pɒpjələ(r)/
safe 🔑 /seɪf/
tiring 🔑 /'taɪərɪŋ/
typical 🔑 /'tɪpɪkl/
unusual 🔑 /ʌn'juːʒuəl/

Adverbs

always 🔑 /'ɔːlweɪz/
hardly ever 🔑 /ˌhɑːdli 'evə(r)/
immediately 🔑 /ɪ'miːdiətli/
never 🔑 /'nevə(r)/
often 🔑 /'ɒfn, 'ɒftən/
sometimes 🔑 /'sʌmtaɪmz/
usually 🔑 /'juːʒuəli/
violently 🔑 /'vaɪələntli/

Phrasal verbs

go out 🔑 /ˌɡəʊ 'aʊt/
go back to 🔑 /ˌɡəʊ 'bæk ˌtuː, tə/

Expressions

check (my email) 🔑 /ˌtʃek (maɪ 'iːmeɪl)/
go snowboarding /ˌɡəʊ 'snəʊbɔːdɪŋ/
go to bed 🔑 /ˌɡəʊ tə 'bed/
have a shower 🔑 /ˌhæv ə 'ʃaʊə(r)/
have time 🔑 /ˌhæv 'taɪm/
hold (a world record) 🔑 /ˌhəʊld (ə ˌwɜːld 'rekɔːd)/
take part (in competitions) 🔑 /ˌteɪk ˌpɑːt (ɪn ˌkɒmpə'tɪʃnz)/

Idioms

my ears are burning 🔑 /ˌmaɪ 'ɪəz ə ˌbɜːnɪŋ/
your heart is not in it 🔑 /ˌjɔː ˌhɑːt ɪz ˌnɒt 'ɪn ˌɪt/
keep an eye on 🔑 /ˌkiːp ən 'aɪ ˌɒn/
look down your nose 🔑 /ˌlʊk daʊn jɔː 'nəʊz/
put your feet up 🔑 /ˌpʊt jɔː 'fiːt ˌʌp/
up to your neck in (sth) 🔑 /ˌʌp tə ˌjɔː 'nek ɪn ˌɪt/

/p/ pen	/d/ dog	/tʃ/ beach	/v/ very	/s/ speak	/ʒ/ television	/n/ now	/r/ radio
/b/ big	/k/ can	/dʒ/ job	/θ/ think	/z/ zoo	/h/ house	/ŋ/ sing	/j/ yes
/t/ two	/g/ good	/f/ food	/ð/ then	/ʃ/ she	/m/ meat	/l/ late	/w/ we

Nouns

Arabic /'ærəbɪk/
art and design 🔑 /ˌɑːt ən dɪ'zaɪn/
bedroom 🔑 /'bedruːm/
bin 🔑 /bɪn/
biology /baɪ'ɒlədʒi/
bording school /'bɔːdɪŋ ˌskuːl/
canteen /kæn'tiːn/
carnival /'kɑːnɪvl/
CD player 🔑 /ˌsiː 'diː ˌpleɪə(r)/
chemistry 🔑 /'kemɪstri/
classroom 🔑 /'klɑːsruːm/
collection 🔑 /kə'lekʃn/
computer room 🔑 /kəm'pjuːtə ˌruːm/
concert 🔑 /'kɒnsət/
corridor /'kɒrɪdɔː(r)/
cupboard 🔑 /'kʌbəd/
design and technology (D.T.) 🔑 /dɪˌzaɪn
 ən tek'nɒlədʒi (ˌdiː ən 'tiː)/
exam 🔑 /ɪg'zæm/
farm 🔑 /fɑːm/
field 🔑 /fiːld/
floor 🔑 /flɔː(r)/
foreign language 🔑 /ˌfɒrən 'læŋgwɪdʒ/
French /'frentʃ/
geography 🔑 /dʒi'ɒgrəfi/
German /'dʒɜːmən/
gym /dʒɪm/
hall 🔑 /hɔːl/
head 🔑 /hed/
history 🔑 /'hɪstri/
information and communications technology
 (I.C.T.) 🔑
 /ˌɪnfəˌmeɪʃn ən kəˌmjuːnɪˌkeɪʃn tek'nɒlədʒi/
interview 🔑 /'ɪntəvjuː/
kilometre 🔑 /'kɪləmiːtə(r), kɪ'lɒmɪtə(r)/
lesson 🔑 /'lesn/
library 🔑 /'laɪbrəri/
maths 🔑 /mæθs/
meeting 🔑 /'miːtɪŋ/
motivation /ˌməʊtɪ'veɪʃn/
music 🔑 /'mjuːzɪk/
noticeboard /'nəʊtɪsbɔːd/
physical education (P.E.) 🔑 /ˌfɪzɪkl
 edʒu'keɪʃn (ˌpiː 'iː)/
physics 🔑 /'fɪzɪks/
plant 🔑 /plɑːnt/
playing field 🔑 /'pleɪɪŋ ˌfiːld/
population 🔑 /ˌpɒpju'leɪʃn/
post 🔑 /pəʊst/
poster /'pəʊstə(r)/
private school 🔑 /'praɪvət ˌskuːl/
public school /'pʌblɪk ˌskuːl/
rule 🔑 /ruːl/
sandwich /'sænwɪtʃ/
science 🔑 /'saɪəns/

secondary school 🔑 /'sekəndri ˌskuːl/
shelf (shelves) 🔑 /ʃelf (ʃelvz)/
snack /snæk/
Spanish /'spænɪʃ/
staff room 🔑 /'stɑːf ˌruːm/
stairs 🔑 /steəz/
state school 🔑 /'steɪt ˌskuːl/
subject 🔑 /'sʌbdʒɪkt/
term 🔑 /tɜːm/
timetable 🔑 /'taɪmteɪbl/
uniform 🔑 /'juːnɪfɔːm/

Verbs

announce 🔑 /ə'naʊns/
argue 🔑 /'ɑːgjuː/
borrow 🔑 /'bɒrəʊ/
chat 🔑 /tʃæt/
choose 🔑 /tʃuːz/
collect 🔑 /kə'lekt/
compare 🔑 /kəm'peə(r)/
deliver 🔑 /dɪ'lɪvə(r)/
discuss 🔑 /dɪ'skʌs/
find 🔑 /faɪnd/
gossip /'gɒsɪp/
interview 🔑 /'ɪntəvjuː/
invite 🔑 /ɪn'vaɪt/
pay 🔑 /peɪ/
prepare 🔑 /prɪ'peə(r)/
revise 🔑 /rɪ'vaɪz/
sell 🔑 /sel/
send 🔑 /send/
shout 🔑 /ʃaʊt/
travel 🔑 /'trævl/
use 🔑 /juːz/
vote 🔑 /vəʊt/
wait 🔑 /weɪt/
whisper 🔑 /'wɪspə(r)/

Adjectives

annual 🔑 /'ænjuəl/
colossal /kə'lɒsl/
compulsory /kəm'pʌlsəri/
enormous 🔑 /ɪ'nɔːməs/
free 🔑 /friː/
friendly 🔑 /'frendli/
huge 🔑 /hjuːdʒ/
important 🔑 /ɪm'pɔːtnt/
isolated /'aɪsəleɪtɪd/
little 🔑 /'lɪtl/
lonely 🔑 /'ləʊnli/
massive 🔑 /'mæsɪv/
minute 🔑 /maɪ'njuːt/
optional /'ɒpʃənl/
serious 🔑 /'sɪəriəs/
special 🔑 /'speʃl/

tiny 🔑 /'taɪni/
unhappy 🔑 /ʌn'hæpi/

Adverbs

over 🔑 /'əʊvə(r)/
quite often 🔑 /ˌkwaɪt 'ɒfn, 'ɒftən/
twice 🔑 /twaɪs/

Phrasal verbs

take apart 🔑 /ˌteɪk ə'pɑːt/
take away 🔑 /ˌteɪk ə'weɪ/
take down 🔑 /ˌteɪk 'daʊn/
take in 🔑 /ˌteɪk 'ɪn/
take off 🔑 /ˌteɪk 'ɒf/
take out 🔑 /ˌteɪk 'aʊt/

Prepositions

behind 🔑 /bɪ'haɪnd/
in front of 🔑 /ˌɪn 'frʌnt əv/
near 🔑 /nɪə(r)/
next to 🔑 /'nekst ˌtuː, tə/
on 🔑 /ɒn/
under 🔑 /'ʌndə(r)/

Expressions

follow (the rules) 🔑 /ˌfɒləʊ (ðə 'ruːlz)/
make friends 🔑 /ˌmeɪk 'frendz/
on their own 🔑 /ˌɒn ˌðeər 'əʊn/
once a week/year 🔑 /ˌwʌns ə 'wiːk,
 'jɪə(r)/
take place 🔑 /ˌteɪk 'pleɪs/
(a) way to do sth 🔑 /ə ˌweɪ tə 'duː
 ˌsʌmθɪŋ/

/i/ happy	/æ/ flag	/ɜː/ her	/ʊ/ look	/ʌ/ mum	/ɔɪ/ noisy	/ɪə/ here
/ɪ/ it	/ɑː/ art	/ɒ/ not	/uː/ you	/eɪ/ day	/aʊ/ how	/eə/ wear
/iː/ he	/e/ egg	/ɔː/ four	/ə/ sugar	/aɪ/ why	/əʊ/ go	/ʊə/ tourist

Nouns

blouse /blaʊz/
boot 🔑 /buːt/
bride /braɪd/
bridegroom /'braɪdgruːm/
camping 🔑 /'kæmpɪŋ/
cap 🔑 /kæp/
cardigan /'kɑːdɪgən/
castle 🔑 /'kɑːsl/
citizenship /'sɪtɪznʃɪp/
diving /'daɪvɪŋ/
documentary /ˌdɒkju'mentri/
dress 🔑 /dres/
drive 🔑 /draɪv/
energy /'enədʒi/
event 🔑 /ɪ'vent/
flight 🔑 /flaɪt/
football match 🔑 /'fʊtbɔːl ˌmætʃ/
forest 🔑 /'fɒrɪst/
guest 🔑 /gest/
headscarf /'hedskɑːf/
honeymoon /'hʌnimuːn/
hot-air balloon /ˌhɒt ˌeə bə'luːn/
invitation 🔑 /ɪnvɪ'teɪʃn/
island 🔑 /'aɪlənd/
jacket 🔑 /'dʒækɪt/
jeans 🔑 /dʒiːnz/
jumper /'dʒʌmpə(r)/
living room /'lɪvɪŋ ˌruːm/
mountain 🔑 /'maʊntən/
nature 🔑 /'neɪtʃə(r)/
outdoors 🔑 /ˌaʊt'dɔːz/
problem 🔑 /'prɒbləm/
reception 🔑 /rɪ'sepʃn/
shirt 🔑 /ʃɜːt/
shoe 🔑 /ʃuː/
shorts 🔑 /ʃɔːts/
skirt 🔑 /skɜːt/
sock 🔑 /sɒk/
sun 🔑 /sʌn/
sweatshirt /'swetʃɜːt/
tae kwon do /ˌtaɪ ˌkwɒn 'dəʊ/
tent 🔑 /tent/
tie 🔑 /taɪ/
top 🔑 /tɒp/
tracksuit bottoms /ˌtræksuːt 'bɒtəmz/
trainer /'treɪnə(r)/
trousers 🔑 /'traʊzəz/
T-shirt /'tiː ˌʃɜːt/
volleyball match /'vɒlibɔːl ˌmætʃ/
wedding 🔑 /'wedɪŋ/

Verbs

arrange 🔑 /ə'reɪndʒ/
book 🔑 /bʊk/
carry 🔑 /'kæri/
celebrate 🔑 /'selɪbreɪt/
chat 🔑 /tʃæt/
cost 🔑 /kɒst/
count 🔑 /kaʊnt/
hand 🔑 /hænd/
ice-skate /'aɪs ˌskeɪt/
invite 🔑 /ɪn'vaɪt/
keep 🔑 /kiːp/
leave 🔑 /liːv/
organize 🔑 /'ɔːgənaɪz/
remember 🔑 /rɪ'membə(r)/
reserve 🔑 /rɪ'zɜːv/
roller blade /'rəʊləbleɪd/
shine 🔑 /ʃaɪn/
smile 🔑 /smaɪl/
stand 🔑 /stænd/

Adjectives

amazing 🔑 /ə'meɪzɪŋ/
black 🔑 /blæk/
blue 🔑 /bluː/
boring 🔑 /'bɔːrɪŋ/
brown 🔑 /braʊn/
busy 🔑 /'bɪzi/
careful 🔑 /'keəfl/
crowded 🔑 /'kraʊdɪd/
different 🔑 /'dɪfrənt/
dishonest 🔑 /dɪs'ɒnɪst/
enormous 🔑 /ɪ'nɔːməs/
enthusiastic 🔑 /ɪnˌθjuːzi'æstɪk/
extravagant /ɪk'strævəgənt/
fascinating /'fæsɪneɪtɪŋ/
formal 🔑 /'fɔːml/
green 🔑 /griːn/
grey 🔑 /greɪ/
honest 🔑 /'ɒnɪst/
impolite /ˌɪmpə'laɪt/
impossible 🔑 /ɪm'pɒsəbl/
incredible /ɪn'kredəbl/
irregular /ɪ'regjələ(r)/
memorable /'memərəbl/
necessary 🔑 /'nesəsəri/
orange 🔑 /'ɒrɪndʒ/
pink 🔑 /pɪŋk/
polite 🔑 /pə'laɪt/
possible 🔑 /'pɒsəbl/
purple 🔑 /'pɜːpl/
quiet 🔑 /'kwaɪət/
red 🔑 /red/
regular 🔑 /'regjələ(r)/
reliable /rɪ'laɪəbl/

simple 🔑 /'sɪmpl/
strong 🔑 /strɒŋ/
terrible 🔑 /'terəbl/
well known 🔑 /ˌwel 'nəʊn/
white 🔑 /waɪt/
yellow 🔑 /'jeləʊ/

Adverbs

abroad 🔑 /ə'brɔːd/
easily 🔑 /'iːzəli/
fast 🔑 /fɑːst/
fluently /'fluːəntli/
hard 🔑 /hɑːd/
loudly 🔑 /'laʊdli/
outdoors 🔑 /ˌaʊt'dɔːz/
quickly 🔑 /'kwɪkli/
slowly 🔑 /'sləʊli/
underwater 🔑 /ˌʌndə'wɔːtə(r)/
well 🔑 /wel/

Expressions

get dressed 🔑 /ˌget 'drest/
get married 🔑 /ˌget 'mærid/
get ready 🔑 /ˌget 'redi/
get tired 🔑 /ˌget 'taɪəd/
get together 🔑 /ˌget tə'geðə(r)/
get well 🔑 /ˌget 'wel/
graduation party /ˌgrædjuˈeɪʃn ˌpɑːti/
have (a) barbecue /ˌhæv ə 'bɑːbəkjuː/
have (a) good time 🔑 /ˌhæv ə ˌgʊd 'taɪm/
have (a) picnic /ˌhæv ə 'pɪknɪk/
look forward to 🔑 /ˌlʊk 'fɔːwəd ˌtuː, tə/
pass an exam 🔑 /ˌpɑːs (ən ɪg'zæm)/
physical appearance 🔑 /ˌfɪzɪkl ə'pɪərəns/
special occasion 🔑 /ˌspeʃl ə'keɪʒn/

Idioms

cost a fortune 🔑 /ˌkɒst ə 'fɔːtʃuːn/
have butterflies /ˌhæv 'bʌtəflaɪz/
make it 🔑 /'maɪk ˌɪt/
on the dot 🔑 /ˌɒn ðə 'dɒt/
take it easy /ˌteɪk ɪt 'iːzi/

/p/ pen	/d/ dog	/tʃ/ beach	/v/ very	/s/ speak	/ʒ/ television	/n/ now	/r/ radio
/b/ big	/k/ can	/dʒ/ job	/θ/ think	/z/ zoo	/h/ house	/ŋ/ sing	/j/ yes
/t/ two	/g/ good	/f/ food	/ð/ then	/ʃ/ she	/m/ meat	/l/ late	/w/ we

Nouns

accommodation ☞0 /əˌkɒmə'deɪʃn/
apartment ☞0 /ə'pɑːtmənt/
bat /bæt/
beach ☞0 /biːtʃ/
bear ☞0 /beə(r)/
bee /biː/
bite ☞0 /baɪt/
blood ☞0 /blʌd/
campsite /'kæmpsaɪt/
cartoon /kɑː'tuːn/
cheetah /'tʃiːtə/
continent ☞0 /'kɒntɪnənt/
cottage ☞0 /'kɒtɪdʒ/
desert ☞0 /'dezət/
dolphin /'dɒlfɪn/
dusk /dʌsk/
eagle /'iːgl/
elephant /'elɪfənt/
forest ☞0 /'fɒrɪst/
fortnight /'fɔːtnaɪt/
giraffe /dʒə'rɑːf/
goat /gəʊt/
grass ☞0 /grɑːs/
half board ☞0 /ˌhɑːf 'bɔːd/
hill ☞0 /hɪl/
hippo (hippopotamus) /'hɪpəʊ
  (ˌhɪpə'pɒtəməs)/
hotel ☞0 /həʊ'tel/
insect ☞0 /'ɪnsekt/
island ☞0 /'aɪlənd/
jellyfish /'dʒelifɪʃ/
kilogram ☞0 /'kɪləgræm/
lake ☞0 /leɪk/
leopard /'lepəd/
lion /'laɪən/
lobster /'lɒbstə(r)/
malaria /mə'leəriə/
metal ☞0 /'metl/
monster /'mɒnstə(r)/
mosquito /mə'skiːtəʊ/
mountain ☞0 /'maʊntən/
mud ☞0 /mʌd/
ocean ☞0 /'əʊʃn/
octopus /'ɒktəpəs/
ox /ɒks/
parrot /'pærət/
per cent ☞0 /pə 'sent/
planet ☞0 /'plænɪt/
prawn /prɔːn/
rainforest /'reɪnfɒrɪst/
resort ☞0 /rɪ'zɔːt/
rhinoceros /raɪ'nɒsərəs/
river ☞0 /'rɪvə(r)/
sailing ☞0 /'seɪlɪŋ/
sea ☞0 /siː/

shark /ʃɑːk/
sightseeing /'saɪtsiːɪŋ/
snake ☞0 /sneɪk/
sprinter /'sprɪntə(r)/
sting ☞0 /stɪŋ/
teeth ☞0 /tiːθ/
tentacle /'tentəkl/
tiger /'taɪgə(r)/
town ☞0 /taʊn/
valley ☞0 /'væli/
villa /'vɪlə/
village ☞0 /'vɪlɪdʒ/
walking ☞0 /'wɔːkɪŋ/
waterfall /'wɔːtəfɔːl/
whale /weɪl/
wildlife /'waɪldlaɪf/
youth hostel /'juːθ ˌhɒstl/

Verbs

book ☞0 /bʊk/
flow ☞0 /fləʊ/
hurt ☞0 /hɜːt/
kill ☞0 /kɪl/
mean ☞0 /miːn/

Adjectives

aggressive ☞0 /ə'gresɪv/
badly-written ☞0 /ˌbædli 'rɪtn/
bad-tempered ☞0 /ˌbæd 'tempəd/
boiling ☞0 /'bɔɪlɪŋ/
comical /'kɒmɪkl/
dry ☞0 /draɪ/
enjoyable ☞0 /ɪn'dʒɔɪəbl/
enormous ☞0 /ɪ'nɔːməs/
fantastic /fæn'tæstɪk/
far ☞0 /fɑː(r)/
first-class /'fɜːst ˌklɑːs/
freezing ☞0 /'friːzɪŋ/
furious /'fjʊəriəs/
friendly ☞0 /'frendli/
furthest ☞0 /'fɜːðɪst/
good-looking /ˌgʊd 'lʊkɪŋ/
hard-working /ˌhɑːd 'wɜːkɪŋ/
heavy ☞0 /'hevi/
helpful ☞0 /'helpfl/
high ☞0 /haɪ/
hilarious /hɪ'leəriəs/
intelligent ☞0 /ɪn'telɪdʒənt/
large ☞0 /lɑːdʒ/
left-handed /ˌleft 'hændɪd/
lively ☞0 /'laɪvli/
painful ☞0 /'peɪnfl/
rainy /'reɪni/
sandy /'sændi/
second-hand /'sekənd ˌhænd/

soaking /'səʊkɪŋ/
terrible ☞0 /'terəbl/
washable /'wɒʃəbl/
well known ☞0 /ˌwel 'nəʊn/
wet ☞0 /wet/
worst ☞0 /wɜːst/

Adverbs

certainly ☞0 /'sɜːtnli/
continuously ☞0 /kən'tɪnjuəsli/
sadly ☞0 /'sædli/

/i/ happy	/æ/ flag	/ɜː/ her	/ʊ/ look	/ʌ/ mum	/ɔɪ/ noisy	/ɪə/ here
/ɪ/ it	/ɑː/ art	/ɒ/ not	/uː/ you	/eɪ/ day	/aʊ/ how	/eə/ wear
/iː/ he	/e/ egg	/ɔː/ four	/ə/ sugar	/aɪ/ why	/əʊ/ go	/ʊə/ tourist

Nouns

accident 🔑 /'æksɪdənt/
airmail /'eəmeɪl/
altimeter /'æltɪmiːtə(r)/
art gallery /'ɑːt ˌgæləri/
bank 🔑 /bæŋk/
birdwatching /'bɜːdwɒtʃɪŋ/
boots 🔑 /buːts/
box office 🔑 /'bɒks ˌɒfɪs/
bus station 🔑 /'bʌs ˌsteɪʃn/
bush 🔑 /bʊʃ/
canoeing /kə'nuːɪŋ/
car park 🔑 /'kɑː ˌpɑːk/
cash machine 🔑 /'kæʃ məˌʃiːn/
climbing 🔑 /'klaɪmɪŋ/
cinema 🔑 /'sɪnəmə/
cord /kɔːd/
department store /dɪ'pɑːtmənt ˌstɔː(r)/
east 🔑 /iːst/
equipment 🔑 /ɪ'kwɪpmənt/
experience 🔑 /ɪk'spɪəriəns/
fishing 🔑 /'fɪʃɪŋ/
frame 🔑 /freɪm/
franchise /'fræntʃaɪz/
garage 🔑 /'gærɑːʒ/
golden eagle /ˌgəʊldən 'iːgl/
goggles /'gɒglz/
ground 🔑 /graʊnd/
harness /'hɑːnɪs/
helmet /'helmɪt/
instructor /ɪn'strʌktə(r)/
jumpsuit /'dʒʌmpsuːt/
leaflet /'liːflət/
library 🔑 /'laɪbrəri/
lung 🔑 /lʌŋ/
mayor 🔑 /meə(r)/
mechanic /mə'kænɪk/
mobile 🔑 /'məʊbaɪl/
mountain biking /'maʊntən ˌbaɪkɪŋ/
museum 🔑 /mju'ziːəm/
national park 🔑 /ˌnæʃnəl 'pɑːk/
painting 🔑 /'peɪntɪŋ/
parachute /'pærəʃuːt/
park 🔑 /pɑːk/
penknife /'pennaɪf/
pilot 🔑 /'paɪlət/
police station 🔑 /pə'liːs ˌsteɪʃn/
post office /'pəʊst ˌɒfɪs/
railway station 🔑 /'reɪlweɪ ˌsteɪʃn/
red squirrel /ˌred 'skwɪrəl/
reef /riːf/
reference 🔑 /'refrens/
return ticket 🔑 /rɪ'tɜːn ˌtɪkɪt/
scenery /'siːnəri/
skiing /'skiːɪŋ/
skydiver /'skaɪdaɪvə(r)/
skyscraper /'skaɪskreɪpə(r)/
snowboarding /'snəʊbɔːdɪŋ/
stage 🔑 /steɪdʒ/
stamps 🔑 /stæmps/
theatre 🔑 /'θɪətə(r)/
tourist information office 🔑 /ˌtʊərɪst ˌɪnfə'meɪʃn ˌɒfɪs/
town hall 🔑 /ˌtaʊn 'hɔːl/
west 🔑 /west/
woods 🔑 /wʊdz/
wrist 🔑 /rɪst/
writer 🔑 /'raɪtə(r)/

Verbs

agree 🔑 /ə'griː/
answer 🔑 /'ɑːnsə(r)/
arrive 🔑 /ə'raɪv/
ask 🔑 /ɑːsk/
borrow 🔑 /'bɒrəʊ/
chat 🔑 /tʃæt/
continue 🔑 /kən'tɪnjuː/
film 🔑 /fɪlm/
hurry 🔑 /'hʌri/
land 🔑 /lænd/
lend 🔑 /lend/
miss 🔑 /mɪs/
park 🔑 /pɑːk/
phone 🔑 /fəʊn/
repair 🔑 /rɪ'peə(r)/
reply 🔑 /rɪ'plaɪ/
ride 🔑 /raɪd/

Adjectives

alive 🔑 /ə'laɪv/
impossible 🔑 /ɪm'pɒsəbl/
main 🔑 /meɪn/
rare 🔑 /reə(r)/
ready 🔑 /'redi/
urgent 🔑 /'ɜːdʒənt/

Adverbs

after that 🔑 /'ɑːftə ˌðæt/
as soon as 🔑 /əz 'suːn əz/
at times 🔑 /ət 'taɪmz/
finally 🔑 /'faɪnəli/
first of all 🔑 /ˌfɜːst əv 'ɔːl/
frequently 🔑 /'friːkwəntli/
later 🔑 /'leɪtə(r)/
on time 🔑 /ˌɒn 'taɪm/
then 🔑 /ðen/

Phrasal verbs

call back 🔑 /ˌkɔːl 'bæk/
run out of (time) 🔑 /ˌrʌn ˌaʊt əv 'taɪm/

Prepositions

between 🔑 /bɪ'twiːn/
opposite 🔑 /'ɒpəzɪt/

Expressions

be in a hurry 🔑 /ˌbiː ˌɪn ə 'hʌri/
be in danger 🔑 /ˌbiː ɪn 'deɪndʒə(r)/
be on holiday 🔑 /ˌbiː ɒn 'hɒlədeɪ/
by hand 🔑 /ˌbaɪ 'hænd/
catch a bus/train 🔑 /ˌkætʃ ə 'bʌs, 'treɪn/
go by car 🔑 /ˌgəʊ baɪ 'kɑː(r)/
go for a walk 🔑 /ˌgəʊ fər ə 'wɔːk/
go on foot 🔑 /ˌgəʊ ɒn 'fʊt/
leave a message 🔑 /ˌliːv ə 'mesɪdʒ/
on the radio 🔑 /ˌɒn ðə 'reɪdiəʊ/
phone someone back 🔑 /ˌfəʊn ˌsʌmwʌn 'bæk/
phone someone on 🔑 /'fəʊn ˌsʌmwʌn ˌɒn/
take your time 🔑 /ˌteɪk jɔː 'taɪm/
waste time 🔑 /ˌweɪst 'taɪm/

Idioms

time flies 🔑 /ˌtaɪm 'flaɪz/

/p/	pen	/d/	dog	/tʃ/	beach	/v/	very	/s/	speak	/ʒ/ television	/n/ now	/r/ radio
/b/	big	/k/	can	/dʒ/	job	/θ/	think	/z/	zoo	/h/ house	/ŋ/ sing	/j/ yes
/t/	two	/g/	good	/f/	food	/ð/	then	/ʃ/	she	/m/ meat	/l/ late	/w/ we

Nouns

(road) accident 🔊 /('rəʊd) ˌæksɪdənt/
aluminium /ˌæljəˈmɪniəm/
brass /brɑːs/
broker /ˈbrəʊkə(r)/
businessman 🔊 /ˈbɪznəsmæn/
cancer 🔊 /ˈkænsə(r)/
childhood /ˈtʃaɪldhʊd/
computer program 🔊 /kəmˈpjuːtə ˌprəʊɡræm/
copper /ˈkɒpə(r)/
court 🔊 /kɔːt/
death 🔊 /deθ/
degree 🔊 /dɪˈɡriː/
experiment 🔊 /ɪkˈsperɪmənt/
garden 🔊 /ˈɡɑːdn/
genius /ˈdʒiːniəs/
governess /ˈɡʌvənəs/
government 🔊 /ˈɡʌvənmənt/
graduate /ˈɡrædʒuət/
iron 🔊 /ˈaɪən/
judge 🔊 /dʒʌdʒ/
laboratory /ləˈbɒrətri/
lecture 🔊 /ˈlektʃə(r)/
lecturer /ˈlektʃərə(r)/
lead 🔊 /led/
leader 🔊 /ˈliːdə(r)/
magnesium /mæɡˈniːziəm/
medicine 🔊 /ˈmedsn/
nationality /næʃəˈnæləti/
neighbour 🔊 /ˈneɪbə(r)/
Nobel Prize /nəʊˌbel ˈpraɪz/
notes 🔊 /nəʊts/
nuclear energy 🔊 /ˌnjuːkliər ˈenədʒi/
operating theatre /ˈɒpəreɪtɪŋ ˌθɪətə(r)/
polonium /pəˈləʊniəm/
present 🔊 /ˈpreznt/
prize 🔊 /praɪz/
professor 🔊 /prəˈfesə(r)/
radiation /ˌreɪdiˈeɪʃn/
radioactivity /ˌreɪdiəʊækˈtɪvəti/
radium /ˈreɪdiəm/
remains 🔊 /rɪˈmeɪnz/
research 🔊 /rɪˈsɜːtʃ/
rest (of) 🔊 /ˈrest əv/
rights 🔊 /raɪts/
speech 🔊 /spiːtʃ/
stadium /ˈsteɪdiəm/
stock exchange /ˈstɒk ɪksˌtʃeɪndʒ/
studio 🔊 /ˈstjuːdiəʊ/
surgeon /ˈsɜːdʒən/
surgery /ˈsɜːdʒəri/
tomb /tuːm/
undergraduate /ˌʌndəˈɡrædʒuət/
uranium /juˈreɪniəm/

Verbs

celebrate 🔊 /ˈselɪbraɪt/
die 🔊 /daɪ/
discover 🔊 /dɪˈskʌvə(r)/
graduate /ˈɡrædʒueɪt/
invent 🔊 /ɪnˈvent/
perform 🔊 /pəˈfɔːm/

Adjectives

awake 🔊 /əˈweɪk/
biographical /ˌbaɪəˈɡræfɪkl/
ill 🔊 /ɪl/
needy /ˈniːdi/
wealthy /ˈwelθi/

Adverbs

early 🔊 /ˈɜːli/
extremely 🔊 /ɪkˈstriːmli/

Expressions

be born 🔊 /ˌbɪ ˈbɔːn/
collect a prize 🔊 /kəˌlekt ə ˈpraɪz/
do a course 🔊 /ˌduː ə ˈkɔːs/
do a degree 🔊 /ˌduː ə dɪˈɡriː/
do research 🔊 /ˌduː rɪˈsɜːtʃ/
get (a job) 🔊 /ˌɡet (ə ˈdʒɒb)/
go round 🔊 /ˌɡəʊ ˈraʊnd/
go to a lecture 🔊 /ˌɡəʊ tu ə ˈlektʃə(r)/
go to school 🔊 /ˌɡəʊ tə ˈskuːl/
go to university 🔊 /ˌɡəʊ tə ˌjuːnɪˈvɜːsəti/
give advice 🔊 /ˌɡɪv ədˈvaɪs/
give a lecture 🔊 /ˌɡɪv ə lektʃə(r)/
grow up 🔊 /ˌɡrəʊ ˈʌp/
have children 🔊 /ˌhæv ˈtʃɪldrən/
take a break 🔊 /ˌteɪk ə ˈbreɪk/
take an exam 🔊 /ˌteɪk ən ɪɡˈzæm/
take notes 🔊 /ˌteɪk ˈnəʊts/
tell a lie 🔊 /ˌtel ə ˈlaɪ/

/i/ happy	/æ/ flag	/ɜː/ her	/ʊ/ look	/ʌ/ mum	/ɔɪ/ noisy	/ɪə/ here
/ɪ/ it	/ɑː/ art	/ɒ/ not	/uː/ you	/eɪ/ day	/aʊ/ how	/eə/ wear
/iː/ he	/e/ egg	/ɔː/ four	/ə/ sugar	/aɪ/ why	/əʊ/ go	/ʊə/ tourist

Nouns

appetite   /'æpɪtaɪt/
apple 🔑   /'æpl/
baked beans   /ˌbeɪkt 'biːnz/
banana   /bə'nɑːnə/
beans   /biːnz/
blackcurrant   /'blæk,kʌrənt/
boredom   /'bɔːdəm/
bottle 🔑   /'bɒtl/
bowl 🔑   /bəʊl/
bread 🔑   /bred/
butter 🔑   /'bʌtə(r)/
can 🔑   /kæn/
cauliflower   /'kɒliflaʊə(r)/
celebrity   /sə'lebrəti/
cereal   /'sɪəriəl/
cheese 🔑   /tʃiːz/
cheeseburger   /'tʃiːzbɜːgə(r)/
cheesecake   /'tʃiːzkeɪk/
chicken 🔑   /'tʃɪkɪn/
chips 🔑   /tʃɪps/
coffee 🔑   /'kɒfi/
coverage   /'kʌvərɪdʒ/
curry   /'kʌri/
dairy product   /'deəri ˌprɒdʌkt/
defence 🔑   /dɪ'fens/
difference 🔑   /'dɪfrəns/
dish 🔑   /dɪʃ/
egg 🔑   /eg/
excitement 🔑   /ɪk'saɪtmənt/
fast food 🔑   /ˌfɑːst 'fuːd/
fat 🔑   /fæt/
fish 🔑   /fɪʃ/
fruit 🔑   /fruːt/
frying pan   /'fraɪɪŋ ˌpæn/
glass 🔑   /glɑːs/
grapefruit   /'greɪpfruːt/
grapes   /greɪps/
hot chocolate 🔑   /ˌhɒt 'tʃɒklət/
isolation   /ˌaɪsə'leɪʃn/
jam 🔑   /dʒæm/
jug   /dʒʌg/
kettle   /'ketl/
lamb   /læm/
law 🔑   /lɔː/
lettuce   /'letɪs/
lobster   /'lɒbstə(r)/
meal 🔑   /miːl/
microwave   /'maɪkrəweɪv/
milk 🔑   /mɪlk/
mind 🔑   /maɪnd/
mushroom   /'mʌʃrʊm, -ruːm/
nickname   /'nɪkneɪm/
olives 🔑   /'ɒlɪvz/
orange juice 🔑   /'ɒrɪndʒ ˌdʒuːs/
oven 🔑   /'ʌvn/

pasta   /'pæstə/
peach   /piːtʃ/
pear   /'peə(r)/
peas   /piːz/
piece 🔑   /piːs/
pineapple   /'paɪnæpl/
pizza   /'piːtsə/
prawn   /prɔːn/
preparation 🔑   /ˌprepə'reɪʃn/
protein   /'prəʊtiːn/
pumpkin   /'pʌmpkɪn/
rice 🔑   /raɪs/
sauce 🔑   /sɔːs/
saucepan   /'sɔːspən/
slice 🔑   /slaɪs/
spider 🔑   /'spaɪdə(r)/
strawberry   /'strɔːbəri/
sugar 🔑   /'ʃʊgə(r)/
sweetcorn   /'swiːtkɔːn/
tea 🔑   /tiː/
toast   /təʊst/
toaster   /'təʊstə(r)/
tomato 🔑   /tə'mɑːtəʊ/
tradition 🔑   /trə'dɪʃn/
vegetable 🔑   /'vedʒtəbl/
water 🔑   /'wɔːtə(r)/
watermelon   /'wɔːtəmelən/
widow 🔑   /'wɪdəʊ/
yoghurt   /'jɒgət/

Verbs

bake 🔑   /beɪk/
boil 🔑   /bɔɪl/
bore 🔑   /bɔː(r)/
compete 🔑   /kəm'piːt/
complain 🔑   /kəm'pleɪn/
complete 🔑   /kəm'pliːt/
continue 🔑   /kən'tɪnjuː/
cook 🔑   /kʊk/
differ   /'dɪfə(r)/
discover 🔑   /dɪ'skʌvə(r)/
excite 🔑   /ɪk'saɪt/
fast 🔑   /fɑːst/
fry 🔑   /fraɪ/
grill   /grɪl/
imagine 🔑   /ɪ'mædʒɪn/
isolate   /'aɪsəleɪt/
participate   /pɑː'tɪsɪpeɪt/
prepare 🔑   /prɪ'peə(r)/
refuse 🔑   /rɪ'fjuːz/
return 🔑   /rɪ'tɜːn/
roast   /rəʊst/
shoot 🔑   /ʃuːt/
stop 🔑   /stɒp/
stretch 🔑   /stretʃ/
weigh 🔑   /weɪ/

Adjectives

baked 🔑   /beɪkt/
bland   /blænd/
brave 🔑   /breɪv/
boiled 🔑   /bɔɪld/
competitive 🔑   /kəm'petətɪv/
defensive   /dɪ'fensɪv/
delicious   /dɪ'lɪʃəs/
equal 🔑   /'iːkwəl/
fresh 🔑   /freʃ/
fried 🔑   /fraɪd/
grilled   /grɪld/
healthy 🔑   /'helθi/
imaginative   /ɪ'mædʒɪnətɪv/
lean 🔑   /liːn/
natural 🔑   /'nætʃrəl/
prepared 🔑   /prɪ'peəd/
raw 🔑   /rɔː/
salty 🔑   /'sɔːlti/
successful 🔑   /sək'sesfl/
sweet 🔑   /swiːt/
tender 🔑   /'tendə(r)/
thin 🔑   /θɪn/
traditional 🔑   /trə'dɪʃənl/
vegetarian   /ˌvedʒə'teəriən/

Phrasal verbs

carry on 🔑   /ˌkæri 'ɒn/
fill in 🔑   /ˌfɪl 'ɪn/
find out 🔑   /ˌfaɪnd 'aʊt/
give up 🔑   /ˌgɪv 'ʌp/
go back 🔑   /ˌgəʊ 'bæk/
pick up 🔑   /ˌpɪk 'ʌp/
push out 🔑   /ˌpʊʃ 'aʊt/

Expressions

take part 🔑   /ˌteɪk 'pɑːt/

/p/ pen	/d/ dog	/tʃ/ beach	/v/ very	/s/ speak	/ʒ/ television	/n/ now	/r/ radio
/b/ big	/k/ can	/dʒ/ job	/θ/ think	/z/ zoo	/h/ house	/ŋ/ sing	/j/ yes
/t/ two	/g/ good	/f/ food	/ð/ then	/ʃ/ she	/m/ meat	/l/ late	/w/ we

Nouns

achievement 🔊 /ə'tʃiːvmənt/
bicycle (bike) 🔊 /'baɪsɪkl (baɪk)/
boarding card /'bɔːdɪŋ ˌkɑːd/
boat 🔊 /bəʊt/
bow /baʊ/
bridge 🔊 /brɪdʒ/
bus 🔊 /'bʌs/
canoe /kə'nuː/
car 🔊 /kɑː(r)/
coach 🔊 /kəʊtʃ/
controls 🔊 /kən'trəʊlz/
dinghy /'dɪŋgi/
disease 🔊 /dɪ'ziːz/
dream 🔊 /driːm/
experience 🔊 /ɪk'spɪəriəns/
ferry /'feri/
freighter /'freɪtə(r)/
guidebook /'gaɪdbʊk/
harbour /'hɑːbə(r)/
helicopter /'helɪkɒptə(r)/
hull /hʌl/
kangaroo /kæŋgə'ruː/
lifeboat /'laɪfbəʊt/
limbs 🔊 /lɪmz/
lorry 🔊 /'lɒri/
mast /mɑːst/
motorbike 🔊 /'məʊtəbaɪk/
opera house /'ɒprə ˌhaʊs/
passenger 🔊 /'pæsɪndʒə(r)/
passport 🔊 /'pɑːspɔːt/
pedal /'pedl/
plan 🔊 /plæn/
plane 🔊 /pleɪn/
port 🔊 /pɔːt/
rail 🔊 /reɪl/
rotor /'rəʊtə(r)/
rudder /'rʌdə(r)/
sail 🔊 /seɪl/
sailor 🔊 /'seɪlə(r)/
scooter /'skuːtə(r)/
ship 🔊 /ʃɪp/
souvenir /ˌsuːvə'nɪə(r)/
starboard 🔊 /'stɑːbɔːd/
stern /stɜːn/
suitcase 🔊 /'suːtkeɪs/
taxi 🔊 /'tæksi/
the Channel 🔊 /ðə 'tʃænl/
tour 🔊 /tʊə(r), tɔː(r)/
train 🔊 /treɪn/
tram /træm/
transport 🔊 /'trænspɔːt/
truck 🔊 /trʌk/
tube 🔊 /tjuːb/
underground 🔊 /'ʌndəgraʊnd/
van 🔊 /væn/

weather 🔊 /'weðə(r)/
wheelchair 🔊 /'wiːltʃeə(r)/
yacht /jɒt/

Verbs

blow 🔊 /bləʊ/
book (a holiday) 🔊 /ˌbʊk (ə 'hɒlədeɪ)/
change money 🔊 /ˌtʃeɪndʒ 'mʌni/
control 🔊 /kən'trəʊl/
design 🔊 /dɪ'zaɪn/
drop 🔊 /drɒp/
lose 🔊 /luːz/
miss 🔊 /mɪs/
move 🔊 /muːv/
pack 🔊 /pæk/
sail 🔊 /seɪl/
spread 🔊 /spred/
steer 🔊 /stɪə(r)/
suck 🔊 /sʌk/

Adjectives

chilly 🔊 /'tʃɪli/
cloudy /'klaʊdi/
cold 🔊 /kəʊld/
confident 🔊 /'kɒnfɪdənt/
disabled 🔊 /dɪs'eɪbld/
exhausted /ɪg'zɔːstɪd/
foggy /'fɒgi/
freezing 🔊 /'friːzɪŋ/
hot 🔊 /hɒt/
humid /'hjuːmɪd/
icy /'aɪsi/
mad 🔊 /mæd/
mild 🔊 /maɪld/
paralysed /'pærəlaɪzd/
rainy /'reɪni/
severe 🔊 /sɪ'vɪə(r)/
showery /'ʃaʊəri/
snowy /'snəʊi/
stormy /'stɔːmi/
sunny /'sʌni/
unsettled /ʌn'setld/
warm 🔊 /wɔːm/
windy /'wɪndi/

Adverbs

over 🔊 /'əʊvə(r)/
suddenly 🔊 /'sʌdnli/
completely 🔊 /kəm'pliːtli/

Prepositions

by the time 🔊 /ˌbaɪ ðə 'taɪm/

Phrasal verbs

come apart 🔊 /ˌkʌm ə'pɑːt/
come on 🔊 /ˌkʌm 'ɒn/
come out 🔊 /ˌkʌm 'aʊt/
come round 🔊 /ˌkʌm 'raʊnd/
take up 🔊 /ˌteɪk 'ʌp/

Expressions

come and go 🔊 /ˌkʌm ən 'gəʊ/
come true 🔊 /ˌkʌm 'truː/

/i/ happy	/æ/ flag	/ɜː/ her	/ʊ/ look	/ʌ/ mum	/ɔɪ/ noisy	/ɪə/ here
/ɪ/ it	/ɑː/ art	/ɒ/ not	/uː/ you	/eɪ/ day	/aʊ/ how	/eə/ wear
/iː/ he	/e/ egg	/ɔː/ four	/ə/ sugar	/aɪ/ why	/əʊ/ go	/ʊə/ tourist

Nouns

accountant /əˈkaʊntənt/
actor 🔑 /ˈæktə(r)/
advantage 🔑 /ədˈvɑːntɪdʒ/
advertisement (advert) 🔑 /ədˈvɜːtɪsmənt/ (ˈædvɜːt)/
airline /ˈeəlaɪn/
animal rescue centre 🔑 /ˌænɪml ˈreskjuː ˌsentə(r)/
application 🔑 /ˌæplɪˈkeɪʃn/
architect /ˈɑːkɪtekt/
artist 🔑 /ˈɑːtɪst/
babysitting /ˈbeɪbisɪtɪŋ/
barrister /ˈbærɪstə(r)/
bricklayer /ˈbrɪkleɪə(r)/
builder /ˈbɪldə(r)/
bus driver 🔑 /ˈbʌs ˌdraɪvə(r)/
chance 🔑 /tʃɑːns/
charity 🔑 /ˈtʃærəti/
chef /ʃef/
cleaner 🔑 /ˈkliːnə(r)/
coach 🔑 /kəʊtʃ/
company 🔑 /ˈkʌmpəni/
computer programmer /kəmˌpjuːtə ˈprəʊɡræmə(r)/
countryside 🔑 /ˈkʌntrisaɪd/
culture 🔑 /ˈkʌltʃə(r)/
customer 🔑 /ˈkʌstəmə(r)/
department store 🔑 /dɪˈpɑːtmənt ˌstɔː(r)/
doctor 🔑 /ˈdɒktə(r)/
dollar 🔑 /ˈdɒlə/
duties 🔑 /ˈdjuːtiz/
engineer 🔑 /ˌendʒɪˈnɪə(r)/
experience 🔑 /ɪkˈspɪəriəns/
factory 🔑 /ˈfæktəri/
factory worker 🔑 /ˈfæktəri ˌwɜːkə(r)/
farmer 🔑 /ˈfɑːmə(r)/
gap year 🔑 /ˈɡæp ˌjɪə(r)/
hairdresser /ˈheədresə(r)/
hospital 🔑 /ˈhɒspɪtl/
inspector /ɪnˈspektə(r)/
interview 🔑 /ˈɪntəvjuː/
journey 🔑 /ˈdʒɜːni/
kitchen 🔑 /ˈkɪtʃɪn/
lawyer 🔑 /ˈlɔːjə(r)/
manager 🔑 /ˈmænɪdʒə(r)/
mechanic /məˈkænɪk/
millionaire /ˌmɪljəˈneə(r)/
minimum wage 🔑 /ˌmɪnɪməm ˈweɪdʒ/
nurse 🔑 /nɜːs/
office 🔑 /ˈɒfɪs/
opportunity 🔑 /ˌɒpəˈtjuːnəti/
overtime /ˈəʊvətaɪm/
passenger 🔑 /ˈpæsɪndʒə(r)/
pay rise 🔑 /ˈpeɪ ˌraɪz/
personal qualities 🔑 /ˈpɜːsənl ˌkwɒlətiz/

photographer 🔑 /fəˈtɒɡrəfə(r)/
plumber /ˈplʌmə(r)/
politician 🔑 /ˌpɒləˈtɪʃn/
post 🔑 /pəʊst/
profession 🔑 /prəˈfeʃn/
public 🔑 /ˈpʌblɪk/
reference 🔑 /ˈrefrəns/
responsibilities 🔑 /rɪˌspɒnsəˈbɪlətiz/
scientist 🔑 /ˈsaɪəntɪst/
secretary 🔑 /ˈsekrətri/
shop assistant 🔑 /ˈʃɒp əˌsɪstənt/
sports centre 🔑 /ˈspɔːts ˌsentə(r)/
teenager /ˈtiːneɪdʒə(r)/
training course 🔑 /ˈtreɪnɪŋ ˌkɔːs/
translator /trænsˈleɪtə(r)/
vet /vet/
visa /ˈviːzə/
waiter 🔑 /ˈweɪtə(r)/

Verbs

apply 🔑 /əˈplaɪ/
attend /əˈtend/
backpack 🔑 /ˈbækpæk/
describe 🔑 /dɪˈskraɪb/
dismiss 🔑 /dɪsˈmɪs/
earn 🔑 /ɜːn/
finance 🔑 /ˈfaɪnæns/
offer 🔑 /ˈɒfə(r)/
promote 🔑 /prəˈməʊt/
resign /rɪˈzaɪn/
restore 🔑 /rɪˈstɔː(r)/
retire 🔑 /rɪˈtaɪə(r)/
serve 🔑 /sɜːv/
show around 🔑 /ˌʃəʊ əˈraʊnd/
volunteer /ˌvɒlənˈtɪə(r)/

Adjectives

allowed 🔑 /əˈlaʊd/
demanding 🔑 /dɪˈmɑːndɪŋ/
extra 🔑 /ˈekstrə/
full-time /ˈfʊl ˌtaɪm/
honest 🔑 /ˈɒnɪst/
ideal 🔑 /aɪˈdiːəl/
local 🔑 /ˈləʊkl/
outside 🔑 /ˌaʊtˈsaɪd/
part-time /ˈpɑːt ˌtaɪm/
reliable /rɪˈlaɪəbl/
rewarding 🔑 /rɪˈwɔːdɪŋ/
voluntary /ˈvɒləntri/

Adverbs

abroad 🔑 /əˈbrɔːd/
outdoors 🔑 /ˌaʊtˈdɔːz/
probably 🔑 /ˈprɒbəbli/

Expressions

be in charge of 🔑 /ˌbiː ɪn ˈtʃɑːdʒ əv/
have an interview 🔑 /ˌhæv ən ˈɪntəvjuː/
take care of 🔑 /ˌteɪk ˈkeər əv/
work part-time /ˌwɜːk ˌpɑːt ˈtaɪm/

Idioms

give someone the sack 🔑 /ˌɡɪv ˌsʌmwʌn ðə ˈsæk/

/p/ pen	/d/ dog	/tʃ/ beach	/v/ very	/s/ speak	/ʒ/ television	/n/ now	/r/ radio
/b/ big	/k/ can	/dʒ/ job	/θ/ think	/z/ zoo	/h/ house	/ŋ/ sing	/j/ yes
/t/ two	/g/ good	/f/ food	/ð/ then	/ʃ/ she	/m/ meat	/l/ late	/w/ we

irregular verb list

Base form	Past simple	Past participle
be	was/were	been
become	became	become
begin	began	begun
blow	blew	blown
bring	brought	brought
buy	bought	bought
can	could	been able to
catch	caught	caught
choose	chose	chosen
come	came	come
cost	cost	cost
do	did	done
draw	drew	drawn
drink	drank	drunk
drive	drove	driven
eat	ate	eaten
feel	felt	felt
fight	fought	fought
find	found	found
fly	flew	flown
forget	forgot	forgotten
get	got	got
give	gave	given
go	went	gone
have	had	had
hit	hit	hit
hold	held	held
hurt	hurt	hurt
keep	kept	kept
know	knew	known
learn	learnt/learned	learnt/learned
leave	left	left
lend	lent	lent
lose	lost	lost

Base form	Past simple	Past participle
make	made	made
mean	meant	meant
meet	met	met
pay	paid	paid
put	put	put
read	read	read
ride	rode	ridden
ring	rang	rung
run	ran	run
say	said	said
see	saw	seen
sell	sold	sold
send	sent	sent
shine	shone	shone
shoot	shot	shot
show	showed	shown
shut	shut	shut
sing	sang	sung
sit	sat	sat
sleep	slept	slept
smell	smelt/smelled	smelt/smelled
speak	spoke	spoken
spell	spelt/spelled	spelt/spelled
spend	spent	spent
spill	spilt/spilled	spilt/spilled
spread	spread	spread
stand	stood	stood
steal	stole	stolen
swim	swam	swum
take	took	taken
teach	taught	taught
tell	told	told
think	thought	thought
understand	understood	understood
wear	wore	worn
win	won	won
write	wrote	written

OXFORD
UNIVERSITY PRESS

Great Clarendon Street, Oxford OX2 6DP

Oxford University Press is a department of the University of Oxford.
It furthers the University's objective of excellence in research, scholarship,
and education by publishing worldwide in

Oxford New York

Auckland Cape Town Dar es Salaam Hong Kong Karachi
Kuala Lumpur Madrid Melbourne Mexico City Nairobi
New Delhi Shanghai Taipei Toronto

With offices in

Argentina Austria Brazil Chile Czech Republic France Greece
Guatemala Hungary Italy Japan Poland Portugal Singapore
South Korea Switzerland Thailand Turkey Ukraine Vietnam

OXFORD and OXFORD ENGLISH are registered trade marks of
Oxford University Press in the UK and in certain other countries

© Oxford University Press 2010

The moral rights of the author have been asserted

Database right Oxford University Press (maker)

First published 2010

2023

17

ISBN: 978 0 19 445300 4

Printed in Spain by Indice, S.L.

This book is printed on paper from certified and well-managed sources.

ACKNOWLEDGEMENTS

*The authors and publisher are grateful to those who have given permission to reproduce
the following extract and adaptation of copyright material*: p.79 'It's given me my
life again' by Sam Wollaston, 5 September 2005, *The Guardian*. Copyright
Guardian News & Media Ltd. 2005. Reproduced by permission.

Source: p.66 Fictitious interview with Sonya Thomas
(www.sonyatheblackwidow.com).

Front Cover: (One Moment Photography-Thomas Hartmann/Moment).

The publisher would like to thank the following for permission to reproduce photographs:
123RF (123RF, VOLODYMYR BURDYAK); Alamy Stock Photo (A ROOM WITH
VIEWS, AF archive, Alexandra Carlile/Elvele Images Limited, Alexey Stiop,
Amanda Ahn/dbimages, Archivart, Big Mama's and Papa's Pizzeria/Nippon
News/Aflo Co. Ltd., Bill Bachman, BRIAN HARRIS, Chris Ison/PA Images,
Colin Fisher/Alamy Live News, Colin Harris/era-images, David & Micha
Sheldon/F1online digitale Bildagentur GmbH, David J. Green - science,
David Robertson, Dennis MacDonald, Design Pics/Radius Images, Dinodia
Photos, Edd Westmacott., Elmtree Images, Enigma, Everett Collection Inc.,
foodfolio, Greg Wright, Homer Sykes, Ian Allenden, Ian Nicholson/PA Images,
Ian Roberts, IMAGEMORE Co., Ltd., Interpix, JGI/Jamie Grill/Tetra Images,
LLC, John Stillwell/PA Images, John Terence Turner, kolvenbach, Kos Picture
Source Ltd, Manfred Bail/imageBROKER, Marion Bull, Mark Boulton, Mark
Eveleigh, Maximilian Weinzierl, Mehdi Taamallah/Abaca Press, Michele
Falzone, Middle East, Momentum Creative Group/JSP Studios, Neal Simpson/
PA Images, Odilon Dimier/PhotoAlto, Paul Bradbury/OJO Images Ltd, Phil
Degginger, Rider Thompson, Robertharding, Sasa Kralj/JiwaFoto/ZUMA
Press, Inc., sébastien Baussais, SETFORDELETION, SOPA Images Limited,
Stephen Emerson, Steve Vidler, Tim Hill, World Pictures, Xpacifica, Zakir
hossain chowdhury zakir); ardea.com (Valerie & Ron Taylor); Arnos Design
(Arnos Design); Corbis (Andersen-Ross, Comstock Select, Corbis, Eleanor
Bentall, Justin Guariglia); Fotolia (Fotolia, Ruta Saulyte, Simone Van Den
Berg, Victor Burnside); Getty Images (945ontwerp/E+, adwalsh/E+, Angelika/
iStock, arlindo71/E+, Bettmann, billberryphotography/iStock, BirdImages/
E+, bluestocking/E+, bonniej/iStock, Carlos Alvarez, Cate Gillon, Coldimages/
iStock, Colin McPherson/Corbis Historical, Daniel Berehulak, dehooks/iStock,
Dejan750/iStock, DIBYANGSHU SARKAR/AFP, Digital Vision, Doug Pensinger,
dpruter/iStock, EcoPic/iStock, esemerda/iStock, fpm/iStock, Gannet77/E+,
guhl/iStock, Hero Images, Hogie/E+, Hulton Archive, izusek/iStock, JacobH/
E+, jgroup/iStock, juanestey/iStock, kevinruss/iStock, krausphoto/iStock,
Leland Bobbe/DigitalVision, leonardophoto/iStock, lisafx/iStock, Luso/iStock,
Michael Goldman/Photodisc, Mlenny/E+, Monkeybusinessimages/iStock,
naphtalina/E+, Nicholas Free/iStock, Owlet/iStock, photonimo/iStock, Roine
Magnusson/Stone, RollingEarth/iStock, RonTech2000/iStock, Snowlizard/
iStock, Sportstock/iStock, SureshMenon/iStock, Taxi, TAXI/Dietmar Busse,
THEPALMER/E+, The-Tor/iStock, tomazl/E+, ullstein bild, vaide/iStock, Veni/
E+, WILLIAM WEST/AFP, Yellow Dog Productions/The Image Bank, YinYang/
iStock); OUP (Corbis/Digital Stock, David Jordan, Haddon Davies, Mark
Bassett, Onoky, OUP, Photodisc, Stockbyte); Photolibrary (Andersen Ross/
Blend Images, Banana Stock, BananaStock, Corbis, Kevin Peterson/Photodisc,
Laurence Mouton/Zen Shui, Ron Nickel/Design Pics Inc); Punchstock
(Punchstock); Science Photo Library (JIM REED, PLANETOBSERVER);
Shutterstock (Alaettin YILDIRIM, AlinaMD, Anderson Matos, Andreas
Altwein/EPA, Andrii Kobryn, Art Konovalov, badahos, bonchan, British Sky
Broadcasting Ltd, Chekyravaa, Elena Ermakova, Featureflash Photo Agency,
GaudiLab, i viewfinder, Iakov Filimonov, Igor Grochev, imageBROKER,
Kyryk Ivan, LightField Studios, Ljupco Smokovski, Markson Sparks, Michele
Vacchiano, Mountainpix, NadzeyaShanchuk, NAN728, Patryk Kosmider,
Peter Foley/EPA, pikselstock, prochasson frederic, Rawpixel.com, Richard
Bowden, RossHelen, Shane Gross, Shutterstock, Sinelev, smuay, Svetlana
Orusova, Take A Pix Media, Timothy Craig Lubcke, Triff, Vergani Fotografia,
WAYHOME studio).

Illustrations by: Claude Bordeleau pp.6, 14, 24, 27, 32, 33, 34, 70, 79, 107,
109, 113; Rebecca Halls/The Organisation pp.67, 95, 99; David Oakley/
Arnos Design p.26; ODI pp.49, 78; Dylan Teague p.25; Fred van Deelen/The
Organisation pp.52, 62.